Journalism

across cultures

Journalism
across cultures

Fritz Cropp
Cynthia M. Frisby
Dean Mills

Blackwell
Publishing

© 2003 Iowa State Press
A Blackwell Publishing Company
All rights reserved

Blackwell Publishing Professional
2121 State Avenue, Ames, Iowa 50014

Orders: 1-800-862-6657
Office: 1-515-292-0140
Fax: 1-515-292-3348
Web site: www.blackwellprofessional.com

Printed on acid-free paper in the United States of America

International Standard Book Number: 0-8138-1999-7

Library of Congress Cataloging-in-Publication Data

Journalism across cultures / edited by Fritz Cropp, Cynthia Frisby, and Dean Mills.
    p. cm.
Includes index.
   ISBN 0-8138-1999-7 (alk. paper)
   1. Minorities--Press coverage--United States. I. Cropp, Fritz. II. Frisby, Cynthia.
III. Mills, Dean.
   PN4888.M56J68 2003
   070.4'493058--dc21

                                                        2003005989

The last digit is the print number: 9 8 7 6 5 4 3 2

For . . .

Mary, Eric, and Marisa Cropp

Craig, Marcus, and Angela Frisby

Sue, Jason, Karen, Jesse, Krista, Maya, Willem, and Macy Mills

Contents

Contributing Authors

Leroy Aarons is visiting professor at the Annenberg School of Journalism at the University of Southern California. He directs Annenberg's Program for the Study of Sexual Orientation Issues in the News (SOIN), which he founded with the support of Dean Geoffrey Cowan in 1999. SOIN is dedicated to being a resource for inclusion of sexual orientation issues in the curriculum at journalism institutions (Web address: www. usc/annenberg/soin). Aarons is a journalist of four decades who served as national correspondent for the *Washington Post* in the 1960s and 1970s, then as executive editor of the *Oakland Tribune*, which won a Pulitzer Prize during his tenure. He is co-founder of the Maynard Institute for Journalism Education (MIJE) and founder of the National Lesbian and Gay Journalists Association (NLGJA).

Judith M. Buddenbaum is a professor in the Department of Journalism and Technical Communication at Colorado State University. She is co-editor, with Daniel A. Stout, of *Journal of Media and Religion.*

She is the author of *Reporting News about Religion: An Introduction for Journalists* (Ames: Iowa State University Press, 1998) and, with Debra L. Mason, the editor of *Readings on Religion as News* (Ames: Iowa State University Press, 2000). Her research on religion news has been published as book chapters and as articles in *Journalism History, Journalism and Mass Communication Quarterly*, and *Newspaper Research Journal*. With Daniel L. Stout, she is also co-editor of *Religion and the Media: Audiences and Adaptations* (Thousand Oaks, Calif.: Sage, 1996) and *Religion and Popular Culture* (Ames: Iowa State University Press, 2001).

A former religion reporter, she has also conducted media research for The Lutheran World Federation in Geneva, Switzerland. She holds an A.B. in chemistry, M.A. in journalism and Ph.D. in mass communication from Indiana University, Bloomington.

Jan Colbert is an associate professor at the Missouri School of Journalism. She teaches classes on women and the media, design, writing, media issues and graduate research seminars. Her research focuses on visual storytelling and gender issues.

She has been the executive director of Investigative Reporters and Editors, the managing editor and art director of *The IRE Journal* and the co-editor, with John Ullmann, of the second edition of *The Reporter's Handbook.* Colbert has worked as a newspaper reporter and editor and has designed numerous magazines and books. She freelances as a book designer and photo editor and is currently writing a book on in-depth reporting, writing and photography methods.

Kent S. Collins, journalist and educator, is the chair of the Broadcast Department at the Missouri School of Journalism. He has served at the Missouri School of Journalism for 18 years. He teaches advanced television reporting technique, television newsroom management, and television research. He has twice served as news director for KOMU-TV, the University's commercial (NBC) station. He is the director of the Missouri Lifestyle Journalism Awards, the nation's largest contest for newspaper feature writers and editors. Collins also is a nationally syndicated newspaper columnist, a consultant to television stations in this country and Europe, and serves as an expert witness in court cases involving libel, slander, trespass and invasion.

Fritz Cropp directs the International Programs office at the Missouri School of Journalism, where he also is an assistant professor of advertising. He has 10 years of experience as a college instructor and professor, and 13 years of professional experience in journalism, public relations and marketing communications. Cropp has taught international workshops in Mongolia, China, Korea and elsewhere. His dissertation involved international advertising and his master's thesis examined perceptions of public relations practitioners among newspaper journalists. His academic work has been published in the *Journal of Public Relations Research*, the *Journal of Communication Management* and the *Handbook of Public Relations.* Cropp earned his Ph.D. in journalism from the University of Missouri-Columbia, his master's degree in public relations from California State University-Fullerton, and his undergraduate degree from the College of Wooster (Ohio).

Cynthia M. Frisby, assistant professor of advertising, joined the Missouri School of Journalism in 1998. Frisby teaches courses in advertising, media planning and media sales. Frisby received a doctorate and her master's and bachelor's degrees at the University of Florida. She has received several awards and honors, including the Provost's Outstanding Junior Faculty Teaching Award, the University of Missouri Faculty Incentive Grant, and the Kappa Gamma and Zeta Tau Alpha "Professor of the Year" awards.

Frisby also has completed several nationally recognized research projects, including studies that are dedicated to helping health organizations understand and develop health communication campaigns for underserved populations. Her research agenda centers on advertising effects and the use of research for concept and message development. Through the use of formative evaluation and other research methods, Frisby's research focuses on creating messages that resonate with particular audiences. It is assumed that this research will help to identify vernacular and other message elements that may be most appropriate for specific audiences in order to address and/or change attitudes and behaviors.

Ronald B. Kelley is currently director of corporate and foundation relations for Miami University in Oxford, Ohio. Dr. Kelley was previously at the University of Missouri-Columbia, where he was Director of Student, Alumni and External Relations for the School of Journalism and a faculty member in the Broadcast News Department. He was the project director for the grant called Strategic Study on Race and News, which was aimed at finding and implementing improved news coverage on race issues and minorities. He also coordinated and co-edited *Guide to Research on Race and News*, a guidebook and comprehensive study on race and media. Kelley has a Ph.D. in higher education administration from the University of Missouri-Columbia, a M.S. degree from Kansas State University and a B.S. from Arkansas State University.

Teresa Trumbly Lamsam, a former mainstream journalist and tribal press editor, is an assistant professor in the Communication Department at the University of Nebraska at Omaha. She teaches print journalism courses and conducts research on the Native American Tribal Press and development communication. Lamsam, an Osage, grew up on the Osage Reservation in northeastern Oklahoma.

Dennis McAuliffe, Jr., a former assistant foreign editor of the *Washington Post*, is the University of Montana School of Journalism's Native

American Journalist in Residence. He is the author of *Bloodland: A Family Story of Oil, Greed and Murder on the Osage Reservation.* McAuliffe, also an Osage, oversees the new college newspaper website for Native American students, www.reznet.com.

Dean Mills has been professor and dean at the School of Journalism at the University of Missouri-Columbia since 1989. He earlier served as vice chair and director of graduate studies at California State University, Fullerton, and as director of the School of Journalism at the Pennsylvania State University.

His research has focused on journalism in the former Soviet Union and Eastern Europe, the coverage of diversity and minority issues in U.S. media, and journalism ethics. He is co-author of *Journalism and Journalism Education in Eastern and Central Europe* (Hampton Press, 1999).

He has a Ph.D. in communications from the University of Illinois, an M.A. in journalism from the University of Michigan, and a B.A. in Russian and journalism from the University of Iowa. He also attended Talladega College. Before joining the academy, he was a Washington and Moscow correspondent for the *Baltimore Sun.*

Wesley G. Pippert is director of the Missouri School of Journalism's Washington (D.C.) Program and an associate professor on its faculty. Pippert formerly spent an extended career in newspapers and wire services. He was Middle East bureau chief for United Press International, based in Jerusalem, as well as a UPI White House correspondent during the Carter administration. Pippert has traveled worldwide as a journalist and educator. He has taught workshops for a variety of audiences ranging from Palestinian journalists in Ramallah to Albanian business editors in Washington. In the 12 years since Pippert took over the School's Washington program (founded in 1969), more than a third of the participants have been international students.

Mercedes Lynn de Uriarte, formerly an assistant editor and writer at the *Los Angeles Times*, now teaches journalism and Latin American studies at the University of Texas, Austin. She received her Ph.D. in American Studies from Yale University. While at the *Times*, she was responsible for expanding coverage of Mexico and Central America, as well as U.S. minority communities. She recently headed the research team that produced *Perpetual Disconnects: Missteps Toward Newsroom*

Diversity, a study of intellectual diversity from classroom to newsroom. She was the first chair for the AEJMC Commission of the Status of Minorities. She is bilingual and bicultural—born in the United States and raised in Mexico.

At the University of Texas, she developed the first course in the nation to teach non-minority journalism students how to cover underrepresented communities. She also pioneered a course in community journalism that for a decade produced *Tejas*, a publication for diverse voice, the first such classroom laboratory publication in the nation. Articles in *Tejas* received the 1996 Robert F. Kennedy Memorial Award for Outstanding Journalism.

Alexander Wissner-Gross has done extensive research in physics and engineering at the Massachusetts Institute of Technology. He has devoted much of his work, including two patents, to exploring revolutionary technologies to ultimately improve the quality and length of human life and to enable people with disabilities.

Elizabeth Wissner-Gross, author of *Unbiased: Editing in a Diverse Society* (Ames: Iowa State University Press, 1999) has worked as a professional writer and editor for more than 25 years. She has taught journalism at Hofstra University, Iona College, and Fairleigh Dickinson University and has run workshops on "Bias in the Media" at New York University, Barnard College, the New School for Social Research and Newsday. She has guest lectured on the elimination of bias and served on panels for media companies, civic organizations, religious groups, secondary schools and elementary schools. Her career has included editing and writing as a staffer for Newsday, the Associated Press, and the *Daily News* of Los Angeles. Her articles have also appeared in the *New York Times*, *Los Angeles Times*, *Washington Post*, *Boston Globe* and hundreds of other domestic and foreign publications. She is a graduate of the Columbia University Graduate School of Journalism and of Barnard College.

Preface

Many obstacles lie in the path of media professionals who want to do a better job of dealing with groups that have historically been undercovered or inaccurately covered. Based on our research and on our experiences with journalists and journalism students, we believe the three main obstacles are these:

- Even the most fair-minded journalists find it difficult to get past the stereotypes that they inherit from their cultures and that interfere with the ability to see people as individuals rather than as stereotypical members of groups.
- Many journalists believe, we think erroneously, that conscious attempts to correct undercoverage or stereotyped coverage of underrepresented groups will result in distorting news content in the name of political correctness.
- Because of the difficulties of covering underrepresented groups, some journalists simply run for cover—and try to avoid covering them for fear of running into some political correctness landmines.

We launched this book project in the hope of helping journalists and journalism students past those obstacles. To that end, we asked each of the authors to help readers understand something about the history or culture of the group covered and the historic problems of journalistic or advertising treatment of the group, and to give some recommendations for improvement. We believe all our authors handled the assignment in ways that should help media professionals better serve their audiences.

As editors, we ourselves got a useful lesson in diversity. When we saw the first drafts of the chapters, we were initially concerned that the authors had taken quite different approaches to the assignment. Some were more scholarly, others more journalistic. Some relied heavily on academic literature, some very little. Some were interested more in print or broadcast journalism, one mainly in advertising. And although there was much overlap in the recommendations, the authors varied widely in their preference for one solution or another.

As we read and reread the chapters, we understood what probably should have been obvious from the outset. Given the complexities of cross-cultural work, different authors will take different approaches in both analyzing the question and in recommending ways to improve media performance. We quickly understood that these differing approaches, like diversity in journalism or advertising, were a strength. As in other areas of journalism, there is no one true path to improvement.

And improvement is what this book is about. As we tell the students at Missouri who take our required undergraduate course in cross-cultural journalism, the goal is not social justice (though we believe good journalism can aid social justice), and it is certainly not political correctness. Our goal is better journalism, achieved through a better understanding of the people we cover and of how better to cover them.

Chapter 1 provides an overview of academic research into the coverage of minorities and a report on an innovative approach to improved coverage through the collaboration of journalists and researchers. Chapter 2 concentrates on the news coverage of women. But it also describes the varying academic theories by which news content about any subject can be studied—a helpful primer to journalists or students who would like to explore new paradigms for analyzing news, many of which challenge our traditional assumptions of what news is and should be. We believe that, together, these chapters provide necessary background on the history of research on diversity in journalism and advertising, and an understanding of how theory can help us systematically analyze cross-cultural journalism.

The other chapters describe individual underrepresented groups, analyze the history of their coverage, and offer recommendations and resources for improved coverage. The authors had impossible assignments, really: to sum up in a few pages the complexities and nuances of the media's interactions with groups that comprise almost infinite members and infinite variations. To take an example, how could the hundreds of cultures that fall under the heading "Asian Americans" be fully and accurately treated in a book, let alone a single chapter? And we offer only one chapter of analysis on covering nationalities beyond U.S. borders. U.S. journalists face some common problems when covering citizens of other nations, and we believe Wesley Pippert, in his analysis of coverage of the Arab world, provides some helpful advice that is applicable to covering many other areas of the world. Yet the challenges of covering Saudi Arabians are different from those of covering Iranis or Chinese or Somalis or Russians.

If we are to make headway in our efforts to provide citizens the coverage they need and deserve, we must begin some place. We hope this book will be a useful start for its readers.

Journalism
across cultures

CHAPTER 1

Covering the Undercovered

The Evolution of Diversity in the News

Ronald B. Kelley and Dean Mills

Since at least the 1960s, journalists and journalism scholars have engaged in efforts aimed at improving or studying diversity in the news. Usually, the two groups have worked independently.

This chapter analyzes what has happened in journalism and journalism research in the last several decades in this area and describes the uncertain progress made in increasing diversity in newsrooms and news content. It concludes with an account of the first large-scale effort by researchers and journalists working together to make news content more diverse and accurate. We believe that experiment offers some useful lessons to both journalists and scholars who want to surmount the hurdles that have impeded better diversity coverage through the years.

An earlier version of the first part of this chapter, dealing with the history of diversity research, appeared in *Guide to Research on Race and News* (Missouri School of Journalism 2000). Both that report and the research distributed in the last half of the chapter were funded by the Ford Foundation.

Despite decades of efforts, the percentage of minorities in newsrooms does not approach the percentage in the audiences they try to serve. And despite some marked improvements, mainstream news media often underrepresent or misrepresent many of society's component groups.

Covering Race and Gender through the Years

U.S. journalists were challenged to examine questions of fairness in news coverage in 1947, when the Hutchins Commission argued that the press should provide a "projection of a representative picture of the constituent groups in the society" (Commission on Freedom of the Press 1947). After 1968, when many U.S. cities erupted in racial disturbances following the murder of Martin Luther King, Jr., journalists in increasing numbers decided their nearly all-white newsrooms and nearly all-white content had to change. A decade later, the American Society of Newspaper Editors (ASNE), reflecting the changing mind-set on coverage of race, challenged its members to set goals for increasing diversity in their newsrooms so that it would match, by 2000, the diversity of the citizenry.

Initial diversity efforts concentrated largely on bringing more African Americans into newsrooms and more content about African Americans onto news pages and news broadcasts. Gradually, efforts broadened to include Hispanics, Asian Americans and Native Americans, women, gays and lesbians, the disabled and others.

Yet, by the turn of the century, after a quarter century of trying, neither newsrooms nor news content approached the diversity of the audiences they were serving. Detailed findings of the 2002 ASNE Newspaper Newsroom Employment Survey show a breakdown of newsroom staffs by minority group of 2.36 percent Asian Americans (1,283), 5.29 percent African Americans (2,879), 3.86 percent Hispanics (2,098), and 0.56 percent Native Americans (307) (ASNE 2002). For broadcast, the 2002 Radio-Television News Directors Association (RTNDA) figures for the minority news force show 9.3 percent African Americans, 7.7 percent Hispanics, 3.1 percent Asian Americans, and 0.5 percent Native Americans for television and 4.1 percent African Americans, 2.4 percent Hispanics, 0.8 percent Asian Americans, and 0.7 percent Native Americans for radio (RTNDA 2002).

Continuing studies of news content, similarly, show increased attention to diverse groups, but they also show continuing problems.

Increasing Newsroom Diversity: Why Does It Matter?

Why is it important to have larger numbers of underrepresented groups in newsrooms and media management positions? Shouldn't sensitive and conscientious white male journalists be able to provide fair and accurate coverage of all groups?

Journalists who have thought about the issue tend to focus on the difference a minority journalist can make in the myriad decisions that go into constituting the daily news product. George Benge, a veteran journalist, says, "There's no substitute, really, for having people on your staff in numbers who have lived a life and who've walked a walk and talked a talk in minority shoes. Until you have that it's very difficult, on a daily basis, [to deal with] the ebb and flow and the give and take of the thousands of things that occur in a newsroom" (Missouri School of Journalism 2000).

Through the decades, many scholars who have studied the relationship between the makeup of news staffs and the makeup of news content have argued that, almost inevitably, mainstream news reflects the world view of the dominant forces in a society. Given that white, affluent males have historically dominated U.S. institutions, they reason, it is natural that news is filtered through a white male prism (Dates and Pease 1994).

Efforts to increase diversity of either news staffs or news content are sometimes criticized on the grounds that the reformers would distort the news in pursuit of "political correctness." William McGowan (2001) sums up these arguments in *Coloring the News*. Journalists in the trenches frequently resist reforms aimed at increasing diversity by using the same argument. Editors who ask reporters to find more minority sources for their stories or to broaden the diet of the day's news by seeking out stories that look at the world from a minority viewpoint are criticized for distorting the news by inserting subjective judgments into the news process.

Such criticisms ignore the evidence of several decades that news is not something that simply happens out there, waiting only to be seized daily in the nets of reporters and editors. Scholars such as Herbert Gans (1980) and Gaye Tuchman (1971), followed by dozens of others, have shown how the personal and professional judgments of individual journalists select and shape those events that become the day's news.

Jessica Fishman and Carolyn Marvin (1998) demonstrated, in a nonracial, nongender context, how these usually unconscious judgments affect the content of news presented daily to readers as the reality of their world. They studied front-page photographs in the *New York Times* in which violence was portrayed from 1976 to 1996 and found that when

U.S. agents were responsible for the violence, the images were "distinctly 'softer' than that associated with non-U.S. agents."

The images used where U.S. violence was involved were much more likely to be implicit, compared to the explicit violence depicted where non-U.S. agents were involved. What's more, even when explicit instances of violence were involved, the differences were impressive. Israeli soldiers were shown firing tear gas at demonstrators. South African police were shown firing weapons at Capetown University. By contrast, photographs showed U.S. federal agents "comforting a wounded colleague, ... covering an inmate with a blanket after a prison riot ... and police rescuing an infant injured during domestic violence" (Fishman and Marvin 1998).

Fishman and Marvin speculate that the journalists responsible for selecting the *New York Times* photographs unconsciously select them in ways that show Americans in a more favorable light, even in moments of violence, than non-Americans. They cite an argument of Herman and Chomsky (2002):

> The raw material of news must pass through successive filters. They fix the premises of discourse and interpretation, and the definition of what is newsworthy. The operation of these filters occurs so naturally that media news people, frequently operating with complete integrity and good will, are able to convince themselves that they choose and interpret the news "objectively" and on the basis of professional news values. Within the limits of the filter constraints, they often are objective; the constraints are so powerful, and are built into the system in such a fundamental way, that alternative bases of news choices are hardly imaginable.

Even when minority journalists make it into newsrooms, even into management positions, they can get caught in a double bind that makes it difficult for them to introduce true diversity into content. Here is the bind: If they adopt the existing, predominantly white values in selecting and covering events, they have not added to diversity. If they don't, they risk career-stalling or even failure for not going along with the dominant values of the newsroom. "Although the debate is framed in terms of participation," wrote Mercedes Lynn de Uriarte (1994, 173), "the real struggle over diversity in the newsroom is a conflict over points of view. Numbers alone won't change perspective. The newsroom structure works against diversity because like all management, media decision-makers often seek to duplicate themselves. It may be that minorities are often hired for their ability to fit in rather than for their ability to provide new or diverse voices."

Journalists and scholars who have the perspective of several decades of attempts to increase diversity understand that, as important as it is, making newsrooms more racially diverse does not automatically result in diverse thinking. A middle-class African American reared in the suburbs and educated at a top university may have much more in common with a white reporter with a similar background than with blue-collar readers, black or white. And the two men may have more in common with each other than either has with the woman, black or white, sitting in the cubicle next to them.

Ruben Rosario, longtime columnist for the *St. Paul Pioneer-Press*, put it this way:

> You can hire a black person, you can hire a Hispanic person, you can hire a Filipino person, you can hire a Somalian, you can hire an Ethiopian, and may not ever get a true diversification in the newsroom. ... My true ideal newsroom would be a newsroom that has—it's almost crazy—but that has a poor person's reporter, that has a working class person's reporter and has a wealthy person's reporter. ... I think many newsrooms across America are cut out of the same mold. We're all college educated, we all make pretty decent money. We're all the same thing. (Missouri School of Journalism 2000)

Nor does all the responsibility rest with white males. Ivan Roman, a Puerto Rican of African descent, is particularly aware of the cross-cultural barriers that face minorities when dealing with other minorities, who he argued also have to work at seeing past stereotypes.

> But starting over is not that easy for many of us who put out the news. The news media create and perpetuate limited views of entire communities: Asian American, African American, Latino, Native American, gay and lesbian, seniors, youth, the disabled. ... And although we complain and focus most of our attention on the white-run and corporate-owned mainstream media, most of us people of color have a lot to learn, too. (Missouri School of Journalism 2000)

Change: More-Diverse Staffs

Although news staffs have not diversified as much or as quickly as many reformers hoped three decades ago, news staffs of today are markedly more diverse than those in the days of the Hutchins Commission. Metropolitan newsrooms that had no, or at most one, minority staff member now have several. News broadcasts that had no minority faces now have at least one. Women journalists have moved in significant numbers from the society pages to the news pages. Many gay and lesbian journalists have emerged from silence to openness. Underrepresented groups of all kinds are now in executive roles in print and broadcast newsrooms—though still not in proportion to their numbers in the population.

It was perhaps inevitable that the change in demographics in newsrooms would lead to problems of a different kind: conflicts between old and new approaches to journalism—and, more personal and more painful, conflicts between demographic groups. Minorities and women often believe they have less of a shot than their white, male colleagues at top management jobs.

A 1996 Associated Press Managing Editors (APME) study found that a substantial majority of minority journalists believed they were not treated fairly in mainstream newsrooms. They believed they struggled longer in entry-level positions than did their white colleagues. They believed they were routinely passed over for promotions that went to less-qualified whites.

And they got discouraged. They were more inclined to leave their jobs and more inclined to leave the field than were whites. So lack of retention of minority journalists can make it even more difficult for newsrooms to increase diversity to levels approaching that of society at large.

A Hispanic respondent in the APME study said that opportunities for minority journalists had changed little during his 20 years with the company: "The CEO recently told a group of minorities while announcing the promotion of seven whites, 'Your time will come.'" An African-American journalist said, "Even though I am at the top of my game and very productive, the white boys still make more, still condescend and still assume their skills are superior. ... Not a single black journalist participates in the Page One meeting" (APME 1996, 8).

For their part, some white journalists have also been embittered in more diverse newsrooms. They, too, felt discriminated against. One white respondent said, "The few minority journalists we have enjoy much greater opportunity for advancement. It's a very enviable position to be in these days, to be a minority with talent." Another white journalist accused his newspaper's managers of reverse racism. He gave the example of an assistant metropolitan editor job for which only minorities were interviewed. "I have found that it is impossible for a white male to participate in a dialogue on these issues without getting his head handed to him by someone who is ready to label him a racist" (APME 1996, 9).

Change: More-Diverse, Less-Biased Content

Despite continuing problems, progress has been made by news organizations in treating minorities. Sins of both commission and omission have been reduced markedly. Blatant examples of racial stereotyping appear much less frequently in today's media than in the pre–civil rights movement era. The social pages of newspapers are no longer routinely closed to minorities. African Americans and Hispanics now appear on television news in roles other than criminals, welfare recipients, entertainers and athletes (though, as we shall point out later, they still appear disproportionately in those categories). And most large news organizations have strived to provide more extensive coverage of minority communities and have tackled head-on, at least once, the issues of race relations in their communities.

But there remains room for pessimism. Although few news organizations would tolerate overt racism in their coverage today, many, if not most, deal with this touchy issue by dealing with it as little as possible. Racist coverage has largely been replaced by no coverage of racial issues. And in the view of at least some researchers, explicit racism has been replaced by "modern racism," a fuzzier concept and one that in some ways is more difficult to combat.

Paul Lester and Ron Smith (1990), in an analysis of pictures in *Life*, *Newsweek* and *Time* from 1937 to 1988, asserted that more positive images of African Americans appeared in the magazines at the end of the period. African Americans in photos increased from 1.1 to 8.8 percent. Lester and Randy Miller (1996) found that, although the number of African Americans in pictures had continued to increase, blacks were still most commonly shown as athletes, entertainers or criminals.

In his pioneering analysis of television news, Robert Entman (1992) argued that "modern racism" has replaced traditional racism in the news. Entman defined "modern white racism" as "hostility, rejection and denial toward African-American aspirations and activities." The presence of African Americans as TV news reporters and new societal norms make blatant racism unacceptable. But the conventions of news perpetuate the new and subtle form of racism, which allows whites to conclude that enough concessions have been made to African Americans, and that

they are justified in being hostile or indifferent to blacks' calls for justice. Black politicians, for example, are portrayed as more confrontational and extreme than their white counterparts.

Marilyn Gist, in her 1990 study of two newsrooms, pinned down
problems that remain common today. The content of the news often parallels the demographics of the newsroom—predominantly Caucasian
and middle class. A few, usually controversial, "spokesmen" are chosen
to represent the minority community. Minorities are seldom seen as typical citizens (Gist 1990).

Time magazine pointed out in a 1997 media analysis a continuing
race-biased approach to reporting, in which only white victims are big
news. A media frenzy surrounded the murder of Jon Benet Ramsey, in a
rich Colorado suburb, while the murder of Girl X in Chicago's Cabrini
Green housing project was virtually ignored.

Relatively little academic research has been done on the treatment of
Latinos in the news. What little there has been suggests a pattern similar to that of news about African Americans. When they appear, it is usually as criminals, welfare recipients, or confrontational politicians. In
addition, because of the heavy immigration into the United States from
Latin America, they often are lumped together as illegal aliens. (On the
other hand, one study of two southwestern U.S. newspapers showed
Hispanics were treated better in news coverage than were whites.)

Formal research studies on Asian Americans have been rare. (That
may be because coverage has been rare, even in urban centers with large
Asian-American populations, as we discuss below). Some anecdotal evidence suggests that Asian Americans may have suffered more continuing stereotypical coverage than other minorities. A multiyear project of
the Center for Integration and Improvement of Journalism at San Francisco State University turned up numerous examples of racist slurs in
stories and headlines and facial stereotypes in cartoons. Asian minorities
can get it from both directions—characterized as unrealistically good
(model student, ambitious shop owner) or bad (Asian gang member).
Asian Americans present a special challenge because the term itself suggests a reality that doesn't exist; there are enormous cultural, historical
and other differences among Korean Americans, Chinese Americans,
Hmong Americans and so on.

The News: Still White?

Given that minorities remain underrepresented in newsrooms, and
given that those who are in newsrooms face continuing pressures, im-

plicit or explicit, to in effect act white, we should not be surprised to find that the content of the media reflects predominantly a white, even a white male, version of reality.

A number of sociologists have shown persuasively how the content of news is affected by the cultural and professional norms of the editors and reporters who produce it. So today's journalists, when they take a moment to reflect, are perhaps less likely than those of the preceding generation to assume that news simply reflects some reality that is out there in the world waiting to be picked up and plunked onto the pages of newspapers or into the six o'clock news. And on those rare occasions that journalists tackle projects—like a major series on race issues—that force them to surface their assumptions, they learn firsthand (and often painfully) that their unspoken assumptions can affect profoundly both the selection and content of news.

Yet, on a day-to-day basis, most journalists still act as if news determined itself. In reality, as a result, most news is being determined by white men, or through the psychological prism of white men.

In an ethnographic study of Hispanic journalists, Don Heider (1996) vividly showed one of the dilemmas faced by minority journalists working in a television newsroom dominated by mainstream values: how to cover their own communities fairly, yet retain professional credibility in the eyes of their non-minority colleagues and bosses. "We're hired because we're different," observed one of the subjects, "because maybe we can speak a different language or whatever and so therefore you hired me. You also have to understand that we're going to have a different approach, perhaps."

Heider (1996, 10) observed, "But by acknowledging that ethnic stories are different, Hispanic journalists to some extent participate in a newsroom culture that identifies and categorizes stories about non-whites as 'different.'"

Several academic researchers have produced content analyses that attempt to show the connections between media content and the underlying mainstream assumptions that shape it. The 1970s struggle between the American Indian movement and U.S. authorities was the subject for a number of such studies. Baylor (1996) used the sociological tool of "frames" to analyze television coverage of the movement. Defining frames as "a set of ideas that interpret, define and give meaning to social and cultural phenomen[a]," Baylor posited that news gatekeepers tend to use "frames that are familiar and resonate with both themselves and the public." In the case of the Indian movement coverage, he found the dominant frame to be the Indian as "militant," surely not surprising given television news's need for visuals and conflict. Other frames included "civil rights" (Indians' struggle for a higher standard of living and more personal rights), "stereotype" (peace pipes, feathers, Indian dances), "factionalism" (quarrels between various Indian groups) and "treaty rights." The last was the one least used by television news people and the one most important to the Indians being covered.

Yet another problematic aspect of the coverage of minorities comes, ironically but probably inevitably, as a result of journalism aimed at improving the conditions of minorities. As Oscar Gandy (1994) pointed out,

> The use of headlines, statistics and graphic examples to attract the attention of politically involved white readers to an investigative report on racial discrimination, for example, contributes to the definition of African Americans as hapless victims at the same time that it leads blacks to overestimate the risks and oppression they actually face.

In sum: Despite years of efforts on the part of well-meaning journalists, white and minority, the content of news continues to distort our understanding of race issues because the content (1) is decided largely by white news managers and (2) is often implicitly produced with a white, middle-class audience in mind.

The challenge to both journalists and scholars who seek diverse and representative news coverage is to find ways to encourage new and different people to enter the newsrooms of the country, and to encourage the journalists already there to take new approaches to news.

A New Research Approach for Diversity

Four researchers* from the Missouri School of Journalism working in collaboration with journalists at three U.S. metropolitan newspapers and one major market television station conducted experimental studies from 1999 to 2001 aimed at developing new ways to cover minority communities. The study was based on two premises that grew out of an extensive review of the academic literature on minority coverage. The review showed that even though some diversity coverage through the years has been excellent, it has been episodic, dependent on the transient interests of individual editors and reporters. The premises were:

---

* Glen Cameron, Esther Thorson, and the authors.

1. Systematic measurement of coverage—a kind of continuing score-card—would help journalists know how they were doing and encourage continued efforts.
2. Systematic measurement of community attitudes would be a useful reality check to journalists, helping them to understand how their perceptions differed from those of the people they covered.

The idea was that social scientists working in close collaboration with journalists in the field could act as both measurers and catalysts of change. That is, by feeding useful and systematic data to working journalists, the researchers might encourage them to try new and perhaps better ways of doing their work. And by measuring the effects of changed approaches on content, the researchers could help the journalists understand what works.

The Research Project

The newsrooms were in a major, high-prestige newspaper in the West and two metropolitan newspapers and one television station in one urban area in the Midwest. All four were chosen because, by their reputation and all anecdotal evidence available to the researchers, they were among the best news organizations in their efforts to make both their newsrooms and their coverage more diverse, accurate and fair.

The western city was ethnically quite diverse, with a large Latino population, a significant though smaller African-American population and a relatively large Asian-American population comprising many different Asian national groups. The midwestern city was dramatically different in composition, with predominantly Anglos, a small African-American population and tiny Asian-American and American Indian populations.

For each news organization, the research team studied (1) staff attitudes toward diversity issues, both in the newsroom itself and in news coverage; (2) the content of the newspaper or newscast; and (3) community attitudes toward diversity coverage by the news organization. The triangulation was aimed at showing the "disconnects" between journalists' perceptions and the actual content of their news products, and between their perceptions and community perceptions. The hope was that these new data would provide the journalists with starting points for strategies for improved coverage.

Negotiating Participation Members of the research team met with members of management of each of the news organizations to get permission to conduct the research. One or more members of the research team had professional or personal contacts with one of the senior-level managers in each case. In some cases, agreement to participate came only after several meetings between the researchers and the media executives. In one case, a senior manager at the news organization initiated the request to participate.

Staff Studies   At each of the three newspapers studied, the research team began with qualitative in-depth surveys of staff. Nearly 100 staffers at the western newspaper were interviewed. At Midwestern Newspaper 1, 26 employees were interviewed. At Midwestern Newspaper 2, 39 were interviewed.

The purpose was twofold. The researchers wanted to assure the staff that they had not come with predetermined agendas other than to study the methods and results of diversity coverage and the possible ways to improve it. And the researchers hoped to use the journalists' own perceptions to help formulate the subsequent quantitative survey of staff.

The second phase of the newspaper staff studies was a quantitative survey. It was based in part on ideas generated by newspaper editors, in part by the results of the in-depth staff interviews, and in part by previous surveys of journalists on diversity issues. The respondents comprised 300 staff members of the western newspaper, 274 of Midwestern Newspaper 1, and 100 of Midwestern Newspaper 2.

At the television station, another qualitative strategy, suggested by station management, was used. Because television news staffs are smaller than those at newspapers and because the news hole is considerably smaller, the managers persuaded the researchers to study their newsroom in action. One member of the senior research team and two experienced doctoral student researchers spent two days in participant observation and interviews at the station.

Content Analyses   Exhaustive content analyses were conducted on randomly selected samples of each of the newspapers to determine differences in quantity and quality of coverage based on ethnicity, gender and age. All news and feature content in all sections of 28 editions of each paper were analyzed. More than 10,000 stories, photos, graphics, columns, and editorials were examined in the case of the western newspaper. For each of the midwestern papers, more than 6,000 separate content units were analyzed. The editions were randomly selected to create four "constructed" weeks of each paper. That is, four copies of an edition from each day of the week, spread out randomly throughout the year, were analyzed. The constructed-week approach aims to minimize peaks and valleys of coverage influenced by individual news events or by weekly patterns (Monday, slow news day; Saturday, coverage of Friday-night high school sports). Five graduate students and one professional journalist coded the data.

Community Surveys   Surveys of each of the two cities were conducted to assess community attitudes toward the news organizations' treatment of gender, ethnicity and age. Many of the questions used in the community survey instruments were identical to those used in the quantitative staff surveys. This technique was useful to editors and reporters who wanted to understand differences between their own and readers' perceptions of their efforts to provide diverse coverage. In the western city, 803 random-digit dialed individuals were interviewed (response rate was 51 percent). In the midwestern city, 1,071 individuals were interviewed (response rate was 56 percent).

The Feedback Loop   Members of the research team kept in contact with representatives of the news organizations throughout the research process. They reported on the progress of the various components of the research and consulted on both research strategies (wording on survey instruments, which staffers to interview, existing data the news organization could provide) and logistics (scheduling interviews, shipping newspapers for analysis, taping newscasts). One or more of the researchers also traveled to the research sites to report back to the journalists on the findings of the staff and community surveys and the content analyses. To reach as many of the staffers as possible, the researchers scheduled several reporting sessions at each site. Approximately two-dozen trips were made to both cities, and almost 20 presentations were made to newsroom staffs.

Findings

In the core project—the newsroom and community study—the goal was to learn about the diversity coverage of three newspapers and one television station through a systematic study of (1) the perceptions of journalists, (2) the perceptions of the community and (3) the contents themselves. Moreover, the researchers wanted to know whether they could find a collaborative, interactive research method that could improve both the quality of journalism and research.

At a macro level, results of the staff and community surveys and the content analyses were predictable. The staffs thought, for the most part, that they were trying very hard to produce better coverage of minorities—even though they conceded that they were still falling short in some areas. The journalists were opposed, for the most part, to anything suggesting diversity quotas in their coverage. They resisted the idea of separate news sections aimed at minorities, the elderly or women.

Citizens thought, for the most part, that journalists weren't trying nearly hard enough. They were quite open to the idea of sections aimed at specific population groups (except for whites, for whom they apparently saw no need). Many citizens failed to report the imbalances that were so dominantly exhibited in the content analyses. They did not realize that African Americans are mostly in the sports sections. They did not realize that males appeared four times more frequently than females in news stories, nor that there were three photos of men for every photo of a woman. They did not realize how children were stereotyped as victims or that teens were stereotyped as victims or perpetrators of crime.

The content analyses suggested the truth was somewhere in between. Some news organizations covered some minorities quite well relative to their number in the population. But for the most part, the picture of their communities offered by these high-quality news operations remains remarkably white, remarkably male, and remarkably upper middle class.

At a micro level, the researchers found many intriguing surprises. The data suggested many questions, some of which might be answered by further research. Why did the ethnicity and gender of journalists at one paper seem to have no effect on the diversity content of photographs and stories, while at another it seemed to make all the difference? Why did the culture at one news organization seem to encourage diversity coverage experimentation, while that of another seemed to discourage it? Why did one news organization have ample coverage of one minority group in its circulation area and so little coverage of another? Why were teenagers and children the unseen citizens in the news content— unless they appeared as criminals or victims? Why do the elderly, who constitute a significant proportion of newspaper subscribers and television news viewers, see so few of themselves in the news?

The study of one television newsroom did not produce sufficient data to draw large conclusions. But it suggested some of the special challenges to accurate coverage of diversity and minority issues for broadcast journalists. Minority coverage gets perhaps even shorter shrift in broadcast, despite well-meant staff efforts, because of the limited staff resources and the limited news holes. Without sustained insistence by top news managers, diversity coverage on television is unlikely to improve. Here, as with newspapers, probably only some external catalyst—ideally a research team—is likely to encourage measurable improvement over the long term.

The study provided many qualitative data and some quantitative data that suggest this collaborative, interactive social scientist/journalist approach to newsroom research can help improve both research and journalism. Here are three examples:

- The researchers were puzzled by the paucity of women and minorities in power positions in the photographs in one of the newspapers. Was there a conscious or unconscious effort on the part of photographers to see women and minorities as passive? When the data were presented to the photojournalists of the newspaper in question, they had a prosaic and more accurate explanation. The newspaper encouraged a high proportion of "mugshots"—pictures that show only the face, with no context. To the extent that they appeared in the paper at all, women and minorities tended to be in mug shots, not full-context photos. There was little opportunity, therefore, for them to appear in more active poses.
- Struck by the extent to which minorities appeared in their newspaper as criminals and victims, the journalists at one newspaper asked the researchers to come up with a way to produce composite profiles of various minorities as portrayed in the paper. In other words, what would the average reader of Newspaper X think a typical Asian American or African American looked like—occupation, income level, education level—based on the content of the newspaper? This idea could be a rich heuristic tool for journalists eager to provide more accurate coverage of minorities.
- Journalists at the television station, in trying to explain their challenges in providing balanced coverage of minorities, asked a question seldom heard by academics: Would the research team consider a more intensive approach? They opened up their newsroom to a team of researchers for two days—they had requested a week—to help the academics better understand the idiosyncratic nature of the

television news product. The result was a richer and more accurate view of the news process than would have resulted from the original, less invasive (and easier for the journalists) approach.

Within the confines of a three-year study, there was little opportunity for quantitative measurement of changes in content that might be related to the social scientist/journalist collaboration. At one of the newspapers, the researchers were able to measure the content of some sections a second time. The first analysis was conducted in the spring of 1998, before the newsroom and community studies and before any changes instituted in the newsroom. The second was conducted in the fall of 2000, after the newsroom's participation in the study. The representation of people of color and of women increased significantly during that period, with particularly impressive gains in the feature section, the section whose editors had concentrated hardest on finding ways to improve the diversity of content. Some other data were also encouraging. Male reporters used significantly more female sources in the "post-innovation" period, for example (Len-Rios et al. 2002).

Discussion

As a tool to improve journalism, we believe this collaborative, interactive research approach has enormous potential. By introducing friendly critics, in the form of social scientists, into the newsroom, it offers new tools to help journalists overcome many of the problems that have stalled most of the best-laid plans for improving coverage through the years. Here are its strengths:

- It gives journalists systematic feedback on how they're doing. The most exciting moments for both researchers and journalists came during the presentation of data on the content analyses. Content analyses are not flawless pictures of the news. But the new and more precise methods worked out for this study provided some concrete evidence that can be compared across time and across news organizations. They give journalists a yardstick to measure what impact, if any, their efforts are having.
- It doesn't require an entire staff to buy into reforms in order for the news organization to move ahead. It enables journalists themselves, singly or as groups, to come up with ideas for improvement. Ideas

for change can come from management or from reporters or editors. The presence of the research team—and its ability to measure the impact of changes—encouraged testing ideas on diversity coverage at each of the four news organizations in the study.
* It lends itself to sustained, continuing efforts to improve over time. Once baseline studies of content and community perceptions have been completed, news organizations can measure improvements (or lack of them) in both content and community or reader perception over time. That provides both the carrot and stick of objective assessment—thus getting beyond the stop-and-start nature of many diversity-improvement efforts.

In short, we believe that sustained research of this kind offers rich promise of effecting long-term improvement in the coverage of diversity. Indeed, we believe it is a model for improving the quality of journalistic processes and products across the board. Many excellent efforts to improve coverage have foundered after initial bursts of optimism and enthusiasm. This model provides two crucial ingredients for success that have been missing from those efforts:

1. *Continuing measurement* to provide motivation and the concrete data needed for midcourse corrections.
2. *A countervailing force*, in the form of a sympathetic research team, to mitigate against the natural tendency of the daily news process to overwhelm efforts at change and reform.

In a market economy, the key lever to change is the economic one. Many advocates of newsroom diversity through the years have emphasized that, in a capitalist society, the only sure-fire motivation for diversity is an improvement in the bottom line. Unfortunately, it is not easy to develop concrete measures that would show (or not show) that diversity improves the bottom line.

As members of the research team, we saw preliminary indications in our measures of content and community perception at the western research site that such connections might be made. A "Latino initiative" for improved coverage had measurable effect on the quality of the content of Latino coverage. Early signs were that Latinos in the community were picking up on the improvements—the kind of change that, when demonstrated through systematic measurement, can make significant differences in the bottom line.

Summary

For decades, the best intentions and efforts of both journalists and social scientists have not resulted in the improvements that they would like to see in the comprehensive coverage of all members of the communities covered. We believe the collaborative journalist/social scientist research model offers a way out of the inertia. The key elements to a nationwide improvement in coverage would be:

1. The ongoing, active collaboration of journalists and social scientists.

2. The double-feedback mechanism, in which research data encourage journalists to test new approaches and testing on the fly sharpens research techniques.

3. Continued, systematic measurement of news content and the perceptions of both journalists and the communities they cover.

The best promise of a truly transformative change in diversity coverage would be a national, multiyear, multisite collaboration of social scientists, journalists and funders engaged in such an enterprise. It could be a solution to the barrier that hinders well-meaning attempts at improvement—the inertia and cynicism (diversity fatigue, as some journalists call it) that often swamp meaningful long-term reform. Social science tools of measurement, if instituted in the newsroom on a continuing basis, could (1) provide the crucial motivation of systematic feedback to those journalists who want to try new approaches to coverage, (2) act as catalyst and reinforcement to encourage further reform experiments and (3) serve as a continuing goal toward improvement for both management and newsroom workers.

Resources

Internet

http://www.apme.com/   Associated Press Managing Editors (APME) is an association of U.S. and Canadian editors whose newspapers are members of the Associated Press.

http://www.asne.org/   The American Society of Newspaper Editors (ASNE) is the main organization of daily newspaper editors in the Americas.

http://www.rtnda.org/   The Radio-Television News Directors Association (RTNDA) is the world's largest professional organization, representing

local and network news executives in broadcasting, cable and other electronic media in more than 30 countries.

http://www.poynter.org/   The Poynter Institute is a school for journalists, future journalists, and teachers of journalism.

http://www.maynardije.org/   The Robert C. Maynard Institute for Journalism
Education (MIJE) helps the nation's news media reflect America's diversity in staffing, content and business operations.

http://www.missouri.edu/~jourcasr/   The Center for Advanced Social Research (CASR) is a nonprofit survey research organization affiliated with
the School of Journalism at the University of Missouri–Columbia.

http://newswatch.sfsu.edu/   News Watch is a project of the Center for Integration and Improvement of Journalism of the San Francisco State University Journalism Department.

Book

Missouri School of Journalism, University of Missouri–Columbia. 2000. *Guide
to Research on Race and News*. Columbia, Mo.

References

APME (Associated Press Managing Editors). 1996. Newsroom Diversity
Study. Minnesota Opinion Research Institute.

ASNE (American Society of Newspaper Editors). 2002. "Newsroom Employment Census." http://www.asne.org/

Baylor, T. 1996. "Media Framing of Movement Protest: The Case of American
Indian Protest." *Social Science Journal* 33:241-255.

Commission on the Freedom of the Press. 1947. *A Free and Responsible Press:
A General Report on Mass Communications: Newspapers, Radio, Mo-
tion Pictures, Magazines, and Books*, edited by Robert D. Leigh.
Chicago: University of Chicago Press.

Dates, J.L., and E.C. Pease. 1994. "Warping the World: Media's Mangled Images of Race." *Media Studies Journal* 8:89-96.

de Uriarte, Mercedes Lynn. 1994. "Exploring (and Exploding) the U.S. Media
Prism." *Media Studies Journal* 8:163-175.

Entman, R.M. 1992. "Blacks in the News: Television, Modern Racism, and
Cultural Change." *Journalism Quarterly* 69:341-361.

Fishman, Jessica, and Carolyn Marvin. 1998. "Pictures of Pain on Page One:
Examining Media Violence." Paper presented at the annual conference of
the International Communication Association, July 20-24, 1998,
Jerusalem, Israel.

Gandy, O.H. 1994. "From Bad to Worse: The Media's Framing of Race and Risk." *Media Studies Journal* 8:39-48.

Gans, Herbert J. 1980. *Deciding What's News.* New York: Vintage Books/Random House.

Gist, M. 1990. "Minorities in Media Imagery: A Social Cognitive Perspective on Journalistic Bias." *National Review of Journalism* 11:52-63.

Heider, Don. 1996. "Completeness and Exclusion in Journalism Ethics: An Ethnographic Case Study." *Journal of Mass Media Ethics* 11(1):4-15.

Herman, E.S., and N. Chomsky. 2002. *Manufacturing Consent: The Political Economy of the Mass Media,* 37-86. New York: Pantheon Books.

Len-Rios, Maria, Esther Thorson, Shelly Rodgers, and Doyle Yoon. 2002. "Analysis of News Content and Newsroom and Audience Perceptions of Ethnicity Coverage and Diversity in the Newsroom: Implications for Social Comparison Processes." Paper presented at the annual conference of the International Communication Association in 2002.

Lester, P.M., and R. Miller. 1996. "African American Pictorial Coverage in Four US Newspapers." Paper presented at the 1996 meeting of the Association for Education in Journalism and Mass Communication, Anaheim, California.

Lester, P.M., and R. Smith. 1990. "African American Photo Coverage in *Life, Newsweek* and *Time*, 1937-1988." *Journalism Quarterly* 67 (Spring): 128-136.

McGowan, William. 2001. *Coloring the News: How Crusading for Diversity Has Corrupted American Journalism.* San Francisco, Calif.: Encounter Books.

Missouri School of Journalism, University of Missouri–Columbia. 2000. *Guide to Research on Race and News.* Columbia, Mo.

RTNDA (Radio-Television News Directors Association). 2002. "2002 RTNDA/Ball State University Annual Survey." http://www.rtnda.org/research/

Tuchman, Gaye. 1971. "Objectivity as Strategic Ritual: An Examination of Newsmen's Notions of Objectivity." *American Journal of Sociology* 77:660.

CHAPTER 2

Women, Gender, and the Media

A Look at Representation, Coverage and Workplace Issues

Jan Colbert

Problems in Coverage of Gender Issues

The rise of the women's movement, beginning in the 1970s, was followed by attempts on the part of women (and some men) journalists to improve the coverage of women in the news. Now, more than three decades later, journalists who debate the coverage of gender issues often cannot agree on what questions to ask, let alone what the answers are.

In this chapter, we describe a variety of ways of framing the questions, some of which depart radically from traditional ways of looking at journalism. These (often mutually contradictory) approaches to journalism scholarship might help journalists rethink their approaches to the coverage of women. Indeed, because many of the theories challenge not just journalistic conventions but the very way journalists understand their world, they could be used to rethink the coverage of any group.

Journalism scholars have begun to confront the issues of sexism only in the last three decades. They have grabbed theories and frameworks from sociology, political science, history, and literature and are just beginning to speculate, develop and formulate frameworks that encompass issues of gender.

Few texts in journalism or women studies confront these issues. Not enough research in the area of women and the media has been done. By not defining categories and by not building a disciplinary framework, both academics and journalists have skirted the issues. Those interested in gender/media issues are just beginning to formulate their own theories—ones that make sense for the kinds of work they do.

Because the issues of women and journalism are so varied, the formation of frameworks and theories of understanding have understandably been based on a variety of ideas. There are cross-cultural theories, feminist theories, African-American theories and general journalism theories as well as other social science theories. Exploring the framework for these theories can help us figure out how they might apply to the practice of journalism.

Empirical Theories

Empirical theories say sexism and racism are biases that can be eliminated by stricter application of certain rules. The system works as it is; it just needs reform. Or MTV is a marvelous network; it just needs to take women more seriously.

Because these theories don't revolutionize the system, just reform it, many journalists like them. Journalists are, by nature or training, reformers: give them the rules and they will uncover and investigate those who don't follow them. This works well sometimes—for example, in covering crime or political corruption or spousal abuse. Most activists don't want to cut off the genitals of perpetrators; they just want the laws enforced fairly. The journalist's job is to get sources to ferret out the problems, explain the issues and propose solutions. Reform, not revolution.

Most journalists took the reformist approach covering the 30th anniversary of Title IX, the federal law banning sex discrimination in all schools that receive federal funding. Journalists explained the law and its ramifications, uses and abuses—how it works and doesn't work. While some journalists reported that some felt the law had run its course or could be modified, the focus was on reforming the law or violations of the laws, not rethinking the whole system.

In the media workplace, reformists would take a don't-rock-the-boat approach. Women should just move into the seats men have occupied for centuries and do the job the same way. In the 1980s women even wore outfits based on men's styles: suits (with high heels, of course), little ties and button-down shirts. Clothes represented some women's ideas that they were in the newsroom to perform as the great male journalists always had. They used white male standards in the creation and production of stories.

In the early years, women journalists were complimented for writing like a man, sounding like a man. We don't use those terms anymore. We use more gender-neutral words to say the same thing, for example, to write or broadcast "with authority." Sometimes "authority" disguises the sexist premise of the comments, and sometimes it just means authority. Do you see why this is hard to figure out?

For example, many news executives (men and women) say they don't have a female anchor because they haven't found one that has the "authoritative presentation" necessary for network television. Does this mean women's voices are not authoritative, or does it mean that right now there are no women who have this quality? Maybe we should ask Gwen Ifill or Judy Woodruff.

Standpoint Theories

There is nothing wrong with learning from the past, nothing wrong with studying antecedents in the rich and varied journalism tradition. This is important, even valuable. Questioning the methods and examining the premises of the past are also important. That is what the standpoint theorists attempt to do. These theories say that knowledge is always influenced by an individual's particular position at a specific time in history as well as a specific class, race and gender. Many of these theories do not reject universal truths altogether. They argue that universal systems can work, but not the way they are now defined.

For example, Jonathan Alter, *Newsweek* columnist, was writing about the career of Minnesota governor Jesse Ventura. In trying to explain Ventura's stands on various issues, including gender issues, Alter called Ventura "so September 10th." Ventura is the same person, but the world changes. Minnesotans are not willing to be so tolerant of a flamboyant, playful guy in the face of terrorism. This is an obvious example, easy for most journalists to figure out. The more time, space and money it takes to explain this kind of thing to readers and viewers the less chance they have of ever seeing it.

A classic example: For years journalists had reported that teenage pregnancy was a problem of ignorance. By the 1980s, story after story was still running with that framework: If young teens just knew the rudimentary rules of contraception, then the problem could be solved. Leon Dash, a writer for the *Washington Post*, decided to write his story by talking with the girls, learning about their families and understanding the complications of class and poverty. What he found surprised most readers: Young girls knew how not to get pregnant, they wanted to be pregnant. They needed someone to love. For them, pregnancy wasn't due to ignorance, it was due to poor self-esteem. The problem of teen pregnancy stayed the same, but the reasons why changed. Dash's efforts paid off; he helped change how readers understood teenage pregnancy. That kind of reporting takes time, money and space.

Another example: A journalist wants to do a story on the formation of a gay studies program at the local university. The proponents of the new program insist that the needs of gay students and scholars are not being met on campus; the opponents say gay-related content can be mainstreamed throughout the curriculum. The journalist is in a dilemma. Reformist solutions don't apply easily because of the interdisciplinary nature of the program. Gay issues run the gamut from literature to sociology to medicine and more.

From a standpoint theoretical framework, the story can be defined as this: New departments have the potential to work, and many have been added over the years, but the system needs to be re-evaluated to fit the new kind of program. Covering these stories proves difficult for reformist journalists because they don't offer rules and regulations that have been broken. They have to add context to the issue, causing editors and producers used to 10-inch and 45-second stories to cringe because it takes time and precious space to go beyond the conventional. To many editors and producers, context means the story becomes more expensive.

After Modernism

One cannot take on the task of understanding theoretical frameworks without facing this pervasive layer—the evolving, swirling and often times excruciatingly dense debate over postmodernism. The arguments, raging in all fields from architecture to sociology, weigh heavily in gender frameworks.

These theories reject the very possibility of universal truth about reality. They advocate a profound skepticism regarding the universal or universalizing claims about the existence, nature and powers of reason. They urge the development of a commitment to pluralism and the play of difference. Postmodernists can be revolutionaries, not just reformists.

We have been schooled and ingrained in the first two theories. We must confront the last one. Modernists, who taught us much of what we have learned and practiced, expect and create universal truths that form our world. Much of the popular research in journalism is premised on the modernist view—an expected way to solve problems, an objective way to present our work. Some of this makes sense. Journalism, by its very nature, requires a set of conventions to get the paper out, the news-cast on the air. If we had no rules, newspapers would come out every year or so. So the rules define the news in many ways. But women are "new" components to the news—for many years even against the rules—and we don't know how to fit women in except through our modernist vision.

Many feminists and postmodernists are confronting those ideas. Journalism critics and researchers, while slow to adopt the cliché-ridden phraseology of postmodernism, are confronting the postmodern issues of objectivity, semiotics, plurality, and meaning. Patricia Hill Collins (1991), a leading scholar and black feminist, argued: "Restructuring knowledge to be inclusive is a long-term historical process. Measuring one's place in the process against some assumed end point is a judgment that is as hierarchical as the systems of knowledge we are trying to change."

We need to define frameworks, theories and paths that can help the theories make sense in the study of women and journalism. Linda Hutcheon (1989) described postmodernism's distinctive character as a wholesale commitment to duplicity. In many ways it is an even-handed process because it reinforces as much as undermines and subverts the conventions and presuppositions it appears to challenge. Difference and eccentricity replace homogeneity and centrality as the focus of post-modern social analysis. Feminist, gay, Marxist, black, postcolonial, and poststructuralist theories have added to the historical scholars' foundations and have effected a merger of their concerns but now with a new focus: the investigation of the social and ideological production of meaning. Hutcheon said this appears to coincide with a general cultural awareness of the existence and power of systems of representation that does not reflect society as much as grant meaning and value to a particular interpretation of society.

Todd Gitlin (1980) said postmodernism "is a way of seeing, a view of the human spirit, and an attitude toward politics as well as culture. It self-consciously splices genres, attitudes, styles. It relishes the blurring forms (fiction/non-fiction), stances (straight/ironic), moods (violent/comic). It neither embraces nor criticizes, but beholds the world blankly, with a knowingness that dissolves feeling and commitment to irony."

However postmodernism is defined or critiqued, it has expanded the theoretical playing field. Postmodernism is inclusive. Victor Burgin (1986) said all cultural forms of representation (literary, visual, aural) in high art or the mass media are ideologically grounded. They cannot avoid involvement with social and political relations.

This is a messy way to do journalism. It involves task forces, brain-storming sessions, meetings and more meetings. Remember the time, space and money argument? Add to that the complaints of reporters who barely have time to cover their assignments. Now we want them to re-think the very premise of how they cover stories, re-examine the usual sources and even redefine topics they know.

For example, until the 1990s, journalists had often relegated day-care stories to the women's sections or light feature sections, if they were done at all. Now journalists see day-care issues as legal stories, corporate-benefit stories, political stories. But in the messy process of re-defining the stories in light of social change, newsroom managers had to rethink the typical placement, the presumed audience and the inherent content of day-care stories. In many towns, some of these stories became more relevant to readers and viewers than the city council stories that had led the news for years.

The Complexities Multiply

Add to the theoretical frameworks the isms of feminism—liberal feminism, cultural feminism, marxist/socialist feminism, radical feminism, lesbian feminism, black feminism, eco feminism, womanist, and many others. To understand gender issues you must understand feminist scholarship, which forms the basis for much of the critique on gender and journalism.

Most feminist theories can be divided into two categories: forms of liberal feminism and forms of radical feminism. *Liberal feminists* are willing to work within systems—political, social, religious, legal. *Radical feminists* believe systems are in need of radical change. As you can see from this explanation, many people can be radical feminists on some issues and liberal feminists on others. Collins (1991) said feminist views provide important but partial visions. These scholars should explore each other's work not just as a corrective of their own but to enhance the overall growth in an increasingly nonracist, nonhomophobic body of feminist thought.

bell hooks (1990) argued that feminists might adopt a linguistic shift from "I am a feminist" to "I advocate feminism," which implies one's commitment to a feminist viewpoint, but does not exclude the possibility of supporting other political movements.

To complicate the matter further, the very nature of gender falls into two camps. One is the idea that men and women are equal in all important aspects and are basically alike. This camp says men and women should have the same roles, rights, privileges, and opportunities. The other camp claims that men and women are essentially different, with separate roles and rights. Combine the previous theories with the specifics of gender and the controversies and complexities expand.

Researchers in any field can be myopic, flawed or irrelevant, so journalists must use the skills developed as journalists to measure the validity of what is being promoted. For years, feminists relied heavily on white, middle-class samples for the research they did (Gilligan 1982). Some say there has been a masculine bias in black social and political theory (Collins 1991). The problems are being rectified, but the existing literature has a chorus of powerful feminist critics.

Even the hierarchy of systems is controversial. Collins (1991) set up a framework with race, class and gender as simultaneous and intersecting systems. And beyond those primary systems there are many others—age, religion, sexual orientation, physical and mental ability, regionalism and ethnicity. Others define the hierarchy differently.

Many scholars complain about how gender issues are approached. The problem-based approach to gender issues tends to portray women primarily as victims with status as "other" (Collins 1991). The words of cross-culturalism are confusing—the very word minority marginalizes groups, making them seem outside the mainstream. It reinforces the idea that there is a majority culture. The word *nonwhite,* rarely seen in magazines or newspapers but often seen in research, assumes whites have universal experiences.

Sociologist bell hooks (1990) said there are cool words to talk about gender/cross-cultural issues and uncool words. The cool words (euphemisms) are *difference,* the *other, hegemony, ethnography.* The uncool words are *oppression, exploitation, domination, black/white.* She said to take racism/sexism seriously, one must consider the plight of underclass women of color, a vast majority of whom are black, and study the problems of displacement, profound alienation and despair. Her work explored the precarious choices academics have of studying the systems or doing something about the systems.

How Can Media Practitioners Best Overcome These Problems of Covering Gender?

Understanding the theoretical frameworks discussed in the first section of this chapter lays a conceptual foundation for thinking one's way out of some of the old traps of biased or inaccurate coverage. But how do we apply them in practice?

Tolerance for others is not the only solution when practicing journalism. We cannot promote we-are-the-world togetherness all the time. It is not yes-and-no, us-and-them polarities. Sometimes those looking for easy answers get caught up in the issues and nonissues of political correctness. Ideas within the rubric of women and journalism confound and confront status-quo thinking.

It comes as no surprise that the problems of sexism in contemporary journalism are hard to define and classify. But the complicated and controversial representations are easier to understand and overcome if the process and conventions that exist in journalism are considered.

Howard Becker's extensive study of journalistic conventions helps explain the motivations behind the editorial decision-making process. Conventions are old solutions to new problems, standardized formats that make order and predictability out of a variety of ways of doing things (Becker 1982). Herbert Gans (1979) has described the particular value system of American journalists and noted that the constraints of time and money contribute to a superficial presentation of the news.

Understanding the systemic limitations of journalism is helpful when a journalist runs into roadblocks on stories. Sometimes the block is impenetrable. At other times, change—usually slow—can happen. Disgruntled and lazy journalists often use these limitations as reasons for not doing important work. The smarter ones change what they can about the system but also realize that it is their own conventional ways of doing stories that might be the problem.

One way to get at these personal conventions is to look at a series of questions developed by Bob Steele (2002) of the Poynter Institute. Think of a story you have seen or read on a gender issue, assume you are the reporter and think about how you would answer these questions:

1. What do I know? What do I need to know?
2. What are my ethical concerns?
3. What is my journalistic purpose?
4. What organizational policies and professional guidelines should I consider?
5. How can I include other people, with different perspectives and diverse ideas, in the decision-making process?
6. Who are the stakeholders—those affected by my decision? What are their motivations? Which are legitimate?
7. What if the roles were reversed? How would I feel if I were in the shoes of one of the stakeholders?
8. What are the possible consequences of my actions? Short term? Long term?
9. What are my alternatives to maximize my truth-telling responsibility and minimize harm?
10. Can I clearly and fully justify my thinking and my decision? To my colleagues? To the stakeholders? To the public?

The first rule of medicine is do no harm. Apply it to journalism. The next step is to not be racist, not be sexist, not be classist—in clear, bureaucratic ways, through overt behavior. That's where the bureaucratic line is drawn. Beyond that, a critical paradigm that would help define the problems of representing class, race and gender in American journalism does not exist. A synthesis of current research on representation and other cross-cultural issues helped with the formulation of the following typology. These categories apply to textual and visual analysis.

1. Managed Multiculturalism

Managed multiculturalism is the quick-fix solution to covering issues of race, gender and class. It is the plea by the guilt-ridden editor to include an Asian-American woman in the photo illustration about a Fourth of July celebration, or the commitment by a magazine publisher to put together a 12-page supplement on where to find day care. While these stories fulfill the commendable goal of being inclusive, they lack the context to be meaningful.

These kinds of inclusions allow readers to be mesmerized by what Derrick Bell (1992) called the racial equality syndrome. These stories serve as reassurances that by "staying the course," racism/sexism will not become a permanent component of American life. Bell said that the goal of racial equality is, while comforting to many whites, more illusory than real for blacks. It certainly applies to women as well.

Some would contend that something is better than nothing, and that may be true. But the consistent use of inclusion without content or context poses a system of assimilation that reinforces the goal of sameness while ignoring cultural differences.

2. Sybaritic Portrayal

Sybaritic portrayal is the aesthetic exploitation that Benetton advertising/publishing epitomizes. It is also practiced by fashion magazines where art directors will design spread after spread with models in exotic locations luxuriating in front of the rice growers or beside beggars in Bombay.

In some of these stories, the reporter is seen as what bell hooks (1990) called privileged interpreters, cultural overseers, authoritative "others" claiming to know them better than they know themselves. The journalist is a member of the privileged group who interprets the reality of members of a less-powerful, exploited and oppressed group. hooks argued cultural products that encourage and romanticize relations rooted in domination dangerously undermine efforts to create critical consciousness of the need to eradicate racism.

An example of sybaritic multiculturalism at its best is *Colors,* "a magazine for and about the rest of the world" (http://www.benetton .com/colors/), hailed by its Benetton originators as an instrument that continues to gain strength on an international level in its ability to penetrate the dominions of race and gender. One issue includes a series on new monuments needed around the world, replacing the Statue of Liberty with Madonna's likeness, replacing the Buddha in Thailand with a golden Mickey Mouse, and adding a giant transparent condom in front of the Vatican. Oliviero Toscani, the original editorial director of the magazine as well as the creative mind behind some of the most criticized Benetton ads, loved the controversy. His communications director, Peter Fressola, said in an interview with Bernice Kanner (1992, 24) in *New York* magazine, "We've become a shorthand for multiculturalism and a progressive world view. Exploitation is not bad if there are no victims and some good is being served. It's art in the service of commerce, positioning Benetton as a concerned, socially active company in a modern global village—on the cutting edge."

One might look to the art critics who have consistently maligned some artists for the heartless vanities that underlie their high-minded gestures. *New York Times* critic Richard Woodward (1989) said these artists will serve up the poor as exotic fare for comfortable voyeurs. In looking to the practice of journalism today, Robert Craig (1992) said one finds much design ornamenting the waste. It often reveals an aesthetic based on profit, the conspicuous display of wealth, visual persuasion and false competition. It is often an aesthetic devoid of social value.

Stephen Heller and Julie Lasky (1993) confronted the historical part of this issue and argued that because of the pressure for alluring identities, journalists must "borrow" multicultural solutions and with that borrowing comes problems. Heller and Lasky pose questions for practitioners that help in the decision-making process of journalism:

1. Is the source treated with respect or disregard?
2. Must it be distorted in the act of assimilation or can it be ennobled?
3. Will it inspire appreciation in the audience in its newfound form, leading to a wider interest in or recognition of the culture that generated it?
4. Or has it been stolen surreptitiously, like an artifact from an ancient tomb, leading to nothing but the greater glory and the profit of the thief?
5. Is it possible for designers to communicate the value of history or culture they appropriate?

3. Polarized Approach

Polarized journalism is the easy solution of using simple black-and-white dichotomies that make issues simplistic—Burka-shrouded women on one side, miniskirted women on the other side of the page. These polarizations force stereotypes. Many scholars have complained that the placing of cultural critiques in a debate of good-versus-bad, this-versus-that effectively silences more complex critical dialog and often defines women as one-dimensional victims.

Larry Gross argued that this mainstream solution offers decision-makers an attractive ethical refuge because it appears to fulfill the basic ethical tenets of journalistic practice in the United States: objectivity and balance, particularly the latter. The logic seems to be that if you balance opposing views, then the truth can safely be assumed to "lie somewhere in between: and thus objectivity is achieved. The fatal flaw in this credo is that how one defines the 'responsible' extremes will determine where the center will appear to be" (Gross 1988, 189).

The most obvious example of this kind of journalism is seen in the coverage of reproductive rights, especially abortion, in the United States. If viewers or readers would have to explain this coverage using only media coverage, they would most probably explain that this divisive issue has divided American into pro-abortion or anti-abortion stances. Does this terminology make you nervous? Newsroom managers have spent months deciding what to call people who believe in the right to abortions (pro-abortion, pro-choice) and those who don't (anti-abortion, pro-life). This labeling then perpetuates the us-versus-them dichotomy. What falls between the cracks is the fact that most Americans don't believe the extremes of either position. Polarization makes for great copy, highlighting conflict and difference. The problem is that we often lose the reality of such complex issues.

4. Generic Multiculturalism

Generic multiculturalism is another easy answer for journalists. Rather than being criticized for using the wrong (racist, sexist, classist) images, we opt for the noncontroversial approach. It is the typographic cover that simply states "Beyond Gender," with a silhouette of a woman and man. It is the headline that says "Black and White" with a close-up on two hands, one black and one white. By not confronting the real images/words these stories need, the journalist effectively skirts any potential problem of racism, sexism or classism. Unfortunately, the journalist also deprives readers of the deep and comprehensive understanding they should expect from the story.

5. Analysis of What's Not There

The phrase "symbolic annihilation," coined by Larry Gross years ago, still is appropriate today. He argued that not all interests or points of view are equal; judgments are made constantly about exclusions and inclusions and these judgments broaden or narrow (mostly narrow) the spectrum of views presented.

Newspapers and magazines have made concerted efforts in the last 25 years to include more stories for, by and about women. All the journalism trade organizations have put time and money into studying the coverage of women's issues. But this is just the start of what needs to be done. And as reported in Chapter 1, even at the obvious level of the percentage of content about women, improvement has been limited.

Improving Coverage

What are some ways you as a journalist can help improve coverage of gender issues? Here are some answers found by scholars and journalists:

- Learn how to engage in critical dissent without alienating the newsroom.
- Check out "She Says: Women in the News," an Emmy–award winning, one-hour documentary that examines the impact of increasing numbers of women in decision-making positions in the news business. Some of the most accomplished journalists in the United States are interviewed.
- Look at the work of the media critics, like Noam Chomsky and Michael Parenti, who question the status quo.
- Peruse the lists of self-censored stories compiled each year and ask yourself how many of them include issues of gender. One good list is put together by Project Censored, an organization started by Carl Jensen.
- Enjoy the theater of journalism by questioning the conventions and working around and beyond the standard new agendas.
- Participate in persistent self-critique.
- Stay connected to the community by getting beyond the bars and movie theaters. The people you will meet will be great critics and marvelous sources.
- Make sure you are not writing great stories on poverty in the Galapagos Islands while ignoring the workplace and portrayal issues in your own backyard.
- Join the journalism trade associations that regularly confront the issues of gender. For example, Investigative Reporters and Editors, Inc., helps journalists get beyond the predictable stories and sources (www.IRE.org); JAWS (Journalism and Women Symposium) looks at workplace and portrayal issues of women; RTNDA (Radio and Television News Directors Association) holds conference sessions on gender issues in broadcasting. Many more listings are available on the Poynter Institute website (www.poynter.org).
- Read feminist journals and political magazines. Make sure you are reading across disciplines and across beliefs.
- Read the scholars and historians of women and journalism. For example, Kay Mills, 1988, *A Place in the News: From the Women's Pages to the Front Pages* (New York: Dodd, Mead); Judith Marlane, 1999, *Women in Television News Revisited* (Austin: University of Texas Press). Check out the JAWS website for a complete list.

Scholars of all races, genders and classes are just beginning to work with all these issues. June Jordan, a poet and black feminist scholar, said (Collins 1991, 28), "Factors of race, class and gender absolutely collapse whenever you try to use them as automatic concepts of connection. They serve well as indicators of commonly felt conflicts, but not as elements of connection. Much organizational grief could be avoided if people understood that partnership in misery does not necessarily provide for partnership for change. The ultimate connection cannot be the enemy. The ultimate connection must be the need that we find between us."

Understanding the problems with the coverage of gender is just the beginning. Scholars must strive to critique and analyze; journalists must be given the freedom to test new ideas in the trenches. While this seems obvious, many times the area of gender is marginalized in academia and the opportunity to test new ideas in the field is jeopardized by a bottom-line argument. Scholars and journalists must not only do groundbreaking work, but they must be able to sell it to their institutions. It's no wonder many journalists and scholars opt for the well-worn paths of predictability.

There are those who don't take the expected route. Their work can be recognized by its originality, its insight and its passion. Check the resource list to find the work of scholars and journalists who understand the complexities of gender and manage to get beyond the status quo.

Resources

Internet

http://www.ncrw.org/   National Council for Research on Women link.

http://www.smartgirl.com   SmartGirl is a website for girls founded by Isabel Walcott. Since 2001, the Institute for Research on Women and Gender at the University of Michigan is the "home" of SmartGirl.

http://www.nisc.com/factsheets/wri.htm   Women's Resources International (WRI) covers the core disciplines in Women's Studies to the latest scholarship in feminist research.

http://www.nisc.com/factsheets/qmsd.htm   Men's Studies Database (MSD) complements NISC's databases on Women's Studies and Sexual Diversity Studies and helps complete the spectrum of gender-engaged scholarship inside and outside academia.

http://www.umich.edu/~irwg/   The Institute for Research on Women and Gender provides stimulation, coordination and support for research on women and gender at the University of Michigan.

http://www.asanet.org/sections/rgcbiblio.html   Race, Gender, and Class Bibliography.

Research Paper

We, Gladys. 1993. "Cross-gender Communication in Cyberspace." A graduate
    paper, Department of Communication, Simon Fraser University, Burn-
    aby, British Columbia, Canada. http://eserver.org/feminism/cross-gen-
    der-comm.txt

Film

"She Says: Women in the News." 2002. Out of the Blue Films. Available from
    PBS Video, 1320 Braddock Place, Alexandria, VA, 22314-1698; 1-800-
    344-3337. An Emmy-award winning, one-hour documentary that exam-
    ines the impact of increasing numbers of women in decision-making
    positions in the news business. Accomplished U.S. journalists are inter-
    viewed.

References

Becker, Howard. 1982. *Art Worlds*. Berkeley: University of California Press.

Bell, Derrick. 1992. *Faces at the Bottom of the Well: The Permanence of
    Racism*. New York: Basic Books.

Burgin, Victor. 1986. *The End of Art Theory: Criticism and Postmodernity*. At-
    lantic Highlands, N.J.: Humanities Press International.

Collins, Patricia Hill. 1991. *Black Feminist Thought: Knowledge, Conscious-
    ness, and the Politics of Empowerment*. New York: Routledge.

Craig, Robert. 1992. "On the Aesthetics of Typographic Style." Unpublished
    paper given at the Association for Education in Journalism and Mass
    Communication Conference, Montreal, Canada.

Gans, Herbert. 1979. *Deciding What's News*. New York: Vintage.

Gerbner, George, and Larry Gross. 1976. "Living with Television: The Vio-
    lence Profile." *Journal of Communication* 26(2):173-199.

Gilligan, Carol. 1982. *In a Different Voice: Psychological Theory and Women's
    Development*. Cambridge, Mass.: Harvard University Press.

Gitlin, Todd. 1980. *The Whole World Is Watching: Mass Media and the Making
    and Unmaking of the New Left*. Berkeley: University of California Press.

Gross, Larry. 1988. "The Ethics of (Mis)representation." In *Image Ethics,* ed.
    L. Gross, J.K. Katz, and J. Ruby, 188-202. New York: Oxford Univer-
    sity Press.

Heller, Stephen, and Julie Lasky. 1993. *Borrowed Design: Use and Abuse of
    Historical Form*. New York: Van Nostrand Reinhold.

hooks, bell. 1990. *Yearning: Race, Gender and Cultural Politics*. Boston: South
    End Press.

Hutcheon, Linda. 1989. *The Politics of Postmodernism.* London: Routledge.

Kanner, Bernice. 1992. "Shock Value." *New York,* August 24.

Sillars, Malcolm. 1991. *Messages, Meaning and Culture: Approaches to Communication Criticism.* New York: Harper Collins.

Steele, Bob. 2002. "Be Prepared. Deal with Ethical Issues Before They Become Problems." Posted September 26 on www.poynter.org (search for A7130 or "Be Prepared").

Woodward, Richard. 1989. "Serving up the Poor as Exotic Fare for Voyeurs." *New York Times*, June 18.

CHAPTER 3

A Problematic Press

Latinos and the News

Mercedes Lynn de Uriarte

Early Roots of Coverage

Press coverage of Latinos,[1] both in the United States and in nations south of the border, remains badly flawed. For more than 150 years—since the mid-1800s when newspapers named the first U.S. foreign correspondents to cover the war with Mexico—accuracy has, more often than not, been distorted by a grid of xenophobia, racism, ignorance and social distance.[2] Although some journalists, especially those assigned by the alternative press, have sought to provide insightful, comprehensive reporting, they are too frequently outnumbered by mainstream reporters and editors or news directors who have not.

The earliest reporting about Mexicans and those who would become Mexican Americans began in a period of antagonism when deteriorating foreign relations between the United States and Mexico led to war in 1846 and the subsequent seizure of almost half of that nation's territory, which became the U.S. Southwest. The war, however, simply made more visible earlier resentments. Among other issues, Anglo-American colonists in Texas resented submitting to governance by people "to whom they believed themselves to be morally, intellectually and politically superior. ... The racial feeling indeed underlay Texan Mexican relations from the establishment of the first Anglo-American colony in 1821."[3]

Journalism, like much of the cultural perspective of the era, reflected the values of *manifest destiny*—a term coined by John O'Sullivan, editor of the *Democratic Review,* to describe the mood of the nation upon the annexation of Texas as the 28th state—a conviction of North American superiority. Only a few publications were able to assign the first foreign correspondents to cover the conflict. Their views of Mexico came to influence U.S. news perspective about Latin America as a whole and of U.S. Latinos in general. Images generated then were widely disseminated and linger in contemporary media and popular culture. They made their way into movies and eventually into a newer medium, television.

But in terms of communications history, the mid-1800s proved to be fascinating. The U.S.-Mexico conflict challenged the best technology of the day, making use of pony express, steamers, railroads and the recently developed, limited telegraph service. So efficient was the 2,000-mile communications link set up by cooperating newspapers seeking to contain cost that it often beat the military couriers and U.S. mail with news from the battle zones. In fact, President James K. Polk first learned of the U.S. triumph at Veracruz in a telegram from the publisher of the *Baltimore Sun.*[4] This first cooperative service became the Associated Press in 1849.

George Wilkins Kendall, editor-publisher of the *New Orleans Picayune*, stationed agents in strategic locations throughout the country, but he is regarded as the top correspondent of the time. About a dozen more reporters followed him into the field. Sixteen editors from various papers also went to Mexico as correspondents. The *New York Sun* sent the only woman war correspondent, the only one to report from behind the lines.[5] Still other journalists, found among the ranks of the military, sent reports to papers back home.[6]

Front-line reports supported U.S. involvement. They told of soldiers' reactions to Mexicans—suspicion and prejudice. Like all enemies, Mexicans were demeaned and scorned. Kendall, whose work appeared in a number of publications, wrote that Mexicans possessed "few of the instincts which govern other races. ... Brave, but often imprudent, [the Mexican soldier] exhibited a 'Mohammed fatalism derived from his Moorish kindred.'"[7] The contrasts between the lifestyles and farming practices in Mexico and the United States were perceived by journalists as substandard, the result of Spanish conquest, the mixing of races and the effect of the Catholic Church.

Even politicians and others who opposed the war fostered similar sentiments. Republican Congressman Columbus Delano of Ohio feared Americans would interact with an inferior people. Mexicans, he said on the House floor, "embrace all shades of color ... and a sad compound of Spanish, English, Indian and negro bloods," which he believed resulted "in the production of a slothful ignorant race of beings."[8] Rev. Theodore Parker, a leading Unitarian minister in Boston, condemned the war but called Mexicans "a wretched people, wretched in their origin, their history and character." The United States was destined to be, he said, "the steady advance of a superior race, with superior ideas and a better civilization ... wiser, more humane, more free and more manly."[9] All these conclusions further supported Anglo ideas of racial, moral and intellectual superiority.

Although Mexicans living in the conquered territory became Mexican Americans, their portrayals remained anchored in the hostile environment. Stereotypes constructed then still resonate in some contemporary news coverage.[10]

Segregation in the South excluded Mexicans and Mexican Americans, and social distance further fueled negative coverage of these groups when they were mentioned at all by "white" publications. However, unlike the case of African Americans, skin tone, class position (and an ability to speak groomed English) often differentiated some Latinos from those defined by prevailing pejorative terms and images. These individuals often made their way into mainstream society and then, based on their personal experience, claimed a validation of the American Dream. Because color and class cut across Latino populations, light-skinned members of these groups, who often were more economically secure, frequently claimed a Spanish ancestry to distinguish themselves from those "Mexicans," who were socially rejected. This accepted group experienced more intermarriage and more assimilation as well. For them, social distance and racial identity diminished. Outside others bore the brunt.

Moving Toward 20th-century Reform

Media treatment of Latinos differs historically from that of African Americans in some significant ways and parallels it in others. Both groups share the experience of exclusion, stereotype, a propensity of negative and distorted coverage, low participation in mainstream media and almost no opportunity themselves to provide alternative points of view. These problems plague Asian Americans and American Indians as well. All four groups have been victims of state oppression—conquest, slavery, internment, dispossession. All suffered portrayal by those, including journalists, who tried to rationalize this unjust treatment, so they were cast by media and popular culture as lesser—as stupid, criminal, lazy, unsanitary or otherwise undesirable. For at least two centuries, minority coverage, when provided, has been framed predominantly through the perspective of institutionalized racism.[11]

A long history of negative news about nations south of the border served to periodically refresh undesirable images of immigrant Americans and their descendants; little distinction was drawn between them.[12] A study of national magazine content between 1890 and 1970 by Félix Gutiérrez revealed a near-absence of coverage about Mexicans or Mexican Americans in the United States except when they were seen as a threat to society. Then coverage included pejorative labels: *zoot suiters, wetbacks, illegal aliens.*[13]

Moreover, recurring media campaigns against foreigners, immigrants and outsiders stimulated racial and ethnic hostilities. Although almost every publication has made serious errors in its minority coverage, gaffes by the largest and most influential remain most troublesome because they reach such a large immediate audience, and then are spread further in reprints. In one infamous case—that of the 1943 Zoot Suit Riots—the *Los Angeles Times* tilted its coverage to blame victims of repeated, organized attacks over several weeks by U.S. Navy men against Mexican-American youth in their own barrios (neighborhoods). Some of those assaulted were among the 100,000 Mexicans sent by Mexico to help in U.S. war defense projects. The term *zoot suiter* became linked to the image of crime and delinquency.

A sampling of coverage indicates repeated patterns. During the civil rights movement and the anti–Vietnam war protests of the 1960s, Latinos were again criminalized by press stereotype. Chicano activists organized protests as Latino military casualties climbed. Although Mexican Americans comprised 10 to 12 percent of the total Southwest population, they were 19 percent of those killed in battle. Texas Chicanos sustained 24 percent of the deaths. The second Annual Moratorium on August 29, 1971, drew an estimated 30,000 to Lincoln Park in East Los Angeles for picnics, music and speeches of war protestors. A minor incident between teenagers and a nearby storekeeper brought police, who surrounded the park and—wielding clubs—charged, trapping men, women and children.[14] Nearby, police surrounded the Silver Dollar Bar where a prominent Mexican-American reporter, Ruben Salazar, had just stopped in for a beer and conversation. Police reports of having issued orders to evacuate are contested. What is known is that they fired a 10-inch tear gas projectile into the bar, killing Salazar instantly. Here too, the *Los Angeles Times*, the paper of record, provided incomplete, negative information framed around police versions.[15]

In 1982, during a drive against undocumented immigration, then-President Ronald Reagan authorized the most extensive raid and deportation projects ever undertaken: Operation Jobs. During the next four months, front-page coverage provided little context about the role of cheap labor in this country. Reporters gave no demographic information about the sorts of jobs held, working conditions, the large number of workers paid below the minimum wage. Nor did they describe the deportation process or its gender-related issues. Despite the existence of a significant amount of scholarship about these matters, reporters quoted virtually no experts.

Those who fall outside mainstream America tend to be covered only during conflicts. This heightens negative impact, especially when there is no access to response. This pattern repeats in international coverage of Latin Americans. Both domestic and international news generally focuses on crime, corruption, incompetence, illegal immigration, violence and drug-related incidents.[16]

Today's negative press generalizations of minority youth as gang members and drug dealers also criminalize an entire group.[17] Indeed, coverage of the 1992 Los Angeles riots repeated old errors. For example, although the area most affected, South Central Los Angeles, was evenly divided between black and Latino residents, the press reported events only in terms of black-white conflict. When Latinos actions were reported occasionally on television news, they were sometimes referred to as illegal aliens without verification of residency status. Neighborhood leaders were seldom quoted, and those who were appeared in coverage after the neighborhood conflict ended.

There has been little opportunity for Latinos to report about themselves or to provide a counterbalanced point of view. As a result, miscomprehension and stereotypical imagery has been frequently reinforced. Social distance erected blinders to Latino contributions and accomplishments. Until the 1970s, this sector of the U.S. population remained largely invisible. Although there was a small group of Latino

publications in the United States by the mid-1800s that protested portrayals of Latinos in print and later in movies, they were ineffective in
changing the course of mainstream media. Mostly they addressed small,
enclave communities.

The Impact of Population Growth

The civil rights movement stimulated creative works among Latinos.
Poetry, murals and a growing body of literature addressed identity. As a
group, they asked in countless conferences, academic papers and conversations, "Who are we?" The dialogue increased as populations grew.
Even the terms by which majority Americans think of this group have
been mostly determined by others. In preparation for the 1980 census,
for example, the term *Hispanic* was coined by Washington bureaucrats
to identify anyone whose ancestry comes predominantly from Spanish-
speaking nations or territories. "As a result, millions of people of a variety of national backgrounds are put into a single 'ethnic' category, and
no allowance is made for their varied racial, class, linguistic, and gender
experiences."[18]

Nor are their political, historical, class or cultural realities taken into
account. For example, Mexico, the largest source of immigration from
south of the border, considers itself a mestizo nation,[19] acknowledging
that a majority of its citizens are also indigenous descendents. That heritage, which Central Americans also can claim, disappears under U.S.
labels. Moreover, no distinction is made between the descendants of
those who became citizens as a result of the U.S. absorbing parts of their
nation, the conquered, the colonized, recent immigrants, political
refugees, or those whose nations were occupied or made into depend-
encies by the United States. This masking of identity both contributes to
press myopia and is reinforced by media misrepresentation.

Regardless of terms used, the census provides a measure of the steady
growth of this population. Growth requires the press to recognize a need
for change. Between 1970 and 1990, the percentage of Latino population doubled from 4.5 to 9.0 percent for a total of 22 million, slightly
fewer than the 29.9 million blacks. By 2000, the census reported 32.8
million Latinos, representing 12.0 percent of the total U.S. population.
Nearly two-thirds (66.1 percent) of the Latinos were of Mexican origin,

14.5 percent were Central and South American, 9.0 percent were Puerto Rican, 4.0 percent were Cuban, and the remaining 6.4 percent were of other Hispanic origins. Forecasters advise that the Hispanic population will soon become the largest minority population and will double by 2020. Even so, these figures are an admitted undercount because of the difficulty in reaching much of this population. Before the middle of the 21st century, by the time today's college graduates are in midcareer, the nation will no longer have a majority population but will be evenly apportioned between minorities and Euro-American groups.

Charged with the responsibility of informing a self-governing citizenry, the press must cover its underrepresented communities more comprehensively and accurately. Because population size determines political representation to meet its social responsibility, newsmakers must overcome a number of obstacles, including ignorance, institutionalized racism and low minority participation in mainstream media. Both print and broadcast newsrooms remain virtually nonintegrated. In 2002, about 12 percent of all print journalists and 14 percent of all broadcast journalists are minorities. Limited interaction with minority populations intellectually, socially, politically or geographically largely determines press failure to provide accurate or representative coverage of minority groups. Additionally, the press has been slow to adopt reformist behaviors suggested by minorities, scholars or journalists.

The Push for Change

Newsroom change came slowly, painfully and was costly. At the end of World War II, considered the dawn of the contemporary press era, media employed few minority journalists. The press provided little coverage; what appeared was mostly negative. The Commission on Freedom of the Press (often referred to as the Hutchins Commission) took note in its three-year examination of media.

The commissioners defined the matter of minority coverage as an issue of ethics when they suggested five standards for social responsibility of the press in a democracy. After hearing from 58 witnesses, interviewing 225 more individuals, holding 17 conferences of two and three days, and reviewing 176 documents, they concluded that the press must be inclusive, comprehensive, interactive and representative. Above all, they said setting the first standard, the press must provide "a truthful, comprehensive account of the day's events in a context which gives them meaning."[20] Additionally, they believed that newspapers had to provide voice for all perspectives. Standard two called for "a forum for the exchange of comment and criticism."[21]

They also noted the power of stereotype. "People make decisions in large part in terms of favorable or unfavorable images," said the Hutchins Commission. "They relate fact and opinion to stereotypes. Today the motion picture, the radio, the book, the magazine, the newspaper, the comic strip are principal agents in creating and perpetuating these conventional conceptions. When the images they portray fail to present the social group truly, they tend to pervert judgment."[22] Standard three required "the projection of a representative picture of the constituent groups in the society." The commission said, "Responsible performance here simply means that the images repeated and emphasized be such as are in total representative of the social group as it is."[23] Had the press heeded these standards, much that was faulted about press coverage 20 years later by the National Advisory Commission on Civil Disorders (also known as the Kerner Commission) would have been eliminated.

On July 28, 1967, President Lyndon Johnson appointed the commission to advise the nation on causes for the more than 100 race riots in the United States that year. He asked that they answer three basic questions: What happened? Why did it happen? What can be done to keep it from happening again? Additionally, he asked, What was the role of the press?

The commission, headed by then-Governor of Illinois Otto Kerner, produced the most sweeping examination of race relations ever provided for the government. The commissioners devoted an entire chapter of their report to the role of the print and electronic press, including a comprehensive analysis of news content to media treatment of race riots in black neighborhoods during 1967. They found that the press had tried to do a balanced job, but that it had failed. "Our second and fundamental criticism is that the news media have failed to analyze and report adequately on racial problems in the United States and, as a related matter to meet the Negro's legitimate expectations in journalism."[24]

For the first time, a government report cited fair, balanced coverage of their communities and concerns as a *legitimate* minority expectation. "The media report and write from the standpoint of a white man's world," the commission found[25] and that perspective had social consequences. "By failing to portray the Negro as a matter of routine and in the context of the total society, the news media have, we believe, contributed to the black-white schism in this country."[26] A change of content was required. "Finally, the news media must publish newspapers and produce programs that recognize the existence and activities of the Negro, both as a Negro and as part of the community. It would be a contribution of inestimable importance to race relations in the United States simply to treat ordinary news about Negroes as news of other groups is now treated."[27] The report called for greater newsroom participation by blacks as a means to improve the news product. It proposed an institute of urban communications that would contribute "toward more balanced in-depth coverage and toward the hiring and training of more Negro personnel."[28] The commission believed that better general coverage was a press obligation for equitable race relations.

Despite the criticism of media treatment of blacks, the press was slow to respond. In fact, with the exception of the *New York Times*, which ran a news column by Joseph A. Loftus, no major media reported the commission's findings related to news coverage. The Loftus article, "News Media Found Lacking in Understanding of the Negro: Less Fault Seen in Riot Coverage Than in a 'White World Through White Eyes'—An Urban Press Institute Is Urged," appeared on the inside pages on Friday, March 1, 1968. Coming as it did on the cusp of the civil rights era, however, *The Report of the National Advisory Commission on Civil Disorders* eventually gained wider recognition. As one result, philanthropic organizations such as the Ford Foundation and the Gannett Foundation (now the Freedom Forum) funded studies and programs designed to generate more newsroom awareness of minority populations, perspectives and issues.

Organized calls for media reform came from Latinos as a result of the civil rights movement and the 1964 civil rights law, which for the first time added the weight of the legislation to the need for change. Pushed by Court rulings in license challenges brought by the United Church of Christ's Office of Communication on behalf of black audiences, the Federal Communications Commission (FCC) developed much more stringent guidelines for electronic media to qualify for broadcast licenses.[29] These reforms were also propelled, at least in part, by major studies that focused on press coverage of blacks, especially the most well known of these—the report of the Kerner Commission.

In 1967, when the Kerner Commission investigated, it found that 1 percent of all journalists were black, mostly working for the black press. No other minorities were reported. These findings and the momentum of the civil rights era also served as catalyst for the organization of minority journalists groups. The National Association of Black Journalists, leaders in advocacy, formed in 1975. The Asian American Journalist Association was organized in 1981. The National Association of Hispanic Journalists, which has emphasized career development, was established in 1984 as an outgrowth of the California Chicano News Media Association, which had formed in 1978. The Native American Journalists Association came together in 1984. The Kerner Commission report gained visibility as other minority journalists drew parallels between media treatment of blacks and themselves. Soon they cited it in their professional activities and in briefs filed in discrimination suits.

Because the FCC could address the question of coverage for electronic media, which uses public airwaves, minority citizens began to challenge license renewal applications by local stations. Integration of print newsrooms and change in network hiring would require actions through the Equal Employment Opportunities Commission. Newspapers do not use public resources; they are privately owned. So lawsuits became a major tool in the push for change to multicultural newsrooms. During the 1970s and 1980s all three major networks and several major mainstream newspapers, including the *New York Times, Los Angeles Times, Washington Post*, New York *Daily News* and the Associated Press faced discrimination suits.

In 1985, almost 20 years after the Kerner Commission's report, labor leader Bert Corona and eight Latino faculty members of California State University, Los Angeles (CSULA), filed a libel suit against the *Los Angeles Times*. They set precedent by citing institutionalized racism as contributory to libelous reporting. The plaintiffs claimed, among other charges, that "institutional racism of the *L.A. Times* is part of the corporate culture of reporters and editors responsible for the article, ... that the *L.A. Times* is pervasively biased against Hispanics because of the economic motives of the *L.A. Times* to attract a white middle-class suburban audience."[30] As one piece of evidence, the plaintiffs introduced a color-coded marketing strategy map, provided to display advertisers, that analyzed every aspect of Los Angeles residents except those in minority communities. Their primary residential sections of the city were left blank.

The case brought by the CSULA plaintiffs was the first to connect libel to discrimination. The case raised key arguments about the environment in which news is produced and, for the first time, attached a cost for racially biased inaccuracy. The lawsuit's contributions to the growing debate about press responsibility to minority populations, however, were limited by media reluctance to cover the story.

The Challenge of Inclusion

Ten years after the Kerner Commission published its findings, and after some significant settlements of discrimination suits, the American Society of Newspaper Editors (ASNE) began to seriously address the issue of participation. In 1978, the association called for newsroom parity by the year 2000. As part of that effort, in 1978 ASNE conducted the first of what would become an annual newsroom census. They found that 4 percent of all print journalists were minorities—a slight increase over the 1968 Kerner Commission findings when 1 percent of all journalists were black, mostly working on black publications. No other minorities then were a large enough group to count. Beginning in the 1980s, media institutes like the Poynter Institute for Media Studies, the Freedom Forum, the Institute for Journalism Education, the Pew Charitable Trust and other organizations provided workshops and seminars to improve coverage of minorities. Some newsrooms invited consultants to work with reporters and editors. But more than 50 years after the civil rights law, the press lags in its effectiveness.

The 2002 ASNE Newsroom Employment Census figures show 12.07 percent minority participation: 54,400 whites (a loss of 2,000 from the year before) and 6,600 minorities—the same number as the previous year. There were 2,984 blacks, 2,068 Latinos, 1,321 Asian Americans and 292 American Indians. The 2002 Radio and Television News Directors Association (RTNDA)/Ball State University Annual Survey of television newsrooms claimed 20.6 percent minority participation: 9.3 percent blacks, 7.7 percent Latinos, 3.1 percent Asian Americans and 0.5 percent American Indians. Radio included 4.1 percent blacks, 2.4 percent Latinos, 0.8 percent Asian Americans and 0.7 percent American Indians.

But studies consistently show a minority attrition rate, sometimes as high as 50 percent of the number hired each year leave the industry.[31] In 2001, for example, 698 minority journalists, nearly 100 more than hired that year, quit print newsrooms.

A 1992 study by the Freedom Forum found that the more educated the journalist, the more dissatisfied. "Some of the most sought after people in U.S. newsrooms," said an Associated Press Managing Editors study, "plan to leave them—the young, minorities and the well-educated."[32] Although exit interviews often cite money and advancement as reasons for departure, many minorities also say hostile environment and double standards drove them out. Surveys by both the National Association of Black Journalists and the International Women's Media Foundation indicate such problems. The gap between minority and white supervisor perception about newsroom environment also shows clearly. In fact, most newsrooms seek to retain traditional perspectives regardless of minority participation.

Lack of committed support for the ASNE goal by journalism educators contributed to slight change. In fact, of editorial journalism BA graduates in 1998, 77 percent were white, 10.3 percent African American (down from previous years), 6 percent Hispanic, 3 percent Asian American and 0.07 percent American Indian.[33] That year, two decades after setting a parity goal, ASNE was forced to admit failure and reconsider its target.

Predictably, participation by minorities in television news only creeps forward. Although television spokespeople insist that they seek to diversify newsrooms, they also cling to known deterrents. For example, they offer mostly unpaid summer internships. This virtually eliminates minority candidates, since the majority of minority students are on financial aid. Only by using student loans can these minorities take advantage of such opportunities. When these loans come from government money, federal funds subsidize private profit—interns become a conduit for federal funding of private enterprise.

The Role of Journalism Education

Throughout the two-decade effort to increase minority participation in newsrooms, corporate executives claimed an absence of qualified candidates. Those statements were largely dismissed by advocates as resistance to change, but a review of the number of journalism graduates[34] during the past two decades somewhat justifies that claim. However, graduate surveys also show that it takes minorities longer to find jobs. Minorities have shown some increase in number of BA degrees received in journalism, but figures remain low. In 1997, the year ASNE admitted that parity could not be reached, 2,896 minorites earned BA degrees, compared to 9,141 whites. In 1999, the figures were 2,724 and

10,083 respectively. This weak track record by the academic sector contributes significantly to the relatively small increase toward newsroom parity.

Much of this was due to slow reaction by journalism educators to the Kerner Commission report and results of the 1990 census. Not until 1984, seven years after ASNE set its parity goal, did the Accrediting Council for Education in Journalism and Mass Communication (ACE-JMC) set a standard requiring educators to seek minority inclusion. But good faith efforts were enough to claim compliance in the accreditation process. There followed a long period of much good faith and little advancement. In 1992, the standard was rewritten to require that "in course offerings across the curriculum, units must help prepare students to understand, cover, communicate with and relate to a multi-cultural, multi-ethnic, and multi-racial and otherwise diverse society."[35] By 1996, the ACEJMC was dismantling the requirements in favor of a softer version. In most journalism programs, the more comprehensive the material on minorities, the less apt the courses were to be required.[36]

Nevertheless, innovative professors sought ways to encourage change. Courses addressing mass media and minorities sprang up in many journalism departments to meet accreditation requirements. Historians like Carlos E. Cortez, journalist Félix Gutiérrez and Professor Clint Wilson II developed materials about Latino media. The first known course to teach non-minority aspiring journalists how to cover underrepresented communities, issues and individuals was pioneered by Mercedes Lynn de Uriarte, a Latina professor at the University of Texas (UT) at Austin in 1987. In 1989, a classroom laboratory publication for diverse voice began after a group of Mexican-American students, representing 15 campus organizations at UT Austin, complained that they were unable in two years of meetings to change racial content in the campus newspaper or to get coverage of minority events on campus. de Uriarte initiated a classroom publication, *Tejas*, with a broad spectrum of diverse voice. Later produced in the classroom of journalist Chuck Halloran, it won the 1996 Robert F. Kennedy Memorial Award for Outstanding Journalism. Other professors, including Federico Subervi and América Rodriguez taught students how to analyze broadcast content and produce better broadcast coverage of Latinos. Loup Langton, assistant professor of journalism and photography at the University of Miami, required diverse representation in materials developed for the *Missourian*, a daily produced on campus that serves as the local newspaper.

A major 2001 study of faculty diversity showed that curricular diversity draws minority faculty. Those universities like the University of Missouri that offered more multicultural courses were most successful at recruiting a diverse faculty.[37]

Latino Landmark Innovations

Meanwhile, innovators offered press alternatives. In 1976, Hugo Morales put together a volunteer group of farmworkers and others to begin a radio news and information service for low-income, hard-to-reach Latinos. *Radio Bilingue* (KSJV-FM) made its first broadcast from Fresno to audiences in California's San Joaquin Valley in 1980. By 1993, Morales had strung together five nonprofit radio stations from Stockton, California, to the border and created a satellite network that produces the only Spanish-language programming in public radio. Seventy-five commercial and public stations in the United States, Puerto Rico and Mexico pick them up. Committed to multicultural understanding, Morales includes programs in English, Hawaiian, Hmong, Mixtex, Portuguese, Tagalo and Tagalong.

In 1980, Charles A. Ericksen, a career journalist, Sebastiana Mendoza de Ericksen and Hector Ericksen Mendoza founded the Hispanic Link News Service, a syndicated service whose sole purpose promoted the work of Latino writers by making it accessible to mainstream publications. Soon thereafter, they published the *Hispanic Weekly Report*, a national newsweekly that covers Latino issues and established a press internship in which young journalists cut their teeth covering government, including participation at White House press conferences.

In 1993, *Latino USA* began a weekly half-hour news and culture program on National Public Radio. The idea, first conceived by a student at the University of Texas, was promoted by Dr. Rodolfo de la Garza, then-director the Center for Mexican American Studies (CMAS) at UT. Later, CMAS director Dr. Gilbert Cardenas, succeeded in acquiring funding, mostly from the Ford Foundation. María Martin soon became its first executive producer and conceptual director. By 2002, it aired on 15 stations in 31 states. In its first year, it won the Corporation of Public Broadcasting Silver Award for public affairs programming, four NPR Gold and four NPR Silver awards and 1994 and 1995 Guillermo Garcia

Marquez Awards for coverage of "Guatemala at the Crossroads." By 2002, it had won 15 prestigious press awards.

The Struggle for Representative Portrayal

But Latino media seems to operate in a parallel reality, with little modeling effect on mainstream media. The Latino struggle for media recognition continues. For more than 50 years, the press has had two key documents addressing the matter of representation, race, accuracy and responsibility. Both the Hutchins Commission and the Kerner Commission reports addressed racial coverage. Since 1970, numerous studies have shown press bias, distortion and inaccuracy when covering news related to minorities. Thus, both the models and the critiques are readily at hand. What has been lacking, perhaps, is the will.

The television news track record also begs improvement. A 1995 study by the National Association of Hispanic Journalists analyzed 12,000 stories aired the previous year. Only 1 percent focused on Latinos or Latino issues. Of these, 35 percent covered crime; 22 percent, affirmative action; and 22 percent, immigration. The next most frequent category was welfare. In other words, more than 75 percent of news about Latinos focused on problems consistently evoking negative images. In 2000, 16,000 news stories aired on ABC, CBS, NBC and CNN; 84 (half of 1 percent) were about Latinos. This is a drop from 1999, when they were 1.3 percent of all news stories—excluding those about Elián Gonzales.[38]

To cover Latinos in context, the press must overcome an ignorance of history. Although newsroom guidelines and press ethics codes abound, neither substitute for in-depth knowledge of the people being covered. Recognition of context requires a good grasp of history. Few schools or universities prepare students to perceive a multicultural America, or to understand that minority groups are neither a new phenomenon nor an insignificant one. But because they do not appear in depth in most textbooks and they still have not been acknowledged in society's major institutions, most minority groups remain invisible. Their past is unknown, their present obscured.

Journalists often approach news assignments about minorities as if the story began in the present tense. But unless all students become knowledgeable about the multicultural history of the nation, neither editors nor reporters—the majority of whom will be non-minorities for some years to come—will recognize context. For example, during the 1980s, as U.S. foreign policy supported a vicious military in El Salvador, its citizens fled. Many came to Los Angeles to move into the large Spanish-speaking neighborhoods there. *Los Angeles Times* reporters, who recognized the different lilt in Spanish, noticed different items on menus and in grocery stores and tried to sell that story to editors of the newspaper. Not until protests about deportation captured press attention did the influx of Salvadorans make the news. By then an estimated 250,000 individuals seeking refuge lived in L.A.

Much that has been labeled American has, in fact, its roots in minority experience. Today those contributions grow, as does a more diverse Latino population. Consider just a few aspects of this. The largest concentration of Latino population is in the Southwest, where Mexican Americans make up the greatest number, although Central Americans live in significant numbers in Los Angeles and San Francisco. The five cities with the largest Latino populations are New York, where the majority are Puerto Ricans; Los Angeles, where the biggest group is Mexican American; Miami, where Cuban Americans still outnumber Central Americans; Chicago, where Central Americans augment a large Mexican-American concentration; and San Antonio, where more than half the population is Mexican American.

Miami, with its large middle and upper-class Cuban population, has felt the impact of this culture, and through them has been revitalized after a long economic decline. Cuban Americans have created a thriving business community and are responsible for a significant international outreach to Latin American financial sectors. Immigration in the 1980s by Nicaraguans, Salvadorans and Haitians has provided a new Latino dimension to the area. Immigration of Haitians and Dominicans, for instance, augment the U.S. black Latino population, which has been mostly Puerto Rican (although Puerto Ricans include whites, mulattos and blacks as well). New York and Florida and, to a lesser extent, New Jersey have growing black Latino populations—perhaps the Latino group most ignored by media.

A thoughtful 1991 piece in the *Washington Post,* "Area's Black Hispanics Torn Between 2 Cultures," provided an overview of that population's identity concerns.[39] But few reporters cover racial diversity within Latino groups. Too often minority communities are still vulnerable to negative generalization. As recently as 1997, for example, the *New York Times* published a map of "Criminal Communities," labeling the seven

New York City areas in which individuals serving time had lived—all were virtually totally minority populated. There was no mention of the inequities of a justice system where a disproportionate number of minorities serve time for the same offenses than do whites.

Politics will increasingly be affected by minority voters. Although the majority of U.S. Latinos register as Democrats, most Cuban Americans are Republican. Latinos range across the economic spectrum, but the largest numbers are clustered in low-income situations; about half of all Latino children live below the poverty line. As a group, Latinos have the highest school dropout rates; infant mortality and health statistics for inner-city Latinos and African Americans rival third world records. U.S. Latino groups include distinctly different backgrounds and experiences. This diversity is largely unseen or misunderstood by the press, which also virtually ignores gender issues, reporting news as if it impacts men and women similarly. However, the *Los Angeles Times, Dallas Morning News* and *New York Times* have greatly improved immigration coverage, specifying not only the origin and distinctions between Latino migrants, but also the implications of these differences.

Media scholars consistently find that the press reports social problems from a middle-class/affluent perspective. But the majority of Latinos are not middle class. Moreover, the press fails to report issues in all lower-income neighborhoods in context. For example, education issues are consistently pinned to test scores. The press rarely mentions the distribution of educational resources and the implications of inadequate preparation on those tested. Although the role of the parent in the accomplishments of the child is sometimes noted, reporters usually fail to take family economic reality into account. Parents holding two jobs, for example, are rarely noted by the press. Yet their economic burden often eliminates their ability to supervise homework, attend Parent-Teacher Association meetings and to fulfill other middle-class roles. The press often labels them irresponsible or uncaring.

Calls for more minority newsroom participation, while useful, are often shortsighted because they imply that a genetic affinity will automatically eliminate coverage flaws. Women, for example, remain the most underrepresented of Latinos. Too often when women's issues are reported, they are generalized as if they are impacted in the same way as men. For example, deportation makes women far more vulnerable to violence and degradation than are men.

When other minorities are mentioned, the same problem emerges. Despite years of advancement, women are frequently overlooked; stories either categorize them as minorities and ignore gender, or categorize them as women and ignore race and ethnic identities. Rarer still is a breakdown of information about the diverse groups within these categories.

For example, a survey of affirmative action coverage during the first six months of 1998 in 15 major outlets (dailies, news weeklies and TV news) found that only seven of 314 stories (2 percent) focused on affirmative action's impact on women. Reporters, editors and news directors framed affirmative action stories as if they concerned only race and ethnicity. Women, the disabled and Vietnam vets were virtually never mentioned.

Of the 101 opinion columns published between January 1 and June 30, 1998, that dealt with affirmative action, only 22 were written by women. Just three of the 101 explored affirmative action's significance for women—and two of those three were written by women. The *Washington Post,* local paper of policy-makers in the nation's capital, ran 13 op-ed pieces on the subject. Only one had a female byline, but as a co-author.[40] Thus the press treatment of Latinos must be analyzed both as it affects the group as a whole and in its coverage of women. Certainly, this requires more inclusion.

However, any assumption that greater newsroom participation will change ideological narrowness deserves close scrutiny. Studies consistently show that socialization and routines tailor reporters to the traditional definitions of *objectivity.*[41] Minorities say that they often feel cramped between what editors expect and the more accurate reality they see.

Noting Improvements

There are, of course, increasing exceptions to the rather dismal track record indicated by the past. But at best, the record is checkered. Major mainstream papers in areas with large Latino populations generally do better jobs than before. More newspapers have undertaken minority coverage projects, reporting at least for a time, in-depth stories about communities and individuals not routinely included. In 1984, the *Los Angeles Times* and 16 of its journalists won a Pulitzer Prize for a series on Latinos. But after its own journalists publicly criticized the *Los Angeles Times* coverage of the 1992 civil disorder, the paper slowly began to systematically confront a need to improve content throughout the paper. By the late 1990s, a broad strategy—the Latino Initiative—sought to include Latinos in all segments of coverage throughout the paper. Other papers have adopted a similar model.

The *Los Angeles Times* and the *Dallas Morning News* perhaps lead all other news sites, providing not only consistent coverage, but also doing a much better job at covering Latino politics. These newspapers rank among the top five in the nation;[42] they are publications of record for California and Texas, respectively. Both have minority news staffs of at least 20 percent. Both have minorities, including Latinos, in top decision-making positions, thus mitigating problems of traditional gatekeeping. Frank del Olmo, a first-generation Mexican American, is Assistant Editor, the top-ranking minority at the *Los Angeles Times*. Gilbert Bailón, also Mexican American, holds the Managing Editor position at the *Dallas Morning News*. Both have strong multicultural staffs.

Generally, there is more Latino coverage than in the past. Reporting moves more often beyond crisis and culture to include the insightful stories as urged by the Kerner Commission. Affirmative action and immigration backlash have motivated closer examination of labor and education issues, though often too superficially. A comprehensive example of immigration reporting appeared in the *New York Times* on November 8, 1999, focusing on the diversity within current immigrant groups and the much larger size of these migrations than those of European-heritage groups in the past.

Diversity within diverse populations began gaining attention in the 1990s. In 1993, a Sunday magazine feature in the *San Jose Mercury News* explored multicultural families. This topic increased in importance as the 2000 census approached, re-igniting debate over categorization of identity. For the first time, individuals of more than one ancestry could identify themselves.

Accountability in education movements generated coverage of bilingualism, graduation rates and proficiency. So did affirmative action backlash, which fostered Propositions 187 and 200 in California and Proposition 209 in Washington, where the *Seattle Times* provided outstanding coverage for more than a year, including major investigative projects.[43]

More holidays are now better described—and flaws are more often reflective of Latino lack of knowledge as well as that of others. (For example, cinco de mayo is almost always incorrectly defined as a pivotal event in Mexican history. It actually is rarely celebrated there, as it marks one minor victory in a war lost to the French that led to four years of French occupation. Overlooked totally is the 1910 Revolution, which did have broad significance for and key participation by Mexican Americans.)

Better analysis is provided to counterbalance the mythology and consumerism of special events. In May 1998, an opinion piece by Vicky Gonzales in the *Los Angeles Times* noted the intense promotion and sale of alcohol at cinco de mayo celebrations. "But in stark contrast to 1862, the real message of Cinco de Mayo [sic] is getting lost in a blitz of marketing tactics of the alcoholic beverage industry."[44]

Mexican-American historian Rodolfo Acuña wrote:

> Recognizing that Latinos comprised the largest beer-drinking market in California, [beer companies] developed a plan to expand sales. According to Jim Hernández, director of the California Hispanic Commission on Alcoholism and Drug Abuse the brewers adopted what is now known as the "Budweiser strategy": make alcohol a staple of Latino life.[45]

They gave away calendars with Mexican icons, sponsored festivals and banquets.

> In 1985, leading Mexican-American national organizations—the National Council of La Raza, the American G.I. Forum and later, the League of United Latin American Citizens—signed an agreement with Coors Brewing company. In return for calling off a long-standing national boycott of Coors [over unfair labor practices] the company promised to give more than $350 million to Latino organizations. ... The deal was known widely among Chicanos as "Drink a Coors for La Raza."[46]

The best resource for better coverage is greater familiarity about Latinos and other minorities on the part of the press. This, of course, requires intellectual investment leading to intellectual diversity. Libraries, historians and other researchers can help provide direction. Narrowing social distance between reporters and editors would contribute to balance. Ongoing, pre-crisis press contact with nonprofits and other community organizations and leaders in the same way in which reporters and editors interact with non-minority contacts would help assure fairness.

Charged as it is, with the responsibility of informing a self-governing citizenry, the press must cover its underrepresented populations more comprehensively and accurately. To do so, it must overcome a number of obstacles, including ignorance, institutionalized racism and low minority participation in mainstream media. Limited interaction with minority populations intellectually, socially, politically or geographically largely determines the press's failure to provide accurate or representative coverage of minority groups.

However, there are indications that news organizations, led by the most prominent among them, make greater efforts to be inclusive and accurate. Since ASNE admitted failure of its parity goal, the press has undertaken a few projects designed to energize new, improved coverage. In May 1999, for example, ASNE began annual sponsorship of "Time Out for Diversity," a project that provided online guidelines and encouraged newsrooms to organize activities aimed at bettering the news product; 150 newsrooms and 43 Associated Press bureaus nationwide signed on as participants. In the more than half-century since the Hutchins Commission first provided standards for news media social responsibility, and in the more than 35 years since the Kerner Commission took the press to task, the press has taken only slow steps toward diversity.

Suggestions for Accurate Coverage

- Take college courses about minority history and life in the United States; the best are those that require research projects or papers.
- Become a regular user of alternative and ethnic presses.
- Spend time in the communities you cover; eat there, go to church, visit the schools, shop.
- Learn the history of the communities you cover.
- Get to know the official and informal leaders.
- Read all the posted notices on local bulletin boards everywhere, including laundromats.
- Become acquainted with all community mediums of communication.
- Volunteer to work with a community organization while you are in college.
- Continually diversify the Rolodex beyond standard source predictability.

Resources

Internet

http://www.nahj.org/   The National Association of Hispanic Journalists
http://clnet.ucr.edu/   Clnet's mission is building Chicana/o Latina/o Communities through networking.
http://lanic.utexas.edu/la/region/hispanic/   Hispanic/Latino Academic Resources
http://www.census.gov/pubinfo/www/hisphot1.html   Census Bureau Minority Links for Media, Hispanic Origin
http://www.utexas.edu/depts/cmas/   Center for Mexican American Studies at the University of Texas at Austin
http://www.ksg.harvard.edu/hjhp/   The Harvard Journal of Hispanic Policy
http://latino.si.edu/   Smithsonian Center for Latino Initiatives

Books, Articles and Manuscripts

Anders, Gigi. 2000. "Talking the Talk." *American Journalism Review* 22(9):30-37.
Martindale, Carolyn. 1993. *Pluralizing Journalism Education: A Multicultural Handbook*. Westport, Conn.: Greenwood Press.
Oboler, Suzanne. 1998. "Hispanics? That's What They Call Us." In *The Latino/a Condition: A Critical Reader,* ed. Richard Delgado and Jean Stefancic. New York: New York University Press.
de Uriarte, Mercedes Lynn. 1996. "Crossed Wires: U.S. Newspaper Construction of Outside 'Others'—the Case of Latinos." PhD diss., Yale University.
de Uriarte, Mercedes Lynn. 1998. "Texas Course Features Barrio as Story Source." *Journalism Educator* 43(2):78-79.

Notes

1. Although no term appropriately defines the group of individuals called Latinos or Hispanics in the United States, *Latinos* is preferred by many. It is the term preferred at the *Los Angeles Times*, for instance, as the more accurate of the two.

   Individuals in nations south of the border do not refer to themselves as Hispanic. In some places, the moniker *guachupin* for Spanish, like the term *gringo* for North Americans, is not one of endearment. Moreover, historically, in the United States, to be light skinned and "Spanish" was considered protection against being thought of as "Mexican" and discriminated against.

2. Mercedes Lynn de Uriarte, "Crossed Wires: U.S. Newspaper Constructions of Outside 'Others'—The Case of Latinos" (PhD diss., Yale University, 1996).

3. Eugene C. Barker, *Mexico and Texas, 1821–1835* (New York: Russell & Russell, 1965), 65, as quoted by Rodolfo Acuña in *Occupied America :A History of Chicano*, 3rd ed. (New York: Harper & Row, 1988), 9.

4. Edwin Emery and Michael Emery, *The Press and America: An Interpretive History of the Mass Media* (New Jersey: Prentice-Hall, 1984), 166.

5. Robert W. Johannsen, *To the Halls of the Montezumas: The Mexican War in the Imagination* (New York: Oxford University Press, 1985), 17-18.

6. Ibid., 149.

7. Ibid., 23.

8. Howard Zinn, *A People's History of the United States* (New York: Harper & Row, 1980), 206.

9. Ibid., 154.

10. de Uriarte, "Crossed Wires."

11. This conclusion has been drawn by a number of experts, including the National Advisory Commission on Civil Disorders (1968); Clint Wilson II and Felix Gutierrez, *Minorities and the Media: Diversity and the End of Mass Communication* (Beverly Hills: Sage Publications, 1985); Clint Wilson II and Felix Gutierrez, *Race, Multiculturalism and the Media: From Mass to Class Communication*, 2nd ed. (Thousand Oaks, CA: Sage Publications, 1995); Carolyn Martindale, *The White Press and Black America* (New York: Greenwood Press, 1996); and Janette L. Dates and William Barlow, *Split Image: African Americans in the Mass Media* (Washington, D.C.: Howard University Press, 1990).

12. de Uriarte, "Crossed Wires."

13. Félix Gutiérrez, "Making News: Media Coverage of Chicanos," *Agenda*, Vol.8, No. 6, November/December 1978, 21-22, as quoted by Clint Wilson II and Félix Gutiérrez in *Minorities and Media: Diversity and the End of Communication* (Beverly Hills, Calif.: Sage, 1985), 47.

14. Rodolfo Acuña, *Occupied America: A History of Chicanos*, 3rd ed. (New York: Harper & Row, 1988), 347.

15. Ibid., 348.

16. de Uriarte, "Crossed Wires," 191.

17. Ibid., 183-227.

18. Suzanne Oboler, "Hispanics? That's What They Call Us" in *The Latino/a: A Critical Reader* , ed. Richard Delgado and Jean Stefancic (New York: New York University Press, 1998), 3.

19. See State of the Union speeches by presidents of Mexico, and the work of Mexico's leading novelists, including Carlos Fuentes, and its renowned poet laureate Octavio Paz.

20. Commission on Freedom of the Press, *A Free and Responsible Press: A General Report on Mass Communications: Newspapers, Radio, Motion Pictures, Magazines, and Books*, ed. Robert D. Leigh (Chicago: University of Chicago Press, 1947), 21.

21. Ibid., 20.

22. Ibid., 26.

23. Ibid.

24. National Advisory Commission on Civil Disorders, *The Report of the National Advisory Commission on Civil Disorders* (New York: E.P Dutton, 1968), 364.

25. Ibid., 366.

26. Ibid., 383.

27. Ibid., 386.

28. Ibid.

29. Clint Wilson II and Félix Gutiérrez, *Race, Multiculturalism and the Media,* 2nd ed. (Thousand Oaks, Calif.: Sage, 1995), 219.

30. Bert Corona, Mary Mendez, Hector Soto-Perez, Mañuel de Ortega, Rudy Holguin, Miguel Dominguez, Jose Elizalde, Emilio Pulido Huiza and Norma de la Peña, Plaintiffs v. Times-Mirror Publishing Co., a California corporation, Claire Spiegel, DOES I-XXX, Inclusive, Defendants; Case # C418542, Superior Court of the State of California for the County of Los Angeles, April 1985.

31. ASNE, the Freedom Forum, the Institute for Journalism Education and the International Women's Media Foundation show a minority exodus in surveys conducted. Additionally, studies by the Associate Press Managing Editors and the Freedom Forum find greater journalist dissatisfaction than in the past.

32. Mark Fitzgerald, "Sinking Morale," *Editor & Publisher*, 2 October 1993, 26.

33. Lee Becker and Gerald Kosicki, "1998 Annual Survey of Journalism and Mass Communication Enrollments," James M. Cox Jr. Center for International Mass Communication Training and Research, University of Georgia.

34. Records kept on journalism graduates include those preparing for public relations and other than press roles, therefore these figures do not reflect only those preparing to enter newsrooms. That figure is lower. All journalism education programs do not respond to the survey inquiry, so even these figures may not be accurate.

35. Accrediting Council for Journalism Education and Mass Communication, "Accredited Journalism and Mass Communication Education,

1991-92," ACEJMC brochure, p. 15, and Standard 12 (revised 2 May 1992), University of Kansas, 1992.

36. Mercedes Lynn de Uriarte with Cristina Bodinger de Uriarte and Jose Luis Benavides, "Diversity Disconnects: From Classroom to Newsroom," Ford Foundation–sponsored report, 14 March 2003.

37. Lee B. Becker, Aswin Punathambekar and Jisu Huh, *Evaluating Outcomes of Diversification Initiatives: Stability and Change in Journalism & Mass Communication Faculties, 1989-1998* (Athens, Ga.: James M. Cox Center, University of Georgia, 2001).

38. These figures are drawn from annual reports by the Washington-based National Association of Hispanic Journalists.

39. Stephanie Griffith, "Area's Black Hispanics Torn Between 2 Cultures," *Washington Post*, 8 October 1991, sec. A, p. A1.

40. Janine Jackson, "Affirmative Action Coverage Ignores Women—and Discrimination," *Extra*, January/February 1999, 6-8.

41. Warren Breed, "Socialization in the Newsroom," Social Forces, Vol. 33, May 1955; Gayle Tuchmann, *Making News: A Study in the Construction of Reality* (New York: Free Press, 1978); Herbert Gans, *Deciding What's News* (New York: Vintage Books, 1979); Herbert Altschull, *Agents of Power: The Role of the News Media in Human Affairs,* 1st ed. (New York: Longerman, 1984); Herbert Altschull, *Agents of Power: The Media and Public Policy*, 2nd ed. (New York: Longerman, 1995); Edward Herman and Noam Chomsky, *Manufacturing Consent: The Political Economy of the Mass Media* (New York: Pantheon, 2002); Robert McChesney, *Rich Media, Poor Democracy* (Urbana and Chicago: University of Illinois, 1999); W. Lance Bennett, *News: The Politics of Illusion* (New York: Longerman, 2001); and Kristina Borjesson, ed., *Into the Buzzsaw: Leading Journalists Expose the Myth of a Free Press* (New York: Prometheus Books, 2002).

42. "America's Best Newspapers," *Columbia Journalism Review*, November/December 1999.

43. Mercedes Lynn de Uriarte, "Raising the Bar," *Newswatch*, Summer 1999.

44. Vicky Gonzales, "Ventura County Perspective: Cinco de Mayo's Message Lost in a Blitz of Alcohol Marketing; Increased Sales Mean More Problems for Neighborhoods and for Individuals. And In the Process, Sacred Cultural Icons are Demeaned," *Los Angeles Times*, Ventura County Edition, 2 May 1999.

45. Rodlofo Acuña, *Anything But Mexican: Chicanos in Contemporary Los Angeles* (New York: Verso, 1996), 31.

46. Ibid. Acuña further wrote (pp. 31-32): "Reports show that nearly one-third of Mexican-American males can be considered 'heavy' or 'problem drinkers.' The U.S. Department of Health and Human Services reports that Mexican born males in the United States have a 40% higher risk of death from alcohol-related cirrhosis of the liver than do white males."

CHAPTER 4

Media Coverage of Arabs and Arab Americans

Wesley G. Pippert

While I was in United Press International's (UPI) Jerusalem bureau in the 1980s, the Israeli Army occasionally would issue a typically terse statement saying, for instance, that a terrorist had thrown a Molotov cocktail at an Israeli civilian bus in Samaria, killing two and wounding three. Soon, the Palestine Press Service would call over a scratchy connection from East Jerusalem to report that a freedom fighter had thrown a Molotov cocktail at an Israeli bus in the occupied West Bank and "25 were killed or wounded."

The challenge was not how to write the initial story. This was simple: "A Palestinian threw a Molotov cocktail at an Israeli bus in the Occupied West Bank today, but reports varied on the number of casualties. The Israeli army said two were killed and three were wounded, but the Palestine Press Service …," etc.

The Israeli count was probably the *accurate* one. What was more difficult for me as a Western reporter to understand was the Arabs' use of hyperbole to communicate what they felt was truth. We will return to this matter later, but for the moment, we can state that it illustrates the lack of Western understanding about Arab culture.

The news coverage of the Arab world is shaped by a lack of information and insight, even ignorance. The result is that the average reader or viewer of broadcast news in the United States has a serious gap in knowledge about an important constituency in the world. The effect on relationships among peoples is destructive. When this gap in knowledge extends to policy-making, it becomes a matter of war and peace.

In this chapter we examine Western stereotypes of the Arab world, the causes of these stereotypes, and what both Westerners and Arabs can do about it. We will try to avoid discussing the seemingly all-consuming political dispute between the Arabs and Israel so as to permit us to focus more intently on the stereotypes of the Arabs themselves.

Stereotypes

Many people associate an Arab with a terrorist, a bearded man wearing a flowing robe and a *kafiye*, or a Bedouin wandering about the desert on a camel. These may be far-fetched examples, but variations of them exist in the minds of many people.

The stereotypes propagated by the mass media are numerous indeed. Tarik Allagany, a Saudi spokesman noting a distinction in the stereotypes, said that Arabs in the oil-rich Gulf area were lumped together as "rich and stumblebums," while those in Palestinian areas, Lebanon and Syria were pictured as terrorists.[1] In general, however, the stereotypes fall roughly into two categories: the inclination of the media to see the Arab world as a menacing monolith, and the typecasting of Arabs as rich and arrogant oil sheiks on the one hand or fanatical terrorists on the other.

Western popular culture feeds and reinforces such stereotypes. Jack G. Shaheen, an American of Lebanese descent, has studied extensively the characterization and stereotypes of Arabs on American television and movies. During the 1975-1976 TV season, he documented more than 100 programs, cartoons and documentaries, totaling more than nearly 200 episodes. He found:

> Television tends to perpetuate four basic myths about Arabs: they are all fabulously wealthy; they are barbaric and uncultured; they are sex maniacs with a penchant for white slavery; and they revel in acts of terrorism. Yet, just a little surface probing reveals that these notions are as false as the assertions that Blacks are lazy, Hispanics are dirty, Jews are greedy and Italians are criminals.[2]

Shaheen also reviewed more than 900 movies for stereotypes of Arabs in his book *Reel Bad Arabs: How Hollywood Vilifies a People*

(Northampton: Interlink Publishing, 2001). It is his contention that long after the movie industry changed its portrayal of other minority groups, the Arab is still pictured as brutal, heartless, uncivilized, and bent on terrorizing civilized Westerners.

The American-Arab Anti-Discrimination Committee, founded in 1980 by former Sen. James Abourezk, D-S.D., issues a biennial report on hate crimes and discrimination against Arab Americans. It also assembled a list of Arab stereotypes. For instance:

- *General*
  Epithets: A-rabs, camel-jockeys, towel-heads, sand-niggers
  "Sheik," harem, desert, camels, oasis, nomads, Bedouin, warriors, tribes, Foreign Legion
  Arab world as exotic arena where Western heroes have romantic adventures
  Arabian nights, genie, magic carpet, princess, evil vizier

- *Arab men*
  Oil sheiks, fabulously wealthy, lavish and wasteful spending, "buying up America"
  Greasy merchants, swarthy, dirty, greedy, unshaven, uneducated, dishonest, manipulative, incompetent
  Mad dictators, ruthless, violent, treacherous, barbaric, hatred of Jews/America/Christians, secret plots to destroy America
  Cruel, deceitful, overly emotional, irrational
  Abduct blonde Western women

- *Muslims*
  Fundamentalists, extremists, militants, fanatics, terrorists
  Cut off hands, oppress women
  jihad as "holy war"

- *Palestinians*
  Terrorists, who blow up airliners, seek to destroy Israel and "drive the Jews into the sea"
  "Good Arabs" as minor characters, passive, culturally Western, dramatically insignificant, subordinate to Western heroes, rarely the main character or action hero

- *Arab women*
  Oppressed by Arab men/Islam

Luxurious harem, scantily clad belly dancers; sensuous, beautiful
woman in love with Western hero, who rescues her from evil
Arab man
Confined to home, veils, head coverings, long robes; passive, une-
ducated, voiceless, faceless, characterless
Older women: hysterical, artificial grief in mourning rituals

These stereotypes play out in news coverage in often blatant but usually subtle ways.

These subtleties are found in the careless, unwitting use of words.
"Your terrorist is my freedom fighter," according to a well-worn example. But the examples are often less obvious. In 2002, geneticist Mazin
Qumsiyeh of Yale University wrote the Associated Press: "Why do you
consistently use the word 'targets' for Palestinian places attacked and
never for hitting Israeli targets (checkpoints, settlements, etc.)? Why is
hitting a Palestinian refugee camp, schools, ambulances, and police stations simply hitting 'targets'?"[3]

Other critics have noted that use of the word retaliation is reserved
most often for Israeli actions. In fact, however, about three times as
many Palestinians have died because of Israeli actions as the reverse.

The stereotypes, if anything, have gotten more grotesque during recent decades. Contrast what the novelist Graham Greene wrote in his
1932 novel, *Stamboul Train*. His protagonist Myatt observes:

But the world was altering, the desert was flowering; in stray corners here
and there, in western Europe, the Jew could show that other quality he
shared with the Arab, the quality of the princely host, who would wash the
feet of beggars and feed them from his own dish; sometimes he could cease
to be the enemy of the rich to become the friend of any poor man who
sought a roof in the name of God.

"The Arab World"

Many correspondents, and hence many people, mistakenly see the
Arab world as a unified whole, Islamic, and a massive patch of desert
sand with countless barrels of oil hidden underneath.

In fact, the 22 Arab nations have different characteristics. Their problems are dissimilar. The problems of Greater Cairo, a city of 15 million
that increases by hundreds, even thousands, every day, are far different

from the problems of a struggling kingdom like Jordan. Even within Arab nations there is great diversity. In the Hashemite Kingdom of Jordan, for instance, about 60 percent of the people are Palestinians. King Abdullah is not a Palestinian; hence, a majority of people in Jordan are of a different Arab background than their monarch.

Nowhere is the internal diversity more pronounced than in Lebanon, which has been torn by civil wars almost from its inception after World War II. Lebanon is so diverse that its top three offices—president, prime minister and speaker of the parliament—are divided legally among a Christian, a Suni Muslim and a Shiite Muslim. Gerald Nadler, a veteran correspondent in the Middle East, wrote with remarkable clarity about the complexity of Lebanon: "Most countries are a people before they become a nation, but Lebanon became a nation before it was a people."

Nor are Arabs and Muslims identical. About one Palestinian in six is Christian. The most populous Muslim countries in the world—Indonesia and Pakistan—are not Arab. And one nation that is commonly associated with the Arab world is not Arab at all: Iran, a country whose Persian people have a distinct language, culture and history.[4]

In stories about terrorism or conflict in the Middle East in the past, Israelis were identified by name, Arabs were not—although this is now changing. The stated reason was that Arab names are difficult to pronounce and to spell. But the not so subtle implication was that an Arab life was not so important as to deserve a name.

One occasionally hears the allegation that oil-rich Arabs are trying to buy up America. In fact, Arab investment in the United States is actually declining, according to one key measurement. In 1992, U.S. companies owned by residents in the Middle East less Israel accounted for a mere 0.053 percent of the U.S. gross domestic product; in 1999, the figure had declined to 0.025 percent.[5]

The Terrorist

The bombing of the World Trade Center in 1993 and then the events of September 11, 2001, stunned Americans. In Israel, bombings and suicide bombings have sharply increased. These events served to cement the stereotype of Arab as terrorist in the minds of many Americans.

Such attacks ought to be covered, of course. But often the other side of the attacks often consisted of little more than columnists and TV commentators raising the question, "Why do they hate us?" The question itself assumed a point of view.

These assumptions often implied that the Arabs were envious of American affluence and lifestyle. Or, like a TV evangelist, the assumptions implied that the Arab world feared the exporting of American hedonism as portrayed in the movies and on television.

Arabs, however, say they do not detest the American people. Rather, what they hate are U.S. policies in the Arab world and, of course, those dealing with Israel. As Adnan Aljadi, Washington bureau chief for the Kuwait News Agency, put it: "We do not hate the way the people in America live; we like the way people in America live."[6]

Causes

Nail A. Al-Jubeir, of the Embassy of Saudi Arabia in Washington, helped with press coverage during the 1991 Gulf War. He said in his experience the American correspondents fell into three camps: those who knew the military thoroughly; the handful, mostly print journalists, who knew about the culture of the Arab world; and the group who knew nothing about either the military or Arab culture.[7]

The war in Afghanistan showed vividly how American correspondents with little knowledge of politics or history or culture of the region "parachuted" in for a few days with the ostensibly pompous purpose of giving the American people a *definitive* report on what was going on. Often reporters depend on the clips of other reporters—and if the first reporters were wrong, then the reporter using those clips merely propagates the errors.

In short, correspondents covering the Middle East need to be prepared. Often such preparation is shallow and superficial.

I did an informal survey of the major American media that have permanent correspondents in the Middle East. The survey revealed that most, if not all, of the media had no systematic training program for the correspondents they send abroad. The *Los Angeles Times* said it did not have special training: "We throw people in the deep end." The Associated Press said that if its correspondent is going into a dangerous spot, it provides special training in first aid and lifesaving. Other respondents included the *Washington Post*, which gave correspondents a few months to prepare on an ad hoc basis, and the *Chicago Tribune*, whose training was "quite de facto," such as sending a reporter headed for Russia to live with a Russian family in Washington for four months.[8]

Television networks, which have greatly reduced the number of their bureaus in the Middle East in the last decade, have a particularly difficult job. They must explain complex developments in a complicated area in 90 seconds, and even that time slot may be lost if no pictures are available.

Jack Shaheen repeatedly emphasizes "the lack of presence" of correspondents of Arab descent in the Western news media. The cause and/or result, of course, is a basic lack of knowledge about the Arab world and Arab culture, especially religion.

Religion

The three great monotheistic religions are grounded in the Middle East. The most sacred spots in these religions are in Jerusalem. For Christianity, it is the Church of the Holy Sepulcher, said to be the site of the death and burial of Jesus. For the Jewish, it is the Western Wall, the remaining remnant of the Second Temple. And for Islam, it is the Dome of the Rock, said to be the place where the prophet Mohammed stepped off on his celestial journey.

We have noted that not \all Arabs are Muslims. So the problem for the reporter becomes twofold: first, in not understanding Islam, and second, in assuming that all Arabs are Muslims. For instance, Lebanon is 38 percent Christian and 58 percent Muslim.[9]

What many American reporters, trained in a nation in which there is a strict line drawn between Church and State, fail to see is the intimate relationship between Arab culture and religion. As Nail Al-Jubeir put it, "Everything in the Arab world revolves around faith. Social issues are strongly entrenched in religion."

Most Western reporters have some rudimentary knowledge of Christianity or Judaism, but few know about Islam. This lack of knowledge of Islam or its sacred scripture, the Koran, extends far beyond the press corps.

The central crisis of President Jimmy Carter's administration was the holding of the American hostages in Iran by a fundamentalist Islamic regime. In writing about this in his presidential memoirs, *Keeping Faith,* Carter himself never once drew a distinction between Shiite and Sunni Muslims, the basic two kinds of Muslims.

History

Long before the seminal events of recent centuries, Arabs had made their mark in intellectual pursuits. Their contribution of our numbering system is but one example.

In many ways World War I was the most important war of the 20th century. It drastically rearranged the geopolitical arrangement of the Middle East.

For 400 years the Ottoman Empire stretched from the Balkans to the Middle East. When World War I broke out, the Ottoman Empire entered on the side of Germany. Britain, however, sought to woo the Arabs away from the Axis onto the side of the Allies.

Then, one of the worst acts of perfidy and betrayal in history occurred. Sir Henry McMahon, the British High Commissioner in Egypt, exchanged a series of letters with Sharif Hussein in 1915 and 1916 in which Britain promised the Arab people their freedom after the war. In one note, McMahon said, "You may rest confident that Great Britain does not intend to conclude any peace treaty whatsoever, of which the freedom of the Arab peoples and their liberation from German and Turkish domination do not form an essential condition."[10]

But at almost the same time, the British and the French signed the 1916 Sykes-Picot Agreement, in which they carved up the Middle East into postwar colonies. The League of Nations confirmed their deal, giving the British mandates over Iraq, Palestine and Trans-Jordan, and giving the French, the northern coastal region of Lebanon and Turkey and North Africa.

Lawrence of Arabia tells one part of this story, in which a British officer named T.E. Lawrence headed a group of Arab fighters who captured Aqaba and marched on Damascus. It is clear their independence was part of the Arabs' motivation.

Another war had to occur before these Arab lands got their independence. One can only speculate how history would have been changed had the British kept their word, telling the Arabs that they would get all of their lands except perhaps for a sliver of land along the Mediterranean that would go to the Jewish people, whose gradually escalating return to the Holy Land had begun in the late 19th century.

Truth and Hyperbole

Perhaps in no other area is the Arab more misunderstood than in the matter of telling the truth.

We have spoken of the difference in detail in how Arabs reported the same incident. In past decades, C.L. Stevenson, a University of Michigan philosopher, articulated a theory of emotive truth. According to this theory, in short, emotional statements can be used to communicate truth.[11] This is a technique used by fiction writers and public speakers to help make a point. Someone once remarked to me that he found more truth in Tennessee Williams' play than in a statistical document from the federal government.

Occasionally a Palestinian boy would throw a stone at a passing bus. The Israeli army would clear out some olive trees along the ditch to increase visibility along the roadsides. The Palestinians would report that the Israelis had bulldozed 500 olive trees, when, in fact, the number might have been far fewer.

Thus, when Arabs say that 25 were killed or wounded or when they say 500 olive trees were cut away, they in effect are trying to communicate how deeply they feel about the incident. "If you knew how we feel," they might say, "then you would know why we say 25 were killed or wounded. Then maybe you will understand, too."

The purpose, then, is to communicate truth, not to exaggerate.

Solutions

The solution—and the responsibility—for inadequate coverage must be assumed by both the Arabs and the Western journalists.

The Western Response

It is very difficult to change attitudes and emotions. But, as we have noted, one way to begin is to be prepared. What is needed is an institutionalized, systematic approach for the training of American journalists who are going abroad or journalism students who aspire to go abroad.

I was assigned to the Middle East with little knowledge of the Arab world. My entire reporting career had been spent in U.S. state capitals and the nation's capital. So I prepared for my hasty transfer, which was accomplished in about two months. I made appointments at as many embassies of Middle Eastern countries as possible.

Soon after my colleagues and I arrived back in this country from the Middle East, I surveyed them about what they wished they had known before they went abroad. They said they wished they had studied a modern history of the region, courses in world economics and international trade, courses in cross-cultural relations (for instance, a course on Islam).

These studies could be arranged on most university campuses in a variety of ways, such as tutorials (for individual correspondents) or classes (for groups of correspondents) stretching over three days, three weeks, or even a full semester.

Another kind of preparation, as Adnan Aljadi expressed, is simply to travel more. Travel puts all people, whether journalists or not, in contact with other people and other cultures, and invariably people come away with a greater understanding and even affection for the countries they have visited.

We might summarize the preparation as follows:

- *Intellectual preparation.* We have noted the need for the study of history, political science, and economics but especially, in a place like the Middle East, a study of cross-cultural relations. The more we know, the better we understand.
- *Psychological preparation.* There is no place among foreign correspondents for persons with rigid views. They must be open-minded—not to abandon their own beliefs but to understand better other persons' beliefs that may differ from their own. They should be skeptical, yes, but not cynical.
- *Experience.* There simply is no substitute for experience as a journalist or for experience that comes from travel.

In *Buying the Night Flight: The Autobiography of a Woman Foreign Correspondent*, Georgie Anne Geyer put it all together. She wrote:

> Being a correspondent is very intricate work. You are called upon every moment and every day to exercise not only your romantic and adventurous propensities but also persistence and judgment. You have to judge constantly—facts and people and why people are telling you things—and you'd better be right. … You absolutely need a tough-minded reading of history, of political science, of anthropology, and of literature. Intuition and training mingle in this work.[12]

Equally important, perhaps, the news media need to recruit more reporters of Arab descent. One hero for all Arab journalists has been Helen Thomas—dean of White House correspondents and one of the most famous reporters in America—who is of Syrian descent. Another is Nora Boustany, who is on the *Washington Post* foreign desk.

Conversely, very few Arab nations have resident Western correspondents.

The Arab Response

The Arab journalists who report in the United States and other countries are a talented group whose skills and dedication match those of any American journalist. But in a criticism that the Arabs themselves would acknowledge, Arab journalists who report locally often lack basic journalistic skills and professionalism.

One result of the *intifada*, or uprising, that began in the Palestinian territories in the late 1980s was the birth of a cadre of increasingly professional Palestinian journalists.[13] This birthing began simply enough. The *intifada* revealed the need for American publications and networks to have better sources in the occupied territories rather than to depend on the Israeli army for information. So, in day-to-day contact with the American papers and networks, Palestinian stringers learned a lot about professional Western standards.

The Arab nations also must extend more freedom to their own journalists. This is imperative. Journalists are subjected to harsh restrictions. Unfortunately, these restrictions are worsening more than they are being alleviated. According to *The Annual Survey of Press Freedom 2002*,[14] Egypt, the Palestinian Authority, Lebanon, Saudi Arabia and Syria all have been rated NF (not free). During the previous year, however, that freedom actually diminished in Egypt, the Palestinian Authority, Lebanon and Syria. Only Saudi Arabia showed improvement. Jordan, considered PF (partly free), remained constant in that classification.

The survey found the government in Egypt proposed new repressive amendments to Egypt's document laws. It said that small media outlets were pressured by authorities to provide favorable coverage of Yasser Arafat and the Palestinian Authority, and official Palestinian television and radio were government mouthpieces. In Syria and Jordan, with new youthful leaders who have succeeded their aged fathers, conditions were not better. In Syria, President Bashar al-Assad had relaxed controls over the news media and promised further reforms, but in 2001 he announced a slowdown in the reform process.

In Jordan, under King Abdullah, laws directly or indirectly restricting press freedom have led to considerable self-censorship. In 2001, in a move attributed to the defense against terrorism, an amendment to the penal code provided for the trial of publishers and journalists in state security courts.

So the problem is manifold. This calls for both institutional and personal changes, none of which will be simple or easy to obtain. Governments—both Western and Middle Eastern—must get rid of the formal barriers to understanding that are created by censorship and governmental manipulation or control. The media in the Western world and the Middle East that send correspondents to each other's world must take more care in preparing the journalists to understand the cultures and peoples they will be covering.

On the personal level, few American correspondents have extensive knowledge of the Arab world, on the one hand, and few American correspondents get on-the-scene information about the Arab world. Few Arabs have infiltrated the Western media, and those who report from their own countries are handicapped by lack of training and the difficulty of coverage in lands where there is little freedom of the press.

Further, the more deep-seated and personal biases of both Western and Arab reporters interfere with understanding. These prejudices may be the most difficult to eradicate. As Lt. Cable said in the song "Carefully Taught" in the 1949 Rodgers-Hammerstein musical *South Pacific*:

> You've got to be taught to hate and fear,
> You've got to be taught from year to year …
> You've got to be taught to be afraid of people
> Whose eyes are oddly made,
> And people whose skin is a different shade.
> You've got to be carefully taught,
> You've got to be taught before it's too late …

Resources

Internet

http://www.arabji.com/ArabGovt/ArabLeague.htm   The Arab League
http://www.freep.com/jobspage/arabs/index.htm   "100 Questions and Answers About Arab Americans: A Journalist's Guide," Detroit Free Press

http://www.students.washington.edu/ledger/current/what_you_see_is_what_you
   _get.htm   Anderson, Karie. "What You See Is What You Get? Flirting
   With Inferential Racism, Electronic News Media Consistently Misrepre-
   sents Arabs."

Books

Hashem, M.E. 1995. "Coverage of Arabs in Two Leading U.S. News Maga-
   zines: *Time* and *Newsweek*." In *The U.S. Media and the Middle East: Im-
   age and Perception,* ed. Y. Kamalipour, 151-162. Westport, Conn.:
   Greenwood Press.
Kamalipour, Yahya R., ed. 1995. *The U.S. Media and the Middle East: Image
   and Perception.* Westport, Conn.: Greenwood Press.
Liebes, Tamar. 1997. *Reporting the Arab-Israeli Conflict: How Hegemony
   Works.* London and New York: Routledge.
Shaheen, Jack G. 2001. *Reel Bad Arabs: How Hollywood Vilifies a People.*
   Northampton, Mass.: Interlink Publishing.
Sussman, Leonard R., and Karin Deutsch Karlekar, eds. 2002. *A Target in the
   War on Terrorism? The Annual Survey of Press Freedom 2002.* New
   York: Freedom House.

Notes

1. Tarik Allagany, information supervisor, Royal Embassy of Saudi Arabia,
   Washington, D.C.; interview with author, 15 May 2002.
2. Jack G. Shaheen, *The TV Arab* (Bowling Green: Bowling Green State
   University Popular Press, 1984), 4.
3. Qumsiyeh is the co-founder of AL-AWDA, the Palestinian Right to Return Coalition. He posted his letter on the website: http://www.miftah
   .org/Display.cfm?DocId=641&CategoryId=18
4. Statistics from Arab League Mission, Washington, D.C.
5. Statistics from the U.S. Commerce Department International Investment
   Division.
6. Adnan Aljadi, Washington bureau chief Kuwait News Agency, Washington, D.C.; interview with author, 15 May 2002.
7. Nail A. Al-Jubeir, deputy director of information for congressional affair,
   Embassy of Saudi Arabia, Washington, D.C.; interview with author, 15
   May 2002.
8. This survey was conducted in the summer of 2001.
9. League of Arab States, 1100 17th Street, N.W., Washington, DC 20036.
10. The perfidy is described in Wesley G. Pippert, *Land of Promise, Land of
    Strife* (Waco: Word, 1988), 127-133.

11. This theory is described in William K. Frankena, *Ethics*, 2nd ed. (Englewood Cliffs: Prentice-Hall, 1973), 106.

12. Georgie Anne Geyer, *Buying the Night Flight: The Autobiography of a Woman Foreign Correspondent* (Chicago: University of Chicago, 1996), 56.

13. Various conversations with Nicolas Tatro, former Beirut and Jerusalem bureau chief for the Associated Press, now AP deputy foreign editor; Howard Goller, deputy editor, Reuters world desk in London, and former news editor, Reuters Jerusalem bureau; and Ed Cody, *Washington Post* Middle East editor.

14. Leonard R. Sussman and Karin Deutsch Karlekar, eds., *A Target in the War on Terrorism? The Annual Survey of Press Freedom 2002* (New York: Freedom House, 2002).

CHAPTER 5

The Changing Coverage of Gay, Lesbian, Bisexual and Transgendered Communities

Leroy Aarons

Gay issues are hot buttons in the 21st century because they reflect deep currents of change in our society that go beyond sexual orientation. To do their jobs well, journalists need to understand this.

For example, the scalding debate within the Catholic Church about priests who sexually abused children broadened rapidly to encompass the issue of whether homosexuals should be banned from the priesthood, pinpointing the complex intersection of sexuality and religion in American life. (See "Getting the Numbers Right—or Wrong" below.)

Gay and lesbian issues affect politics and governing. In late June 2002, front-page stories heralded the fact that President Bush would sign a bill allowing death benefits to be paid to domestic partners of firefighters and police officers who die in the line of duty. This extended a federal death benefit to same-sex couples for the first time.

This is remarkable for the sign of progress it represents for gays and lesbians who petition for recognition and acceptance. Just as interesting, perhaps more, is the unexpected and intriguing course the Bush administration has taken with regard to gay and lesbian issues. Bush, the church-bred friend of the political right, has taken a markedly middle of the road, if not subtly friendly, posture toward gay expectations and ambitions.

What does this mean? Is it a nod to political clout of gay conservatives? Is it the influence of Vice President Dick Cheney, whose daughter is openly lesbian? While we see the "dots" in this mosaic showing up in the press, there is very little information connecting the dots to reveal the big picture.

Therein lies a theme of this chapter: Gay and lesbian issues (and bisexual and transgender issues to round out the latest terminology), like so many other issues in today's media, are too often treated as stand-alone curiosities at the expense of history and context.

In this instance, the *Washington Post* has been almost alone in chronicling and following the Bush administration's ambivalent actions vis-à-vis the gay movement.

The radically conservative John Ashcroft amazed media watchers in April 2002 with an incredibly gay-friendly, though little-noted, statement the day that a federal grand jury indicted, under the national hate crimes act, the alleged killer of a lesbian couple. The *Washington Post*, for which it was a local story, played it front page on Thursday, April 11, 2002.[1]

The *Post* continued to monitor the administration's mixed signals as Gay Pride Month approached in 2002, including a comprehensive piece on the subject by Ellen Nakashima, "With Gay Pride, a Balancing Act," on June 12. The story balanced a variety of views without resorting to shrill rhetoric by extremes on either side. It began: "'We're Here! We're Career!' That's the slogan of this year's annual gay pride celebration at the Justice Department. That would be the same Justice Department led by Attorney General John D. Ashcroft, a social conservative. Ashcroft has publicly equated homosexuality with sin. ... Ashcroft's No. 2, Deputy Attorney General Larry D. Thompson, will speak at the [event]."

On the other hand, the article notes, President Bush turned down for the second straight year a government employee group's request to issue a proclamation recognizing June as Gay and Lesbian Pride Month. (As the *Hartford Courant* noted in an editorial July 5, the president in the previous six months had issued proclamations designating National African American History Month, Irish-American Heritage Month, Women's History Month, Older Americans Month and Asian-Pacific American Heritage Month.)

Documenting other you're in–you're out signals, the *Washington Post* article quoted David Smith of the Human Rights Campaign gay lobby saying that the Bush administration has been "very careful not to take any significant steps backward" in its treatment of gay citizens and federal workers. "It has not rescinded Clinton's executive orders banning sexual orientation as a criterion in establishing security clearances, and barring discrimination in the nonuniform federal workforce on the basis of sexual orientation."

Still left unexplained, however, other than a reference to the balancing act of politics, is the context: What effect exactly is the administration's internal machinations in this arena having on policy and legislation about gay issues, such as the extension of hate crime law, and why?

Those dots still needed connecting.

In another area, who would have thought that the September 11, 2001, tragedy would have a so-called gay angle? It had many, in fact.

Exactly four weeks after September 11, the AP ran a picture worldwide of an unidentified sailor preparing to load a bomb onto a plane designated for the Taliban, bearing the graffiti legend, "High Jack This, Fags." A single picture taken tens of thousands of miles away created a stir at home.

Following protests, a day later AP removed it from the wires. The service even apologized, as did the US Navy for letting it happen.[2] These rapid apologies were unusual in the context of what not so long ago was common usage in all news media.

In the 24 hours it circulated, the "High Jack" (note misspelling) photo crossed the desk of many newsrooms, several of which printed it, as did many websites. Let's suppose a green young photo editor on a small-town paper received it just before deadline. Might she have run it? If so, where and how big? She might have asked, just how bad taste is the word *fag*—kids in high school used it all the time. But what if the words had been "High Jack This, N-word"? When AP withdrew the picture should the news outlets that used it have printed a retraction?

These are questions any working journalist can be and is called on to answer no matter how small the market, and usually without much prep time.

Presumably most readers would get it that *fag* is the N-word to gays and lesbians. On the other hand—*queer*, once only pejorative, has become a rallying cry for young activists. Regardless of one's personal views, it is important for journalists to know in what terms minorities choose to be known by or addressed. And it is not always simple. (See the Appendix.)

Many younger journalists are probably unaware of the history of so-called fag headlines and stories: that prior to the late 1960s the media commonly referred to gays in stories and headlines as perverts, pansies, fairies, queers, sissies, dykes, queens, degenerates, inverts, and so on.

That's what I grew up with in the mid-20th century. Most of the time, there was no visible manifestation of homosexuality. An adolescent discovering his or her sexual orientation felt as if a transparent isolation capsule had descended around him or her. No Will and Grace, no MTV, no gay youth centers, no pro-gay lobbyists, no known gay legislators. What clues there were in the media, in books or in "polite" conversation referred to pitiful limp-wristed caricatures or in the case of lesbians, man-hating butches, outcasts condemned by law, family and God.

Of course, every adolescent at one time or another feels like the outsider. These displacements are sharpened for people of color, the disabled, and those identified as the "other" in society. Interestingly, a person of color subjected to insults or prejudice most often has available the supporting embraces of family, relatives and peers to whom to turn for solace. For gays, lesbians, transgenders and bisexuals especially at a young age—this is rarely an option, even to this day. Coming out to one's family and friends remains an agonizing and slow process, with the very real risk of rejection.

Nonetheless, the world has come a long way in five decades (see "A Brief Chronology" below). Visibility of and tolerance for alternative sexual orientation have expanded at seemingly warp speed, especially since the 1969 "rebellion" at Stonewall, a gay bar in New York, that is the benchmark of the beginning of the modern gay civil rights movement.

Gay issues have moved from virtual invisibility to the front pages and lead news stories in broadcast. They show up in films, music, situation comedies on TV, and on the Internet. An oft-quoted quip has it that Oscar Wilde's "love that cannot speak its name" has become the love that can't stop shouting.

So these issues impinge on American life with far higher octane than accounted for by the numbers of people who share that orientation. Why? One reason is the issues cross all lines, touching on millions of lives: gay, lesbian, transgender and bisexuals, but also—with so many coming out—their straight friends, families, relatives, employers, employees, colleagues, fellow students. It crosses all barriers of demographics, race, religion, geography and age.

No journalist will be on the job long without confronting tough ethical and journalistic decisions regarding public understanding of these issues. Who gets to decide what is moral or immoral? How do we define or redefine family in the modern era? What, for example, is becoming of the traditional role gender has played in our culture as women demand equal autonomy, shifting the modality of the dominant male, the submissive female? Gay people no longer accept stereotypes that feed the contempt of a society that recognized only rigid separation of gender roles.

The point is these issues require more, not less, sophisticated coverage, analysis and explanation.

The news business doesn't always connect the dots. Even further behind is journalism education, which is turning out graduates who are largely clueless about the long and varied history of sexual difference, the subtleties of the gay movement and the impact it's had on religion, education, entertainment, advertising, and the news industry itself. No less an institution than the Medill School of Journalism at Northwestern University, always listed in the top 10, recently took the time to examine the syllabi of its 58 course offerings: Only two mentioned sexual orientation.[3]

Another significant story given less than in-depth treatment is the phenomenon of those gays and lesbians who are creating a wide variety of unorthodox family models. In 2002 the American Academy of Pediatrics announced a new policy urging its 55,000 physician members to support adoption by same-sex parents, that is, the partner of a biological parent should have a legal right to adopt and co-parent his partner's child. If you have any idea how conservative medical associations have been, this is another astounding measure of the growth of public acceptance.

I read the news remembering that in my 20s and 30s, struggling with sexual identity, the notion of parenting a child was in the realm of science fiction. Three decades later it is happening all over; gay men and lesbians are parenting and raising children through donors, co-parenting agreements, through surrogates, through adoption, and even foster care. It has come to be called the "gaybe" boom.

These new families make a darn good story, as is obvious to anyone who has followed Rosie O'Donnell's coming out as a lesbian adoptive mother and defending the right of gay people to raise families. Celebrity-focused news media readily pick up on the Rosie angles. But they rarely convey that the adoption–donor–foster care dynamic is part of a larger picture—the changing meaning of relationship, marriage and family in contemporary society.

One can choose to zero in on family, but the same dynamic applies to the church, the military, health care, the workplace, the schools, the Boy

Scouts and neighborhood social networks. All organizations are grappling with issues of sexual orientation and gender identity. These are issues that defy the common boundaries of interaction we once thought we all agreed on.

The challenge for journalists and journalism educators is to examine preconceptions when tackling these issues, and, most important, *be prepared with history and context to recognize rhetoric when they see it on any side of the issue, to make sense, not stereotype, out of some very complicated situations.*

Let's examine some of the ways the press handles contemporary issues to see which perspectives are honored, which ignored.

Lack of History and Context, and Plain Old Ignorance

The debate over gays and lesbians in our society has burned its way into the American psyche as a result of the attention it has received in the media. The emphasis, however, has been more on "debate" than "society," partly because the news business goes for both the moment and the momentous in its coverage. There are sufficient signs that for all the information beamed at the public in print, on the airwaves, by satellite, cable and Internet, there remains a lot of plain old ignorance.

For example, *Time* magazine's coverage of gays and lesbians has ranged from blatantly derisive from the 1930s to the 1960s to increasingly sensitive and balanced from the 1970s to the 1990s. In spring of 1997, *Time* ran a cover of a broadly smiling Ellen DeGeneres with the headline "Yep! I'm Gay!" Yet, less than a year later in its special issue devoted to a review of *Time*'s 75 years of publication, it failed to include a single story about the gay and lesbian movement or the AIDS epidemic. (Its one nod in the gay direction was mention of playwright Tony Kushner's "Angels in America.") When queried, a *Time* editor said the gay topic was on the storyboard but had somehow got lost in the shuffle.[4]

In 1998, the nation recoiled in horror at the savage murder of college student Matthew Shepard in Laramie, Wyoming. The national press did a superb job of covering the big story, but seemed at a loss about what to do next. At the *Washington Post*, then-new managing editor Steve Coll acknowledged he did not know where to take the story until one of his gay reporters informed him that gay bashing up to and including murder existed in Washington, D.C., and elsewhere in America.[5] Coll assigned him, and the reporter turned out an excellent piece with history and context that the *Post* bannered across page 1.

Something similar happened at the *Dallas Morning News* (DMN), Texas's largest and most powerful newspaper. Unlike the *Post*, the DMN did not staff the Wyoming story. It used wire copy. When many days had passed with no staff-written effort, Robert Dodge, reporter in the paper's Washington, D.C., bureau, sent urgent e-mails to several editors. Texas is notorious for a series of brutal gay murders committed in the last decade. Dodge, who is gay, urged a localized story; one was assigned to a gay reporter, whose piece ran at the top of page 1.

Does this mean only gay and lesbian journalists are capable of finding and writing these stories? Of course not. But too often they are the primary resource for managers who remain uncognizant of the complexities of the story and the need for advance preparation. (For an example of first-rate advance planning, see "Be Prepared" below.)

We've already discussed the "high jack" photo above, but there were other September 11 stories with gay angles that eluded the media for days and weeks. Mark Bingham was an apparent hero on United Flight 93 on which passengers overwhelmed terrorists, diverting the plane from its potential target and forcing it down in Somerset, Pennsylvania, at the loss of all on board. Bingham was well known in his hometown of San Francisco as a leading player in a gay Rugby league. The local *Chronicle*'s first story failed to note the connection to the gay community. The omission was more than rectified in subsequent editions, including the story of Bingham's funeral, at which Sen. John McCain spoke. But it took the Associated Press, which had produced hundreds of features about the victims of September 11, nearly seven weeks to catch up to the Mark Bingham story.

Its excellent feature, headlined "Gay Hero Emerges from Hijacking," moved on the very day that Robert Dodge, president of the National Lesbian and Gay Journalists Association (NGLJA), was taking to task some news organizations for "selectively" choosing "to obscure or ignore the sexual orientation of some of those who also lost their lives."

The admonition came after Moral Majority's Rev. Jerry Falwell had pronounced that the September 11 terror was cosmic punishment for America's tolerance of immorality, including homosexuality along with abortion and the ACLU. His widely reported and condemned remarks—which he later tried to recant—slandered the gay firefighters, passengers, office workers, airline stewards, and at least one pilot who died in the tragedy, as well as hundreds of their survivors.

Dodge noted in his letter to the press, "Some journalists may embrace outdated ideas that identifying openly gay and lesbian heroes will cast a negative image on their memory. This decision is based on a presumption that being gay or lesbian is wrong [and] is the same as withholding information about the spouse, children and other features about the heterosexual heroes."

Good point, and still a delicate one. Journalists ought to respect privacy and wishes of family. Being "outed" can still cost jobs and sometimes family. But increasingly, as acceptance and protections grow, gay and lesbian people want to be identified *in the full context of their lives.* Thus a recent story in *USA Today* about retired couples that spend their time RV-ing or trucking about the country included an interview with a pair of women described simply as "a couple" and that was that. It's called *mainstreaming* and is welcomed by gay and lesbian people weary of being depicted solely as victims or problem cases.

In the extraordinary events of September 11, America took to its heart the dead heroes and heroines and their surviving families. That some of these were identified gay, lesbian, bisexual or transgendered contributed to the national bonding that was one of the good legacies of the tragedy.

Reversion to Old Habits: Tabloid Journalism

During the dramatic saga of serial killer Andrew Cunanan in 1997, many television and newspaper outlets pulled out all stops on sensation and unattributed speculation. Cunanan's five-person killing spree included famed fashion designer Gianni Versace. Cunanan's short notoriety ended with his own suicide. His motivations were not known and may never be. Nonetheless, throughout the press characterized him as a "gay serial killer," linking his murderous rage to his gayness, although two of his five victims were not gay. It depicted him as a creature of the so-called gay underworld of "boy-toys," drugs and hustling, although no motive connection was ever made. The press repeatedly reported that he was a murderously angry AIDS victim (in fact, he was uninfected). Even Tom Brokaw resorted to flip alliteration, dubbing Cunanan the "homicidal homosexual." In the heat of a juicy breaking story, the media reverted to old stereotypes, sacrificing careful, solid reporting and neutral language.

More odious was a news magazine feature on the FOX network the following year. The "FOX Files," a kind of "60 Minutes" for bottom-scramblers, presented a segment purporting to expose the seamy side of gay life. With images of gay "gang" thugs, transgender hookers on crack, "circuit" riders on Ecstasy, and low-life glory-hole parlors, the segment would have been laughingly over the top were it not feeding the picture many Americans are led to believe typifies gay people.

GLAAD, the gay movement's anti-defamation league, was so alarmed that it undertook an investigation of each element of the program's content. It concluded:

> GLAAD does not object to journalists examining controversial or even problematic issues facing the lesbian, gay, bisexual and transgender community. However, as a journalistic agency, FOX has a responsibility to provide its viewership with the context in which their stories occur. ...
>
> Imagine a segment on a small part of the African-American community [that] explores gang violence, a high frequency of drug use and sexual behavior that puts members of the community at greater risk for HIV infection. In spite of a few passing comments defensively noting that this doesn't represent the "entire" community . . . the story serves up a scathing look at the African-American community and culture. No commentary is provided by leaders within the community, and no mention is made of comparative statistics. . . . How far would this segment get in a newsroom? Not far.
>
> While organizations such as GLAAD offered themselves as resources to the producers, *FOX Files* did not see fit to allow . . . the opportunity to challenge assertions made. . . . Balance was not FOX's concern—ratings were.[6]

The role of ratings in television news cannot be overestimated—just watch the crime-violence-scandal content of most late-night local news broadcasts, including the commercial break promos. Gay issues are no exception. They often show up in these programs as lurid sequences during sweeps weeks. Many local stations across the country have cloned a surefire formula to snare audiences: hanging out with hidden cameras in rest stops and bathrooms known to be meeting places for a certain segment of gay male culture. These stories are usually hyped with headlines and announcements suggesting that children are at risk in these locales, although none of these shows has documented a single case of anything of the kind happening.

Getting the Numbers Right—or Wrong

As we all know, statistics are tricky. They can be used to prove both sides of an issue. When that issue is as inflammatory as the case of clergymen's sexual abuse of minors within the Catholic Church, you can be sure that dueling statistics flew like darts at an Irish pub.[7]

The goal of this section is to tell you: Be careful. Be skeptical. Demand that you have chapter and verse info on the source of the numbers—and put them in the story. And let the reader or viewer know of significant disclaimers in the research.

From the time the *Boston Globe* broke the scandal in the winter of 2002, the news was full of the tragic multidecade cover-up by the Catholic hierarchy of priests' sexual abuses of young parishioners. When several church apologists sought to deflect the storm in the direction of gay priests, it set off a wave of media stories and opinion pieces.

"People with these inclinations just cannot be ordained," declared Vatican spokesman Joaquin Navarro-Valls. Philadelphia Cardinal Anthony J. Bevilacqua said, "We feel that a person who is homosexually oriented is not a suitable candidate ... even if he did not commit an act [of gay sex]."

The message being conveyed by church fathers was that domination of the priesthood by gay priests had somehow corrupted the system, creating a climate that encouraged sexual excesses.

One intriguing question hanging over the debate was just how many gay priests are there? Since all but a few are closeted (especially since the scandal broke), there is no reliable count. So journalists had a field day citing experts who estimated, variously, from 20 to 60 percent, take your choice. A careful reporter would want to ask: On which statistical base is the charge made that gays hold too much sway in the clergy?

A second challenge came in the controversy about whether what had happened was pedophilia or not. The libel of pedophilia has been aimed at male homosexuals for centuries (see the Anita Bryant reference in the 1970s portion of the chronology). It is a very sensitive point for gay people.

Dictionaries define a pedophile as an adult who actively fantasizes about or engages in sexual activities with prepubescent children. The vast majority of abuses in the clergy cases were of adolescents. Pedophilia is classified medically as a disorder associated neither with homosexuality nor heterosexuality. The religious conservative press used the label freely (and wrongly) in describing the cases, as we'll see in the examples. In its effort to counter that, the gay activist response confused the issue by citing counterstatistics relevant to pedophilia but failing to address gay priests' importuning of postpubescent youths.

Since most of the abuse was by adult priests toward postpubescent youths (a criminal act in most states if one of the partners is below age 18), the implication was that the priests who did most of the molesting are homosexual.

Assuming for now that that is the case, we'd anticipate the press would inquire as follows: Does it mean that all molesters are gay? Does it mean that all gay priests are inclined to molest young choirboys? If not, how many? Is the percentage equal to the percentage of preadolescent molesters among heterosexuals? How many gay priests are sexually active, how many celibates? Should all homosexuals thus be barred from the priesthood?

Some journals and programs did a better job of explicating this tangled conundrum than did others. Mostly, it was a battle of unchallenged statistics from so-called experts.

Let's look at two opinion columns published in June 2002 while the controversy still simmered. On June 12, the *Washington (D.C.) Times* ran a piece by Peter Sprigg, of the conservative, fundamentalist Family Research Council. It was provocatively headlined:

A Missing Moral Link?
Homosexual Men May Evolve into Molesters

Sprigg cited a study in the *Journal of Sex and Marital Therapy* to support his thesis that a disproportionate percentage of youth molesters are homosexual. The study allegedly found that 36 percent of male sex offenders targeted male children. Sprigg said, "Logic thus suggests that in proportion to their numbers, homosexual men are far more likely to be child molesters than are heterosexual men."

Sprigg's logic is based on the assumptions that male homosexuals constitute 3 percent of the population, and that all molestations of male boys or youths are committed by homosexuals. Both assumptions are challengeable.

Journalists should be on the alert to examine closely such syllogisms. First step: *Check the original study.* Was the citation in the article accurate and in context? What of the scientific relevance of the sample (who were the respondents, was the sample scientifically random, how large a sample?) and of the reputation of the journal? How solid are the conclusions?

They should also ask, How many gay men are there? It makes a difference in analyzing Sprigg's calibrations. He uses 3 percent, but the figures on gay population, male and female, are contested: They run from 1 to 10 percent and are only estimates.

Another point: Were the molestations in the sample against prepubescent or postpubescent youth? Molestation of children is widely held to be a dysfunction unrelated to gender sexuality (check policy statements to that effect by the American Psychological Association, the American Academy of Child Psychiatrists and others who claim there is no connection between homosexuality and child sex abuse.)

Assume for argument's sake that 3 percent of the population is homosexual and that gay men are the sole molesters of children and youths. The implication by Sprigg and others is that *anyone who is homosexual* is predisposed to molest children and therefore is a danger to church, school, Boy Scouts, etc. This reverts to the darkest age of gay stereotyping: equating all homosexuals with child abuse. It ignores the possible conclusion that a small percentage of self-identified homosexuals—equal to the proportion in the heterosexual population—might also be pedophiles or *psychosexually arrested,* a term sometimes used in the cases of abuse of postpubescents.

Sprigg also cited a study by the Archives of Sexual Behavior that found "86 percent of [convicted] offenders of males described themselves as homosexual or bisexual." This negates, says Sprigg, the argument that child molestation is a separate "sexual orientation unrelated to homosexual identity." Journalists should make all the same checks—context of citation, sample size and quality, scientific relevance, definitiveness—on this study before allowing it to be printed or cited.

Sprigg went on to cite unnamed "experts" to make the case that molested boys are likely to become homosexuals who later in life molest other kids. This undocumented assertion in the 10th paragraph prompted a copy editor to extrapolate the scare headline that inaccurately paraphrased what was in the story. Sprigg *alleged* that molested boys could evolve into homosexual adults who molest other boys. He did not *say* that "homosexual men may evolve into molesters." This egregious example of distorting a distortion should stand as caution about the frequent disconnect between stories and headlines. It is the headline that many people store in their mental computers.

NLGJA's Robert Dodge, in a letter to the press, had this to say about the debate:

> When news organizations cover instances of sexual abuse by heterosexual adults against children of the opposite sex, they are not cast as stories about sexual orientation. They are accurately reported as crimes against children. Without including balancing comment in the Catholic Church story, news organizations allow themselves to be spun by church officials.

The second article was by Elizabeth Birch, executive director of the Human Rights Campaign, a pro-gay lobbyist organization. It appeared in the *Dallas Morning News* on June 10, 2002, bearing the headline:

Priest's Abuse Problem Isn't a Gay Issue

In arguing against targeting gays as part of the priest scandal, Birch posited that "the research regarding pedophilia is clear—98 percent of the molestation cases [in secular society] are at the hands of a known heterosexual adult, usually male." She cited a 1994 study by researcher Carol Jenny (no further reference given) that "a child's risk of being molested by his or her relative's heterosexual partner is 100 times greater than by someone who might be identified as a homosexual."

She asserted from an unnamed source that of the 93,000 sexually abused kids in the United States in 1999, half were abused by parents, 18 percent by other relatives. (No figures on the other 32 percent).

Birch concluded that with these "incontrovertible facts," church leaders were distorting the truth to take the heat off their culpability.

The conclusion may be independently true, but the foundation is weak. In citing "secular" statistics, the argument fails to account for the special conditions of an internally focused church that stresses conformity, celibacy and secrecy, where young girls do not interact as much with clergy. She also surfs past the fact that pedophilia is not the issue in most of these priest abuse cases.

The facts, based on the well-sourced stories that have appeared, are that some priests who are same-gender attracted have indeed been guilty of importuning postpuberty young males, some over long periods of time. The error in the reporting reflected in newspapers, on the airwaves and on the net is not questioning statements that attribute this behavior, directly or by implication, to all gay priests—and by extension to all gays.

It is true the above pieces ran on opinion pages, where people expect to read differing points of view. But this is too often used in an attempt to absolve editors, copy editors, and headline writers from responsibility for the accuracy and fairness of what they present on their pages.

One of the better reports on the subject turned up on the Web in the online magazine *Salon* ("The Gay Purge," March 27, 2002; www. salon.com). Even here, however, there are red flares.

Reporter Cheryl Reed challenged the orthodox line on gay male priests, raising issues not discussed elsewhere, such as the extent of abuses of young girls that may not get reported.

She stated accurately, "No one, including the church itself, seems to know exactly how big the sex scandal really is, who it involves or what role homosexuality plays in child abuse by priests. ... In order for any concrete conclusions to be drawn, the church would need to assemble its own comprehensive list of abuses. So far, the church has not done so."

Reed's story quoted interviews of several individuals who counsel the church on such issues as sexual abuse, among them, Gary Schoerner, who with his staff at the Minneapolis Walk-In Counseling Center, has consulted in more than 2,000 clergy sexual abuse cases.

Schoerner argued in Reed's piece that more "women and girls" are abused in the church than are young males. "Schoerner says in his practice he sees six times more female (both adolescent and adult) than male victims of abuse from priests." He calls the link between homosexuality and male youth abuse in the church "bullshit." "There are plenty of cases of girls and they are just not getting the visibility," he said.

While Schoerner's credentials seem solid, it must be noted that Reed failed to distinguish the number of cases Schoerner has handled of adult women being abused by priests vis-à-vis female minors. It makes a big difference in the argument if the bulk of male to female abuse involves adults, whereas the bulk of male to male abuse involves children or adolescents.

A. W. Richard Sipe, another interviewee, a Catholic priest turned therapist, agreed with Schoerner that females are victimized more than males but said that most female victims are adults.

Sipe, described as author of three books on priests, sex and celibacy, estimated that "boys are victimized by priests four times more than girls." Estimates based on what empirical data?

The article quoted Sipe on his research that purportedly shows one-third of priests are gay, but "just as many remain true to their vows of celibacy as heterosexual priests, i.e., 50 percent." Where is this reported and how can a reader find it?

Complicated, even confusing? We'd assume most news consumers would be confused. Journalists were playing catch-up on a highly complex story that had been hatching for years with very little journalistic surveillance. Those who report, write and edit stories about the Catholic issue would do well to do the homework of researching the history of the priesthood, the origins of celibacy, and the effect over the years of religious prejudice and biblical admonitions on minorities such as gays and lesbians. It may seem a large order, but fairness demands informed journalism more than ever today.

This sounds a second theme of this chapter: Preparation. One of the maxims of good journalism, it is observed more often in the breach than in the doing.

Be Prepared: A Case History

On September 22, 2000, a gunman entered the Backstreet Cafe, a gay bar in the Bible-belt city of Roanoke, Virginia, and opened fire, fatally shooting one man, injuring seven others.

The local *Roanoke Times* of course went big with the story, which was soon determined to be a hate crime.

Ordinarily, such a story would run out in a few days, reviving briefly during the trial (the assailant was held and later convicted.) But for the editors of the *Times*, the strong public reaction of gay and lesbian citizens who had never dared surface before confirmed what they and their staff had been discovering quietly for several months.

As it happened, earlier in the year a lesbian reporter on the staff, reacting to what she saw as stereotypical handling of wire stories and photos, brought this to the attention of a diversity committee that had been established by management. This led to a roundtable discussion among the full staff with members of the gay and lesbian community about what the paper was missing.

"We realized perhaps we were not really covering the gay community in Roanoke in a very comprehensive way," said Rich Martin, managing editor. "We covered AIDS, violence and Virginia's controversial anti-sodomy law, but we really didn't understand our own community."

Martin assigned several reporters to begin contacting gay sources to discover "who were the gay people who live here. What were their or-

dinary lives like?" At the time, there was no specific plan of writing anything—just getting sources and background as a route to understanding.

When the shooting occurred, the reporting team had been collecting
material for several months.

"We realized when we began to report how little we knew," said team
leader Mary Bishop. But by that time, they had done the groundwork.
The editors decided to go beyond the spot crime story and prepare a
thoroughgoing series on the lives of gays and lesbians in Roanoke and
environs.

The four-day series in January-February 2001 dominated the front
page and the inside "Extra" section with numerous photos, stories and
sidebars. The series disclosed a vibrant subculture of gays, lesbians, bisexuals and transgenders (GLBT) living mostly ordinary lives, struggling to make a life in a hostile, even dangerous environment.[8] It also
made the point that Roanoke (pop. about 100,000) was a magnet center
for gays and lesbians living secluded lives in towns and rural areas
within its orbit. Although the series made an effort to reflect opposition
views in this highly fundamentalist churchgoing populace, nothing quite
like this had ever appeared in the town's daily newspaper. (One photo
depicted two men hugging and kissing.)

"Roanoke is fairly tolerant," Martin told a panel at the Association for
Education in Journalism and Mass Communication (AEJMC) national
convention in August 2001, "but it is also a don't ask, don't tell kind of
community. Seeing gays and lesbians living real lives in their town
touched a lot of people in the wrong way."

He put it mildly, judging from the outraged, bitter, even vicious bar-
rage of mail, e-mail, and phone calls the paper received. Hundreds can-
celled subscriptions to the 110,000-circulation newspaper.

The *Roanoke Times* demonstrated courage. But more than that, it
acted responsibly and deliberately when it identified an important gap in
its coverage. It acted in accordance with high journalism standards
based on the notion of being a mirror to all aspects of a news organization's community. And it made sure it was prepared. The tragedy at the
Backstreet, committed by a man who despised gays, could now be seen
in context. The gay community, as portrayed now in the *Roanoke Times*,
was a cross section of all aspects of life in Roanoke, including religious
devotion, whose major difference was its sexual orientation.

The *Roanoke Times*'s work caught the attention of Ted Koppel and
"Nightline," which produced a five-night special May 20-24, 2002, on
homosexuality, centered primarily in Roanoke.[9] It culminated in a

2-hour live town meeting in Roanoke led by Koppel. The series was the most ambitious and concentrated focus on gay life ever attempted by "Nightline," and perhaps by any commercial network news program.

Koppel made sure to cover every conceivable nuance of opinion—radical right, conservative, moderate, liberal—for a series that beamed out to millions of Americans from every corner of the country. This caution was reflected in the program's title, "A Matter of Choice?" which drew fire from gay advocates as implying there might be a choice. (Some also contended that Bible literalists got too much airtime.)

Religious and other social conservatives argue that homosexuality is a preference that can be changed and should not come under civil rights protection. In fact, the town hall session included a questioner who claimed he succeeded in converting from gay to heterosexual.

The live session was the highlight. It was immediate and dramatic, fueled by Koppel's mix of soft lobs and knuckle ball pitches. Was there a bias to the program? Perhaps, but where it tilted depended on one's point of view. If anything, the inclusive approach discouraged drawing easy truths from the proceedings.

But that is not far from the reality in a nation of contradictions about its sexual self, where sexuality can be both obsession and anathema.

With that said, the "Nightline" series captured a fascinating profile of the varied threads that make up our social tapestry. It ranks for this writer as one of the finest pieces of television journalism on the topic.

The argument in this chapter has been that as the world grows more complex, news media are obligated to anticipate and prepare for events that require them to explain and illuminate tough issues.

Certainly with regard to GLBT issues, a sense of history is critical. Let's take some space for a brief tour of the last several decades to explore what transpired and how news media reflected events.

A Brief Chronology

The 1940s

Until the 1940s, gays and lesbians lived in quiet if not desperate isolation (or somehow managed in heterosexual marriages). They had no sense of identity as a group, movement or social construct—in fact, at the time it would have seemed to them ridiculous and dangerous. Then came WWII. Millions of new GIs poured into urban centers and military bases. Thrown together from all corners of the country, men and women with same-gender attraction connected like iron filings to magnets. The experience revealed the explosive truth that while they may have been isolated, they were not the only ones in the world.

Despite the military's new policy to discredit, imprison, and discharge known homosexuals (still in effect 60 years later), gays and lesbians discovered one another.

> Since all psychiatrists ... viewed homosexuality as a pathology, [they] helped formulate regulations that banned all those with "homosexual tendencies" from the military. In 1943, the final regulations ... were declared [that would] lead to untold injustices and horrors in later years.[10]

When the war ended they stayed in the safer, anonymous urban centers, creating the nucleus of a postwar underground gay culture in most mid-size and large cities in America.

The 1940s also produced the "Kinsey Report," probably the most notorious scientific study of the century, published as *Sexual Behavior in the Human Male* in 1948. A companion study of sexuality and the female appeared five years later. The first report (on males) created a sensation, capturing the imagination of the nation's public and press. It and the female volume shook up America's Puritan image of itself and set the stage for the sexual revolution 15 years later. In addition to provocative statistics of heterosexual adventures, Kinsey reported that 37 percent of American males had had at least one homosexual experience and that an estimated 6 percent of males were gay (albeit invisible). The figure for lesbians in the 1953 volume was 4 percent. It was a revelation for homosexuals and a rare example of gay sexuality displayed in media in scientific context. While many of the data were later challenged, the implications for the nation's images about sex and morality reverberate to this day.

The 1950s

An era of repression set off by the Cold War. A climate of fear and suspicion reigned, aimed ostensibly at Communism but snaring homosexuals (real or alleged) in its net. Sen. Joseph McCarthy and others of his ilk manipulated public anxiety to wage a smear campaign against suspected government communists. The impact destroyed careers of thousands of loyal employees, among them gays and lesbians—called perverts and degenerates in headlines and stories, including in the venerable *New York Times*. The assumption was that these individuals would betray their country rather than be exposed as homosexuals.

The hysteria spread to cities, where "clean-up" campaigns driven by editorials demanded that "our streets be cleansed of degenerates and pedophiles." Rounded up in bars and in cruising neighborhoods, gays stood to have careers and private lives destroyed. In Des Moines, Iowa, 20 gay men were incarcerated in mental institutions as psychopaths after being unjustly linked to a never-solved child murder case.

In reaction to the oppressive climate, 1953 saw the beginning of a movement by a small group of gay men in Los Angeles, the first known organized attempt to address discrimination against gays. The Mattachine Society, as it named itself after masked jesters who spoke out against authority in medieval times, represented a historic shift in that it sought to identify homosexuals for the first time as an interest group sharing a common cause. Two years later, four lesbian couples in San Francisco created a lesbian counterpart, the Daughters of Bilitis, named after a poetess who supposedly lived on Lesbos in the time of Sappho. The homophile movement, as it was known, expanded over the coming years, spawning the first gay periodicals. It presaged the tumultuous struggle that lay ahead.

The 1960s

A decade as radically different from the 1950s as Snoop Doggy Dog is from Snoopy. The era of the sexual revolution, the feminist revolution, the hippie phenomenon, the black civil rights movement, the urban ghetto rebellions, the anti-Vietnam protests, the dump-LBJ movement, and so on. A time of vocal and violent challenge of status quo. But the gay movement—such as it was—was to be a late 1960s bloomer. The homophile groups raised their voices a few decibels and actually took to street demonstrations—very polite, with lesbians in dresses and gay men in suits, jackets and ties. It was enough, however, to awaken the news media to the existence of yet another claimant on the horizon. Stories, many of them frankly patronizing, began to appear. I remember as a (totally closeted) assistant city editor at the *Washington Post* getting a call from our police reporter in 1965: "Guess what, a bunch of queers is picketing the White House."

"What?" I cried.

"Yeah, I got names and everything."

I thought to myself: "What are they, crazy? This will only stir things up against us. And giving out their names. They must be crazy!" In truth, I feared for my career and livelihood should gay people begin to be identified. Nonetheless, I recall that a small article did appear in the paper.

June 28, 1969: the day of the event that would forever change the gay movement. Police raided Stonewall, a gay bar frequented by hustlers, drag queens and other clientele in Greenwich Village. Raids on gay bars were routine for New York. But on this night the clientele—led by a gutsy phalanx of drag queens—fought back, resisting arrest and attacking the police. Soon they were joined by gathering crowds of other gays, who pelted cops with stones, ash, trash cans, ultimately setting fire to the bar, inside which cops had retreated. About 1,000 people participated, then returned for an encore the next night. Although the press gave scant attention, gay people had taken a leaf from the 1960s protest manual, reversing the age-old pattern of meekly submitting. (The New York *Daily News* ran a piece, several days late, with a clever but condescending headline: "Homo Nest Raided: Queen Bees Stinging Mad.") Nonetheless, word spread quickly and widely, lighting the torch to a national bonfire waiting to happen.

The 1970s

The *new* gay movement: activist, militant, driven by young gays and lesbians schooled on the front lines of 1960s protests. No apologies, with the slogan Gay Is Good, they demanded the right of gay and lesbian people to define who and what they are. The Gay Liberation Front and its successor, the Gay Activists Alliance, invented the "zap"—noisy invasions of live TV and radio programs, public forums, city councils— to demand press coverage and rights for homosexuals. The strategy was to create maximum visibility, and it worked. Broadcast and print started covering this loud and colorful new movement.

The momentum built: Soon states and municipalities were passing anti-gay bias measures, the American Psychiatrists Association discarded its designation of homosexuality as a disease. The gay movement was on a roll. (In 1975, while the West Coast correspondent for the *Washington Post*, I "bravely" wrote my first gay-related story, about how gay political clout was likely to help elect George Moscone mayor of San Francisco.)

But, as Oscar Wilde learned 70 years earlier, homosexual visibility invariably generates severe backlash. Gays' and lesbians' advances raised alarm among political and morality-based conservatives, who responded with an array of strategies aimed at reversing the tide of liberalization. The so-called religious right employed well-financed campaigns, via ballot initiative, lobbying, advertisement, and support of conservative candidates, to attack gay civil rights initiatives.

It can be argued that this cycle got its impetus from a single source: Anita Bryant, an ex-beauty queen, orange juice hawker on TV, vocalist and religious fundamentalist. In 1977, Bryant challenged a pro-gay ordinance just passed in Dade County, Florida (Miami). Bryant came up with an old but effective pitch: "Save our children from homosexual predators who don't reproduce and thus must recruit." The ploy triggered a vicious fight that the media amplified with national coverage. The voters overwhelmingly recalled the measure in a June ballot, casting Bryant as a symbol for the now-revived political religious right. The lines were drawn for a leviathan political struggle between gay advocacy and Bible-based orthodoxy that has lasted to the present day. It set the stage for the event-driven, conflict-flavored portrayal now common in the press.

A year later, San Francisco Mayor Moscone and Supervisor Harvey Milk, the great hope of the gay movement, were shot to death by an addled right-winger who had lost his own supervisor seat. The end of the decade was somber, but the gay movement seemed resilient enough to recover.

The 1980s

Then came AIDS and the era of Ronald Reagan. Mainstream news media's ignoring of AIDS is a lasting stain on their reputation. They watched the lethal epidemic escalate for five years with a minimum of coverage. (Exception: the late Randy Shilts of the *San Francisco Chronicle,* the only publicly out mainstream journalist writing courageously about the epidemic. See the Resources list.)

Not until 1985, when Rock Hudson announced he had AIDS, did the press begin to pay serious attention.

For the gay movement, AIDS meant retrenchment and implosion. With obituaries of men in their 20s and 30s running every day, gays and lesbians across the country organized new community institutions to deal with fund raising, education, prevention and treatment of the disease.

While the press ran stories from the religious right that AIDS was God's punishment for gay excesses, the public was also digesting news accounts of loss, heroism, courage, families reunited or split apart by revelations of the disease. The AIDS quilt became emblematic of the humanizing of the disease and, in the process, of gay people, their friends and families.

Ultimately, the disease galvanized and politicized tens of thousands of gay men and women who had never joined a protest march, but took dead seriously the slogan "Silence Equals Death." They went public in droves, ran for offices and boards, sued in the courts, petitioned the legislatures and the foundations, and lobbied Congress. Just as significantly, joined by many nongay sympathizers, they raised and donated millions. It represented in the late 1980s the maturing of the movement as a potent political force.

In 1989, then-publisher Loren Ghiglione assumed the presidency of the American Society of Newspaper Editors (ASNE), a powerful voice of the news industry. Among the first things he did was mandate the first-ever survey of gay and lesbian journalists on mainstream newspapers. I was executive editor of the *Oakland Tribune* at the time. Asked to coordinate the survey, I accepted, with the intuition that my life would never be the same thereafter.

The 1990s

Lesbian and gay mainstream journalists were itching to go public. I did not know that fact when I reported the results of the survey before hundreds of my peer editors in April 1990—a survey that showed the vast majority of such journalists were closeted. In delivering those results, which found widespread perceptions of poor coverage of gay issues, I came out as gay. It drew national attention. Flooded with phone calls and letters from lesbian and gay journalists, I decided we must find a way to organize ourselves. With five colleagues, we formed the NLGJA in my dining room the following August. The response was electric: Within the first year there were six chapters across the country. Clearly the AIDS epidemic had convinced these journalists they could no longer afford to play it safe and invisible.

Now 1,000 strong in 23 chapters, the organization plays a key insider role in guiding news executives and staffs toward balanced and unbiased reportage. It helped make newsrooms hospitable to gay and lesbian employees as well as helping domestic partner couples obtain equal health benefits.

Three other events typify the 1990s, a seesaw era in which the press chronicled battles between gays and conservatives at many levels.

- Bill Clinton, elected partly on massive support from gays and lesbians who responded with dollars and votes, rewarded them by trying in 1993 to end the military's 60-year policy of kicking gays and lesbians out of the services. He failed, wilting under pressure of conservatives in the military and Congress, settling for the cobbled together "don't ask, don't tell policy."
- In the spring of 1998, Ellen DeGeneres pulled a double whammy, coming out as lesbian simultaneously in her off-camera and on-camera personas. Despite the mega-hyped media circus accompanying it—with cameos by Oprah, Diane Sawyer, and Anne Heche—DeGeneres' action constituted an enormous breakthrough in the realm of pop culture, which until then had never had a gay lead character in prime time. Many gays and lesbians see it as a watershed, from which flowed Will and Grace and other gay images now crowding the airwaves.
- Barely six months later, the pendulum swung to the dark side with the vicious hate slaying of 21-year-old gay Wyoming student Matthew Shepard. Time, place and circumstance combined to make the media accounts of the death of this gentle young man a shocking morality tale for everyone, regardless of politics or persuasion. The century ended with the indelible message that gay people risked lethal consequences for being themselves.

The 2000s

I've tried to show the connection between history and the concerns of today. For example, the ongoing debate in the military is best understood against the backdrop of 60 years of the policy of gay exclusion. The debates over how many gays and lesbians there are, and of genetics versus nurture as the cause of homosexuality, hark back to the first disclosures of the "Kinsey Report."

What of the future? In 2000, the University of Southern California Annenberg School of Journalism and the NLGJA collaborated on a 10-years-later follow-up survey of perceptions of gay and lesbian mainstream journalists, showing that from their perspective many things had changed for the better, others not. The Clinton, Ellen and Shepard stories above and others about celebrities, political juggling or sensational crime got saturation coverage, the study found. Underattended, it reported, are the local issues of concern to gay communities.[11]

Quantity of coverage proliferated, but what of quality? The tendency of journalism to focus less on stories that enlighten, educate and explain has affected the quality of coverage in general and GLBT coverage in particular. ASNE, which has fretted for a decade about the loss of credibility among newspaper readers, reported in 1999 results of a far-reaching credibility survey of public attitudes. The study made the point that there is a huge disconnect between readers and newspapers, driven by perceptions of bias, sensationalism and inaccuracy. More than 80 percent of those surveyed believe that newspapers overdramatize news to sell papers. The public demanded more fact-based exposition as well as more local news.[12]

Guidelines for Covering Sexual Orientation Issues

How does this translate to specifics in coping with covering and teaching about sexual orientation issues? Here are a few guidelines that sum up the thrust of this chapter:

For all in the field:

- *Invest in excellence.* Strive for inclusive curriculum in journalism education and much more attention to training on site at news organizations. In 2002, the results of a survey of 2,000 journalists showed that lack of training was the number one complaint of U.S. news practitioners.[13]
- *Develop sources before the crisis happens.*
- *De-emphasize the easy sensational story.*
- *Stress top down inclusion of all its communities.* Management must reflect this on diversity committees, infuse it into beat reporter assignments, and encourage "mainstreaming" of stories throughout the news budget.

For editors and producers:

- *Assign responsibility to someone on staff to scrutinize local gay publications regularly* for early warning on developing stories.
- *Educate staff routinely to mirror gay and lesbian lives in the full scope of its report.*
- *Reinvigorate communication with gay and lesbian staff members,* signaling that input about coverage would be hospitably received

and acted on appropriately. Include gay and lesbian voices on diversity committees.

• *Develop lines into the gay and lesbian community beyond the obvious spokespeople* as a way of (a) expanding understanding of issues, (b) instilling confidence in that audience in your institution's credibility, and (c) developing a new and richer vein of sources.

For staff reporters and field producers:

• *Be as alert for stories about gay and lesbian people or issues as they would for those of other minorities.* Pursue those stories on a regular basis, for example, the ongoing debate over education about homosexuality in schools, ongoing violence against gays, and the presence of gays and lesbians in pulpit and pew of congregations. Do so especially before and after the glare of controversy has flared.

• *Resist falling into a pattern of covering problem and conflict issues in terms of charges and countercharges,* such as cameras trailing the itinerant rabble-rouser Rev. Phelps. Look beyond the rhetoric for the more complex and telling factors as well as human stories, including the views of ordinary people in the so-called middle.

• *Be sensitive to those areas least covered:* the lives of lesbians, the lives of gays and lesbians of color; the growing transgender rights movement.

• *Remember that there are tens of thousands of nongay people whose lives are entwined with gay people* through family ties and friendship, in worship, on the job and in dozens of other ways.

It is only with commitment that tomorrow's journalists can be prepared to grapple with thorny issues with intelligence and context. Journalism education, for its part, can benefit the practice of good journalism only if it keeps pace with the seismic social change in our society. Billions of pixels of information bombard us from every direction, with news media courting celebrity and the bottom line.

It requires diligence, courage, foresight and hindsight to sustain the historic role of our profession. In return for our protected status under the First Amendment, we journalists and those of us who prepare journalists have an obligation to the public, indeed an unwritten contract, to be correct, contextual, clear and complete.

Bob Maynard, the late publisher of the *Oakland Tribune*—a great journalist and inspirational leader—described that role best when he called on the press to be "an instrument of community understanding [that] provides everyone front-door access to the truth."

Resources

Internet

www.nlgja.org   The National Lesbian & Gay Journalists Association
http://newswatch.sfsu.edu/journal/su2001/070201newsroom.html   Williams, Dara. 2001. "National News Coverage of Gays, Lesbians Increases, But Local Coverage Still Lacking." News Watch link.

Books

Alwood, Edward. 1998. St*raight News: Gays, Lesbians and the News Media*. New York: Columbia University Press. The first and still definitive history of how the news covered lesbians and gays from the 1940s to the 1990s.

Bull, Chris. 1999. *Witness to Revolution: The Advocate Reports on Gay and Lesbian Politics, 1967-1999*. Los Angeles: Alyson Books. A compilation of articles from the country's first, and still extant, national gay news magazine.

Duberman, Martin. 1994. *Stonewall*. New York: Dutton/Plume. Historian Duberman created a novelistic but accurate account of the watershed moment in gay activism.

Gross, Larry. 2001. *Up from Invisibility*. New York: Columbia University Press. Covers much of the same ground as *Straight News* but includes entertainment and advertising as well.

McGarry, Molly, and Fred Wasserman. 1998. *Becoming Visible: An Illustrated History of Lesbian and Gay Life in Twentieth-Century America*. New York: Penguin Studio.

Shilts, Randy. 1999. *And the Band Played On: Politics, People and the AIDS Epidemic*. New York: St. Martin's Press. A classic history of the first years of the AIDS epidemic from 1976 to 1985. Rich with detail of the press's role.

Streitmatter, Rodger. 1995. *Unspeakable: The Rise of the Gay and Lesbian Press in America*. London: Faber and Faber. The book of record on the gay/lesbian press through 1995.

Notes

1. Ashcroft said, "Just as the United States will pursue ... terrorists, we will pursue, prosecute and punish those who attack law-abiding Americans out of hatred for who they are. Hatred is the enemy of justice, regardless of its source. We will not rest until justice is done." (The federal hate law on which the indictment was based applies only to crimes on federal property. Legislation to expand hate crime penalties to any locale where they happen was opposed by Justice and still bottled in Congress in March 2003 by Republican allies of the president.)

2. "It was journalistic error and the editing process didn't work the way it should have," AP spokesman Jack Stokes told Hank Stuever of the *Washington Post*. Rear. Adm. Jockel Finck told Steuver, "We've gotten word to our commanders saying, 'That's not up to our standards, guys.'" ("The Bomb with a Loaded Message," *Washington Post*, 27 October 2001, Style sec.)

3. Dean Loren Ghiglione, talk at the preconvention workshop of the annual meeting of the Association of Educators of Journalism and Mass Communication (AEJMC), 4 August 2001. Tape available from C-Span.

4. Based on an interview by the author for an article in *The Advocate*.

5. Leroy Aarons, "The Matthew Shepard Story: From Bloodshed to Watershed," *NewsWatch* magazine, Spring 1999. For a copy: (415) 338-2083, or dara@sfsu.edu.

6. GLAAD (Gay and Lesbian Alliance Against Defamation), 1998. Search FOX Files in www.glaad.org.

7. One of the finest teaching tools on the interaction of press and clergy on a gay issue is the report, *Media Coverage of Religion, Spirituality, and Values*, published in 2000 by the Garrett-Medill Center for Religion and the News Media, Evanston, Ill., in collaboration with a Chicago ecumenical study group. Pay special attention to the analysis of media treatment of the 1999 church trial of Methodist Rev. Gregory Dell for performing a union ceremony of a gay male couple. Auditing a mass of print and television coverage, this multidimensional study focused on how each interested party in the dispute sought to (and succeeded) in spinning the press to advance its position. The study asks these concluding questions: Could the story have been told in other ways, reflecting views from other sources, or in a "less media-friendly religious tradition" and even a different cultural climate? Ask for both the study text and accompanying content review by journalism students. E-mail Roy Larson, director, at rlarson@Garrett.edu or write Garrett-Medill Center, 2121 Sheridan Road, Evanston, IL 60201.

8. Archived at www.roanoketimes.com; or get editors e-mail online to request them.
9. Tapes or transcripts of back "Nightline" shows may be purchased from www.abcnewsstore.com.
10. Randy Shilts, *Conduct Unbecoming* (New York: St. Martin's Press, 1993), 16-17.
11. "Lesbians and Gays in the Newsroom—10 Years Later" can be downloaded in entirety via PDF from two sites: www.nlgja.org and www.usc.edu/annenberg/soin, the site of the Program for the Study of Sexual Orientation Issues in the News at USC Annenberg. Hard copies are available from the National Lesbian and Gay Journalists Association, 1402 K St. NW, Suite 910, Washington, D.C. 20005.
12. "Examining Our Credibility," ASNE site (Archives) www.asne.org
13. "Newsroom Training: Where's the Investment?" survey released in April 2002 by the Council of Presidents of National Journalism Organizations and the Knight Foundation. Full text available at Poynter Institute website: http://www.poynter.org/centerpiece/newsroomtraining.htm

Appendix

Gay, Lesbian, Bisexual and Transgender Terminology*

ACT UP: The acronym for AIDS Coalition to Unleash Power, an activist organization with independent chapters in various cities. ACT UP acceptable in first reference. **See AIDS.**

AIDS: Acquired Immune Deficiency Syndrome, a medical condition that compromises the human immune system, leaving the body defenseless against opportunistic infections. Some medical treatments can slow the rate at which the immune system is weakened. Do not use the term "full-blown AIDS." Individuals may be HIV-positive but not have AIDS. Avoid "AIDS sufferer" and "AIDS victim." Use "people with AIDS" or, if the contact is medical, "AIDS patient." **See HIV.**

---

*From the NLGJA Stylebook Supplement, © 2002 National Lesbian & Gay Journalists Association.

bisexual: As a noun, an individual who may be attracted to either sex. As an adjective, of or relating to sexual and affectional attraction to either sex. Does not presume non-monogamy.

civil union: The state of Vermont began this formal recognition of lesbian and gay relationships in July 2000. A civil union provides same-sex couples some rights available to married couples in areas such as state taxes, medical decisions and estate planning.

closeted, in the closet: Refers to a person who wishes to keep secret his or her sexual orientation or gender identity.

coming out: Short for "coming out of the closet." Accepting and letting others know of one's previously hidden sexual orientation or gender identity. See **closeted** and **outing.**

commitment ceremony: A formal, marriagelike gathering that recognizes the declaration of members of the same sex to each other. Same-sex marriages are not legally recognized in the United States. (In April 2001, The Netherlands became the first nation to offer legal marriage to same-sex couples who are citizens or legal residents.)

cross-dresser: Preferred term for person who wears clothing most often associated with members of the opposite sex. Not necessarily connected to sexual orientation.

cruising: Visiting places where opportunities exist to meet potential sex partners. Not exclusively a gay phenomenon.

domestic partner: Unmarried partners who live together. Domestic partners may be of opposite sexes or the same sex. They may register in some counties, municipalities and states and receive some of the same benefits accorded married couples. The term is typically used in connection with legal and insurance matters. See **gay/lesbian relationships.**

don't ask, don't tell: Shorthand for "Don't Ask, Don't Tell, Don't Pursue," the military policy on gay men, lesbians and bisexuals. Under the policy, instituted in 1993, the military is not to ask service members about their sexual orientation, service members are not to tell others about their orientation, and the military is not to pursue rumors about members' sexual orientation. The shorthand is acceptable in headlines, but in text the full phrase adds important balance.

down low: Term used by some bisexual men of color to refer to men who have sex with other men without the knowledge of their female partners. Sometimes abbreviated as DL. See **MSM.**

drag: Attire of the opposite sex.

drag performers: Entertainers who dress and act in styles typically associated with the opposite sex (drag queen for men, drag king for women). Not synonymous with transgender or cross-dressing.

dyke: Originally a pejorative term for a lesbian, it is now being reclaimed by some lesbians. Caution: still extremely offensive when used as an epithet.

ex-gay (adj.)**:** The movement mostly rooted in conservative religions, that aims to change the sexual attraction of individuals from same-sex to opposite-sex.

fag, faggot: Originally a pejorative term for a gay male, it is now being reclaimed by some gay men. Caution: still extremely offensive when used as an epithet.

FTM: Acronym for "female to male." A transgender person who, at birth or by determination of parents or doctors, has a biological identity of female but a gender identity of male. Those who have undergone surgery are sometimes described as "post-op FTMs" (for post-operative). See **gender identity** and **intersex.**

gay: An adjective that has largely replaced "homosexual" in referring to men who are sexually and affectionally attracted to other men. Avoid using as a singular noun. For women, "lesbian" is preferred. To include both, use "gay men and lesbians." In headlines where space is an issue, "gays" is acceptable to describe both.

gay/lesbian relationship: Gay, lesbian and bisexual people use various terms to describe their commitments. Ask the individual what term he or she prefers, if possible. If not, "partner" is generally acceptable.

gender identity: An individual's emotional and psychological sense of being male or female. Not necessarily the same as an individual's biological identity.

heterosexism: Presumption that heterosexuality is universal and/or superior to homosexuality. Also: prejudice, bias or discrimination based on such presumptions.

HIV: Human immunodeficiency virus. The virus that causes AIDS. "HIV virus" is redundant. "HIV-positive" means being infected with HIV but not necessarily having AIDS. AIDS doctors and researchers are using the term "HIV disease" more because there are other types of acquired immune deficiencies caused by toxins and rare but deadly diseases that are unrelated to what we now call AIDS. See **AIDS.**

homo: Pejorative term for homosexual. Avoid.

homophobia: Fear, hatred or dislike of homosexuality, gay men and lesbians.

homosexual: As a noun, a person who is attracted to members of the same sex. As an adjective, of or relating to sexual and affectional attraction to a member of the same sex. Use only if "heterosexual" would be used in parallel constructions, such as in medical contexts. For other usages, see **gay** and **lesbian.**

intersex (adj.): People born with some combination of male and female genitalia. Parents and physicians usually will determine the sex of the child, resulting in surgery or hormone treatment. Many intersex adults seek an end to this practice.

lesbian: Preferred term, both as a noun and as an adjective, for women who are sexually and affectionally attracted to other women. Some women prefer to be called "gay" rather than "lesbian"; when possible, ask the subject what term she prefers.

LGBT: Acronym for "lesbian, gay, bisexual and transgender."

lifestyle: An inaccurate term sometimes used to describe the lives of gay, lesbian, bisexual and transgender people. Avoid.

lover: A gay, lesbian, bisexual or heterosexual person's sexual partner. "Partner" is generally acceptable. See **gay/lesbian relationships.**

MSM: Acronym for "men who have sex with men." Term used usually in communities of color to describe men who secretly have sex with other men while maintaining relationships with women. Not synonymous with "bisexual." See **down low.**

MTF: Acronym for "male to female." A transgender person who, at birth or by determination of parents or doctors, has a biological identity of male but a gender identity of female. Those who have undergone surgery are sometimes described as "post-op MTFs" (for post-operative). See **gender identity** and **intersex.**

openly gay/lesbian: As a modifier, "openly" is usually not relevant; its use should be restricted to instances in which the public awareness of an individual's sexual orientation is germane. Examples: Harvey Milk was the first openly gay San Francisco supervisor. "Ellen" was the first sitcom to feature an openly lesbian lead character. "Openly" is preferred over "avowed," "admitted," "confessed" or "practicing."

outing: (From "out of the closet.") Publicly revealing the sexual orientation or gender identity of an individual who has chosen to keep that information private. Also a verb: The magazine outed the senator in a front-page story. See **coming out** and **closeted.**

pink triangle: Now a gay pride symbol, it was the symbol gay men were required to wear in Nazi concentration camps during World War II. Lesbians sometimes also use a black triangle.

Pride (Day and/or march): Short for gay/lesbian pride, this term is commonly used to indicate the celebrations commemorating the Stonewall Inn riots June 28, 1969. Pride events commonly take place in June. See **Stonewall.**

queen: Originally a pejorative term for an effeminate gay man. Still considered offensive when used as an epithet.

queer: Originally a pejorative term for gay, now being reclaimed by some gay men, lesbians, bisexuals and transgender people as a self-affirming umbrella term. Still extremely offensive when used as an epithet.

rainbow flag: A flag of six equal horizontal stripes (red, orange, yellow, green, blue and violet) signifying the diversity of the lesbian, gay, bisexual and transgender communities.

safe sex, safer sex: Sexual practices that minimize the possible transmission of HIV and other infectious agents.

seroconversion: Scientifically observable alteration of blood or other bodily fluids from HIV-negative to HIV-positive. The verb is "seroconvert." See **HIV.**

seronegative: Synonymous with HIV-negative. See **HIV.**

seropositive: Synonymous with HIV-positive. See **HIV.**

sexual orientation: Innate sexual attraction. Use this term instead of "sexual preference." See **lifestyle.**

sexual preference: Avoid. See **sexual orientation.**

sodomy: Collective term for various sexual acts deemed illegal in some states. Not synonymous with homosexuality or gay sex. The legal definition of sodomy is different from state to state and can apply to sexual practices by heterosexuals.

special rights: Politically charged term used by opponents of civil rights for gay people. Avoid. "Gay civil rights," "equal rights" or "gay rights" are alternatives.

Stonewall: The Stonewall Inn tavern in New York City's Greenwich Village was the site of several nights of raucous protests after a police raid on June 28, 1969. Although not the nation's first gay civil rights demon-stration, Stonewall is now regarded as the birth of the modern gay civil rights movement.

straight (adj.)**:** Heterosexual; a person whose sexual and affectional at-traction is to someone of the opposite sex.

transgender (adj.)**:** An umbrella term that can include preoperative, postoperative or nonoperative transsexuals, female and male cross-dresses, drag queens or kings, female or male impersonators and inter-sex individuals. If an individual prefers to be called transsexual, drag queen or king, intersex, etc., use that term.

transition: The process by which one alters one's sex. This may include surgery, hormone therapy and changes of legal identity.

transsexual (n.)**:** An individual who identifies himself or herself as a member of the opposite sex and who acquires the physical characteris-tics of the opposite sex. Individual can be of any sexual orientation. To determine accurate use of names or personal pronouns, use the name and sex of the individual at the time of the action.

transvestite: Avoid. See **cross-dresser.**

Additional information on terminology and contact information for lesbian, gay, bisexual and transgender organizations are available at *www.nlgja.org.*

CHAPTER 6

Just Don't Call 'em "Old Folks"

Kent S. Collins

"Just don't call 'em 'old folks,'" the newspaper editor joked years ago, before he was old folks.

Today you can call them "old folks" and not offend if the context is right. Unlike writing about other minorities and other matters of identity sensitivity (a.k.a. cross-cultural journalism), writing about this minority is changing for the better. Writing about aging is easier now; it is not so politically charged.

What's changing is the realization that the same cross-cultural shift that happened to that newspaper editor happens to all of us. We all become a part of this minority, this societal segment that has suffered from stereotyping and prejudice and distorted news coverage. When we write about older people we are, potentially, writing about our future selves. That is not usually true when writing about other cross-cultural segments. People don't often change their religion or ethnicity or gender. But people change their age. People grow old. Thus, journalists write about old age with some inkling they will be the subjects one day. This is the new cross-cultural realization for journalists.

Yet, writing about older people still has its challenges. One of them is the flip side of the distinction we have just discussed: Journalists may self-censor their stories because they know that the characteristics of old folks that foster stereotyping and prejudice are now or some day will be characteristics of themselves.

The New Face of the Old Faces of America

Covering news about the aging population is difficult for many reasons. Here are nine problems that get in the way of accurate and representative news reporting.

The Crystal Ball Factor

Journalists may have a skewed view of stories about older people because their stories are a crystal-ball look at themselves. What journalists write about old people, they are writing about people they will some day be. A journalist writing about saving Social Security is writing about his/her own financial future.

Predictions of Social Security troubles 20 years away, estimates of Medicare bankruptcy in the future, relief from the high-cost of prescription medicines or cures for Alzheimer's disease years away all relate to us, the journalists. We will be there some day. Indeed, debates on today's aging issues affect how we will live in retirement and old age. Few story assignments in cross-cultural journalism carry that constant risk of conflict of interest.

All in the Family

Few relationships are as universal as that between child and parent. Virtually all of us will experience the aging of parents. The nature of that experience directs in part how we approach aging for ourselves and our associates, our readers and our audiences. How is it that our parents grow old? At what point do we realize it? How do we react—if at all—to it?

Before we acknowledge our own aging, we witness the aging of our parents.

Researchers have not yet studied it, but probably most of our perceptions, stereotypes and prejudices about aging develop from experiences with our parents. If we see our own parents growing into some glossy magazine–style golden years, playful and active, and well-enough off, then our image of aging is positive. As journalists, we can easily write on the golden years theme.

Retirement is the new good times for Americans—with RVs and IRAs, continuing-care retirement communities and community service projects. Organizations to serve retirees, marketing opportunities to attract retirees, magazines to tempt them are all multiplying in America. To see parents aging into these kinds of lifestyles is cause for joy and for optimism.

But there is a dark side to growing old, and it can affect both the people aging and their loved ones. Journalists who see that in their own families might paint more pessimistic portraits of older people.

Adult children whose parents struggle with the dark side of aging find their efforts expensive and time consuming, sad and threatening. This, too, is a different relationship for a journalist. It is not like the relationships that more commonly develop between journalists and other minority groups addressed in this book.

Stories about people in retirement and people of age are stories about our parents. That cuts both ways. Especially negative or positive feelings about aging parents can influence a journalist's approach to a story about the aging of others. Stories about aging are stories about the good and bad experiences in our own families.

Talk to any young or middle-aged adult about growing old or older people, and you hear responses prejudiced by the personal experience of that young or middle-aged adult. That's because those stories cut so close. We are either especially protective or especially repulsed by the subject matter and its closeness to people we love or are responsible for or both.

Thus a journalist's story about threats to Social Security is a story about the financial well-being (or maybe even the financial dependence) of our older parents. If Social Security does not pay enough, will I have to subsidize my parents?

More emotional are the stories about the diseases that ravage some people in old age. No journalist interviews people with Alzheimer's disease without wondering how to handle the disease if it should come to his/her family. If we are not aware of it, we might write with prejudice.

For journalists, and the people who employ them and read or watch their work, there is a natural conflict of interest. Consider these examples:

- Should editors balk at assigning stories about neglect in nursing homes to a staffer with a parent in a nursing home?
- Can newspaper readers trust stories about investing Social Security funds in the stock market that are written by the adult children of retirees who were hurt by a recent market decline?

- Will young and middle-aged journalists react without prejudice to elderly people who exhibit the same problems as their own parents?

Journalists can usually distance themselves from these conflicts of interest—intellectual as well as material—by applying Walter Williams' "clear thinking and clear statement, accuracy and fairness"[1] when writing about people of race, creed or color that they will never be. But the aging demographic is much more universal. And this demographic eventually encompasses all who live long enough. That reality is without situational peer in all other cross-cultural journalism.

Denial and Avoidance

In Western cultures, where the specter of death looms large, to grow old is to grow fearful. A 73-year-old woman who continually complained about aches and pains and had endless reasons for her own lethargic living visited an assisted living center in Missouri. In deciding to move there to live among other retired and elderly people, she asserted cheerfully: "I think it would be good to live in that place. I can help all those old people. I really like them."

She was old of spirit and body, but believed herself to be younger to the point of being able to be helpful to senior citizens of very similar circumstances, and in some cases of better circumstances. She denied her age.

This is not akin to vanity efforts to continue looking young. Hair color products and makeup are of only passing concern to people growing old. This is a matter of intellectual mind-set. Some retirees do not think of themselves as old. Even those well into retirement and relatively long in years don't necessarily equate themselves with the aging population.

Denying true age is partly a defense mechanism and partly an unconscious effort to be forward-thinking. We are conditioned to plan ahead, schedule a future. And we all expect to grow or improve, to get richer and happier. That's the American way, the American dream. It may take a life-altering episode to snap us to the reality of our age. When illness or the death of a spouse or loved one crushes the spirit, then the notion of being old comes clear. The acceptance of growing or being old too often comes with impact rather than with gentle transition.

Our culture makes it difficult sometimes to grow old gracefully. There are few facilities and precious little conditioning for the lifestyles of old age. And so, the shift from middle-aged to old is difficult.

Other minorities addressed in this book are not at all likely to deny their race, heritage, gender, whatever. But some older people deny being older. And more important to the issues of journalists and journalism: People in the younger demographics don't necessarily accept that they will some day be part of the older segment of the population. Someday they might be one of those old folks, act like their cantankerous mother-in-law, suffer like an old man tied to his wheelchair in a nursing home, or whatever the stereotype might be.

In order to write of the aging population to this young demographic, journalists need to use humanized examples and health care statistics to indicate that younger old people could become like the subject matter of the story.

Rocking Chairs on the Porch

The old stereotypes of old age are giving way to new ones: Rocking chairs on the front porch give way to adult-size tricycles at Sun City, black wingtips to rubber-cleated athletic shoes, wire-rimmed bifocals to sunvisors with sports insignia, Norman Rockwellesque paintings of grandmas and grandpas acting noble and stable at home to scenes of raucous retirees cruising down the interstate highway in an RV with bumper stickers claiming "We are spending our children's inheritance."

The stereotypes and even the framing contexts and facets of old age in America are much more diverse than ever before. That's good, but confusing. The diversity of stereotyped images extends from frail people suffering in nursing homes to young-looking seniors at play in retirement resorts.

Once, stereotypes of the elderly were few and easy to note. Now, they are far more numerous, thus not easily remembered, and hence confusing for journalists to use—or to avoid.

If stereotypes about age even had any validity, they seldom, if ever, apply today. That's because old age is bigger and broader and more diverse than ever before. The folklore of old age is a picture of Grandma waiting. The media lore about old age today is often that Grandma is busy.

Further, with more of the population living to older ages, there is more than one kind of older person, and the same person may live through several different kinds of old age. The lives of 60-year-olds differ from most 90-year-olds. Americans are just beginning to understand that.

Gathered in the coffee room of a daily newspaper, any group of journalists can cite stories about their parents and grandparents. Their stories are of people living much longer than mankind knew even 100 years ago. According to the 2000 Centers for Disease Control and Prevention (CDC) report, the U.S. life expectancy reached a record high of 76.9 years, while in 1900, the average life expectancy for white men in the United States was 48.2 years (51.1 years for white women).

Age 80 was a novelty before World War II. It is routine today. "World War II was a pivotal point in the development of medical care. Penicillin, discovered in 1928, was used by military doctors to battle infection during the war; then it came into widespread antibiotic use,"[2] writes journalist Guy Keeler in the *Fresno Bee* Time Capsule from January 2000.

"Americans on average are living longer than ever before, and much of this is due to the progress we've made in fighting diseases that account for a majority of deaths in the country," said Tommy G. Thompson, Secretary of Health and Human Services in 2002.[3] Gray hair was the hallmark of old age not so long ago. Now the gray is often dyed.

People who lived past 70 in earlier generations often lived badly, burdened with ailments and handicaps, aches and pains. Now people past age 70 get revolutionary new medicine to control many of their aches and pains. According to Ruth Kirschstein, Principal Deputy Director, National Institutes of Health, "Our longer lives have a great deal to do with knowledge gained through medicine and science. … Medical technology has given us remarkable diagnostic tools, such as MRIs, medications, and complex surgical procedures. Our understanding of risk factors and disease prevention has increased; death rates from stroke and coronary heart disease have decreased dramatically in the last 25 years. All these advances may improve life and prolong a healthy life."[4]

Behind many of the old stereotypes of the elderly is this: Old people used to be dependent for finances and caregiving on family and government. Out of the workplace or with children grown out of the home, older people were seen to be needy of all sorts of assistance. Pensioners needed either government or family financial support. Widows and widowers needed sympathy or health care. True still for some, but less true for most. The United Nations Volunteers Organization press release from April 2002 stated, "The dearth of information … has fuelled the stereotyping of older people as unproductive, dependent and subject to irreversible decline. This myth needs to be broken, as older persons today are active, healthy, and independent for many more years than at any time before." The shades of gray between independence and care-giving defy easy stereotyping.

"Greedy Geezers"

Twenty years ago, some journalists began to joke about greedy geezers—although they didn't necessarily publish the term. They reported how retirees were demanding from Congress more benefits, demanding from community agencies more services, and demanding from society more respect.

Social Security became a news story. Older people marched, wrote books, pestered congressmen and senators.

Seniors made the American Association of Retired Persons (AARP) one of the biggest, richest and most vociferous lobbying groups in the country. A dozen other advocacy and lobbying groups were developed by seniors for seniors. This new lobby argued old people were due more because they were veterans who protected our country, they were teachers who taught our children, they were workers who built our economy.

As the baby boomers add their huge numbers to this group, the demands on the rest of the nation will grow. The baby boom generation consists of approximately 76 million people born between 1946 and 1964. The first of the baby boomers will turn 65 in 2011. In 1995 there were about 24 million people over the age of 70. By 2030, when the baby boom generation is fully retired, this figure will have nearly doubled to 47.8 million.[5] The ratio of retirees to workers will change dramatically. In 1965, when Medicare began, 5.5 workers were paying into the system for every beneficiary. By 1995 that ratio had fallen to 3.8 workers per enrollee, and by 2030 it is projected that there will only be 2.2 workers per enrollee.[6] Social Security taxes will rise. Worker benefits may decrease. If some critics of the system prove to be prophetic, other social services will be constricted to pay for the demands of the aging. Services for older Americans will be more and more in budget competition with services for the rest of the citizenry. Today, approximately 38 million people are enrolled in Medicare. By 2010, this will grow to 47 million, and by 2030 over 75 million people will be enrolled in Medicare. In 1996, Medicare spending as a percentage of gross domestic product (GDP) was 2.7 percent. By 2010, the Congressional Budget Office projects that this will grow to 4.4 percent, and to 7.4 percent by 2030, under current policies.[7]

The challenge for journalists will be covering the broad issue fairly and completely. The future controversy will be whether spending such a high percentage of the GDP to support the aging population is a feasible option. Attitudes may shift from encouraging budget spending to support old people toward a more reserved tone reflecting concern for the growing chunk of public money required by Medicare, Medicaid, or similar programs.

She Acts Like She's 84, But She's Only 69

"She acts like she's 84, but she's only 69," wrote a distraught middle-aged daughter of her mother. The letter appeared in a 1999 advice column for seniors, "The Senior Forum," published by Tribune Media Services in newspapers around the country.

"In everything she does and says, Mother is old before her time," the daughter's letter continued. "She's almost totally senile. There's no sense trying to reason with her. And she's endlessly complaining about all sorts of imaginary aches and pains. I swear, she's like some really old person in a nursing home."

And to make matters more confusing for this daughter, her husband's mother, age 73, was far more vibrant and connected to activities and events, family, and friends.

Research has made it clear: We age in different ways, in different stages. The ways and stages are clear, but the progression is not. People suffer them differently: senility, episodic or pervasive; arthritis, mild or severe; isolation, a little or a lot. Some people skip some stages altogether as they grow old. Some people experience them as they grow older; some never experience them before they die.

News reporters like to ask people who turn 100, "How did you come to live so long?" The answers—more to amuse than inform—include one drink of whiskey and branch water every day, church every week, a smile all the time. Oh, if only life—and the end of it—were so easily managed. Whiskey may, instead, hasten the decline into ailments in old age. Church doesn't keep the good from dying young. And smiling won't ease arthritis pain.

But the question of why people age at different rates in different ways is the subject of considerable scientific and sociological research. This is a study that journalists and society will find especially valuable in years to come, as the population of retirees grows and becomes more demanding of news coverage. Although not yet close to explanations of the environmental influences on aging or on the genetic reason for fast-or-slow aging, science has isolated some causes. Bad health habits accelerate aging in most people. Isolation accelerates aging in most people. Genes trigger ailments that in turn accelerate aging.

The mantra of the self-proclaimed experts on the elderly is that wellness practices—exercise, diet, and social interaction—all contribute to a healthier life and may even prolong life. In this examination of cross-cultural journalism relating to aging, the reasons for the varying pace of aging are critical. Understanding this can quash many of the stereotypes that plague reporting, producing, and delivering news about people of age.

Senior What?

If old and aging are different things in different people, then what do we call this group, this demographic, this growing minority demographic? What is the name?

It probably isn't *old folks,* as the newspaper editor warned. But then, some self-deprecating older folks don't mind being called *geezers* in the correct context. It is geezers who slap bumper stickers on the back of their RVs that boast "I'm spending my children's inheritance." The label geezer expresses a defiant or couldn't-care-less attitude.

Probably the most polite, but not totally accurate, title for this large and diverse age group is something like *retiree, retired, retired folks.* Retirement is generally seen as something positive. It is a time of life not defined exactly by time and dates and age. But as more people keep working, at least part time, well into their 70s or even 80s, those terms can't be used for all older people.

The great financial institutions of Wall Street and Main Street have spent millions of dollars in advertising to make retirement akin to Xanadu. They have raised the stock of retirement because it is in their best financial interests to do so. People who feel good about retirement—dreamy views of handsome and healthy younger old people with gray hair and handsome automobiles—are more inclined to invest their money in it. And the financial institutions get rich.

This enrichment of the theme of retirement was not due to the efforts of policy-makers or sociologists bent on improving a segment of the American population. The financial institutions saw it as a good investment.

That, in turn, has caused articles and special sections, magazines and books, television broadcasts and syndicated radio shows portraying older Americans as the nouveau rich—people who can turn home equity and pension payouts into portfolios of stock market winners. Indeed, once upon a time, older Americans were viewed predominantly as poor. Now they are frequently portrayed as wealthy, or near wealthy. Their spending power is a marketer's target. The money of the golden years is changing the nomenclature of aging.

The American Association of Retired Persons, which has changed its official name to the acronym AARP, markets memberships to people as young as 55. Age 55 is not a retirement age date set by Congress or ordered by the courts. The 55th birthday is relatively nondescript for most people.

Emperor Bismarck of the German Empire ordered an old age pension for his soldiers and workers at age 65. Why 65? Most of Bismarck's people didn't live that long, so his pension promise was economical, while sounding benevolent.

But age 65 has remained fixed in Western cultures as some sort of coming-of-late age. The basic age for Social Security benefits was long 65. Employer-based pensions also have been pegged to the traditional age of 65.

Beginning with people born in 1938, the full retirement age for benefits will gradually rise until it reaches 67 for those born in 1960. The Senate's plan would conform Medicare eligibility with the normal retirement age for Social Security by gradually phasing in, over the next 30 years, a rise in the eligibility age from 65 to 67.[8]

So, what are journalists to do, given the shifting concepts of what old is and when it begins? Our experiences with people of age are so varied and diverse as to be confusing to relate in our journalism products.

The TV cameraman videotapes the stark image of an elderly woman, listless in her wheelchair, held fast and safe by soft ties. The writer describes the spiritual survival of a woman in round-the-clock caregiving of her husband. The radio producer broadcasts interviews with pensioners demanding gimme, gimme, gimme. Those images of picture and word and sound need to be put in perspective. They need to be placed in context of all others in the demographic of retirees. No image can be presented as more than it truly represents.

Lifestyles of the Rich and Famous, the Meek and Mild

This is the contrast of the "haves" and the "have-nots." The contrast is in assets and income, but it is also in attitude. Some retirees flaunt their status as free of work and rich of pension. But others are less pronounced about it. Maybe it is only the common differences of personality, no matter the age.

But reporters get caught up in the presentation of those who flaunt their position and those who subjugate it to the other elements of their lives. Sources in, experts on and victims of the issues of old age and retirement posture themselves in various ways: rich and famous, meek and mild. They do it to sell the message that serves their interest: well-being, success, gimme-gimme-gimme, fearful, desperate, or grateful in their role of being older and elderly.

Part of this problem is that some retirees like, and need, to brag. They leave their workplace bragging to co-workers left behind about the leisure and the income they will soon enjoy. They brag about golf and cottages at the lake. They overstate the reality in their enthusiasm. Sometimes, they brag to counterbalance the fear of what will become of them in retirement. Sometimes they brag in hopes of leaving behind in the workplace a bigger image of themselves.

The moment of retirement—leaving work and joining the pension crowd—is a sensitive one. Forty or 50 years of career-building are difficult to dislodge from, at least intellectually. Some older people try to ease the difficulty with boasting. It makes them feel better. It also makes them unreliable sources.

Truly reliable sources are difficult to find on subjects of the personal attitudes and the happiness quotient of older people. The two best sources are the scholars who research old age development and lifestyle, and the older people who have gotten past the boasting about retirement and come to realizations about their careers and retirement and aging. Their hindsight is good. But finding people with hindsight and a willingness to share it is a shoe-leather effort. Social work and mental health professionals can provide perspective into the attitudes of people retiring and aging. But their experiences tend to be of the negative kind, thus coloring the story. Some books written in recent years have mixed the boasting of older people, the hindsight of experienced retirees, the observations of professionals, and the frustration of adult children to be valuable sources for journalists. (See the resource list.)

When the Practical Clashes with Your Emotions

One final problem area for journalism about old age is that issues associated with aging are both of great emotion and matters for regulation. Death is an emotional topic, but it is also enmeshed in state and federal laws and regulations involving wills and estate taxes. Illness causes emotional reactions of fear and sympathy but is also tied up with regulations on insurance, Medicare, hospital days and stays, nursing homes, and home health care. Moving an elderly person into a nursing home is charged with emotion and loaded with regulation. Ending a career is a great intellectual transition and also a complicated financial situation.

Growing old is a time of reward and adventure. But it also requires hard-nosed attention to budgets and health and consumer affairs.

Both the people growing older and the younger people who love them get caught up in this contrast between emotions and regulations. And they transfer that confusion to the journalists who write about them.

Any story about state budget cuts could be a story about cuts in care to the elderly. Any story about the excitement of the "golden years" is also a story about approaching old age.

Summary

No other demographic group is quite like this one. All people's ages change. And then, their age changes them. And it is not just the journalists, but also their readers/viewers who are or should be sensitive to insensitive reporting and writing about people of age, seniors, retirees, and the elderly.

There is another special quality about the aging minority: Our own loved ones become a part of it. We serve them and sometimes suffer with them in this late stage of life. Experiencing this group so intimately is unlike associations that journalists experience with many other minorities.

In addition, the minority of older people is fast becoming a powerful minority—large and wealthy and political. And most important of all, society's prejudices about growing old are complicated by the fact that the phenomena we often associate with old age do not come to all of us at the same age nor in the same pattern. The degree of aging or oldness varies markedly from one human being to the next, despite his or her chronological age.

So how does a journalist write for readers, produce for viewers or deliver for listeners news about a demographic so diverse and so intertwined with our own experience? How does a journalist avoid the generalizations and the negative images of people in so changeable a group?

There are frequently shifting crosscurrents in this particular category of cross-cultural journalism. A journalist must understand these shifting crosscurrents to write, produce and deliver about them, to get the facts straight and get them in a truthful context.

The "Old Folks" Beat—A Moving Target

How then can journalists cover issues of retirement and aging without discrimination? They can employ the basic rules of sourcing and fact gathering to a higher level to overcome the kinds of prejudice already noted. And journalists can follow these six guidelines for reporting on retirees and the elderly:

Guideline 1: *Humanization* (using anecdotes about specific issues) *can be risky.* The diversity within the demographic is so great that humanization might mask the contrast between the actual group at issue and the many other subsets of the whole. Stereotyping is an obvious journalistic pitfall. Any one example used in humanization does not serve to describe or represent more than a specific group within the demographic.

Any attempt at humanization in a news story must be balanced by details and qualifiers of the age and income, the state of wellness and the state of mind of the specific story subjects.

Conversely, with good attention to detail and qualifiers to contrast one subset from all the others of older Americans, humanization could be an especially valuable technique. And in the context of a news story, possibly the sooner the humanization is written the better. It will give both the human interest and point-of-reference of a subject, and also the distinguishing characteristics for the exact target of the story. Editors should be wary of storytelling humanization that is not concretely detailed and cast in a larger context. For example, one of the most popular subjects now for stories about older people relates to their interest and ability to return to work months or even years after official retirement from a career.

Only details of age and income, wellness and state of mind make such stories accurate:

- New retirees can be more anxious to parlay their success and experience into a new workplace adventure.
- Other new retirees think "good riddance" to the workplace and scoff at the suggestion of a retirement-time job.

- Younger retirees relish the idea of leisure time and 401(k) money to finance it, thus rejecting work opportunities—or needs.
- Some older retirees worry their savings are dwindling and they need new income.
- Some of those same older retirees, however, have health problems that prevent a return to work.

No one of these competing examples should be offered as typical of retirees as a group.

During the stock market boom of the 1990s, financial planning magazines published endless stories glorifying early retirement. The theme was that rising stock prices gorged 401(k) plans and other retirement savings programs so as to make early retirement easy. Not only have times changed with the stock market decline at the turn of the century, but more important, the number of early retirement candidates was restricted by two realizations: Advances in health care could mean even well-to-do retirees could outlive their savings, and the psychological benefits of a structured workplace are critical to some personalities.

Those details and qualifiers will pinpoint the exact persons affected and thereby define the specific subset of the specific demographic group the story refers to. Social Security is basic to all retirees, but it is critical to only those of modest means—those with few personal assets and no private pensions.

Health care is important to the older subset, while wellness is more important to the younger ones. Adult children are good company or bad to young retirees. But the emotional value and the caregiving value of adult children and grandchildren may be critical to those closer to the end of life.

The upper middle-class retirees pictured in slick magazines, especially in this day of retirement resorts and investment frenzy, are but a fraction of the post-60 population. And those retirees who will someday live in a nursing home are of critical societal concern, but still are only a part of the demographic. "An estimated 53 percent of all elderly will need nursing homes at some point. That figure rises dramatically for people over 85 years old, according to AARP."[9]

Guideline 2: *Beware of those who claim to represent and those who are eager to profit from senior citizens, retirees, and the elderly.* Their motives are hidden if our stories are not properly sourced. And their messages are subtle.

The AARP has a political agenda and political clout in the federal and state capitals. The AARP portrays older Americans in whatever manner might suit the political issue of the day:

- Old and frail and in need of government protection
- Relatively young and willing to take responsibility for their own financial well-being if the government will give them a tax break
- Unified and of one mind to vote in a block for the politicians and the issues that serve the AARP agenda

Other organizations do the same.

Slick magazines portray a richer retiree, flush with special retirement accounts and savings plans. The magazine ads would have journalists believe that growing older offers great opportunity to pick lifestyle and win rewards for long careers and hard work. Slick magazines on retirement even deny old age, portraying and glorifying instead the so-called 50-plus subset.

Guideline 3: *Beware of the editors and publishers, news directors, and general managers who would prefer a younger, more energetic older person in stories and visuals.* That approach may please advertisers, but it is far from representative of the great variations in the demographic. Much is made these days of the wealth of the younger subset of older people. They are "economically correct" for the image and the financial needs of the newspaper and broadcaster. Old and gray, sick and worried do not lure advertisers.

Guideline 4: *Beware of the inclination to sensationalize. The demographic of post-60 offers endless opportunities.* Television, particularly, likes to sensationalize the darkest side of aging—the poor elderly. Television news programming profiles their economic woes, their loneliness, and their nursing home terror. Television advertising often portrays them as gray, wrinkled, and cranky—for presumed comic effect. The negative images on television are captivating but should not be portrayed as typical more than any other subset.

In a 1996 ABC news documentary on bad nursing homes, the producers gave three minutes of eye candy off the top to good nursing homes, then launched into a 40-minute segment on the worst. The totality of the report was to leave a terribly negative impression of nursing home care in America.

Marketers, particularly those selling travel or luxury and financial products, are inclined to glamorize young and handsome older people, but seldom the elderly, and never the frail and infirm. These sensationalized images might or might not fit the needs of a journalist producing copy on some other senior citizen subset.

Guideline 5: *Older people would be best defined by their lifestyle and income, ability and mind-set instead of their age.* These are the determining factors in older people—not so much their years. And these factors are more difficult to pin down than chronological age. Researchers note in myriad studies that activity level does more to define life and dictate longevity and control happiness. Volunteering, for example, is part of the story of aging in America.

More complex yet for journalists is that many retirees and older people are best defined by their views, opinions, and outlook. Those are, of course, often dictated by many interacting variables, including their actual age but also income, state of wellness, political leanings, and family-social environment. Thus there is a great mixing of conditions in each individual retiree, which makes old people a valuable heterogeneous group to write about. Not all elderly ladies are or are destined to be widows and poor and sad, but some very happy elderly ladies are widows.

Journalists would be wise to be attentive to the attitudes of America's aging population. Stories about Social Security changes, Medicare fixes, health care availability, family relationships, financial services, and social activities will be told best by reporting not the numbers but the emotions of the people involved. On any of these subjects the attitudes of a 60-year-old could be the same as those age 80. And attitudes could be the same regardless of income or social standing.

Guideline 6, possibly the most sensitive guideline: *Writers and editors, producers and anchors should write about America's aging populations mindful that they and their readership/viewership will someday be the same.* No other demographic or minority group addressed in this text presents the risks or opportunities for the working journalist. The risks are twofold: One, that our deeply personal involvement with the aging of friends, parents, and ourselves will skew the objectivity of the writing. Two, that the growing diversity of the demographic will not be adequately defined in the news writing. The great opportunity is that so much of America is a stakeholder in the aging process, journalists will find an eager audience and readership for these stories. Topically, growing old is as universal as breathing air. Everyone has to do it, and wants it to be good. It is a closeness-to-subject that most journalists cannot ever achieve. The older people we write about experience what we all will experience in 10 or 20 or 30 years. That makes the writing about them more difficult.

Journalists and those they write for can and should feel a sense of pending empathy with the subjects of our reports on people growing older.

As the newspaper editor said: "Just don't call 'em 'old folks.'" What he meant was, "Just don't call me that."

Resources

Internet

http://www.aarp.org/   AARP (American Association of Retired Persons)

http://www.census.gov/population/www/socdemo/age.html   Age data link.

http://www.globalaging.org/   Global Action on Aging is an international grassroots citizen group that works on issues of concern to older people. It advocates by, with and for older people worldwide.

http://www.democracygroups.org   A project to create an online directory of U.S.-based electronic mail discussions and e-newsletters related to social change and democratic participation.

Books

Hayflick, Leonard, Ph.D. 1994. *How and Why We Age*. Ballantine Books.

Koenig, Harold G., M.D. 2002. *Purpose and Power in Retirement*. 2002. Radnor, Pa.: Templeton Foundation Press.

Rowe, John W., M.D., and Robert L. Kahn, Ph.D. 1998. *Successful Aging*. New York: Pantheon Books.

Savishinsky, Joel S. 2000. *Breaking the Watch*. Ithaca, N.Y.: Cornell University Press.

Notes

1. Walter Williams, "The Journalist's Creed," 1908. Missouri School of Journalism homepage: http://www.journalism.missouri.edu
2. Guy Keeler, "Medicine Gains Weapons: An Arsenal of Vaccines and Antibiotics Revolutionized Medical Care in This Century Bringing a Dramatic Rise in Life Expectancy," Time Capsule, *Fresno Bee*, 1 January 2000. http://www.fresnobee.com/man/projects/timecapsule/body/weapons.html
3. National Center for Health Statistics, "Life Expectancy Hits New High in 2000; Mortality Declines for Several Leading Causes of Death," news release 10 October 2001. http://www.hhs.gov/news/
4. Ruth Kirschstein, "Perspectives on Aging: Societal Issues," *Proceedings: Technologies for Successful Aging, Journal of Rehabilitation Research and Development*, January/February 2001 (Supplement), 38(1):S26–S29.
5. "Raising the Eligibility Age for Medicare," Issue Brief, 2 July 1997. http://www.concordcoalition.org/entitlements/medicare_elig_age0797.html
6. Ibid., 4.
7. Ibid.
8. Ibid.
9. SF Financial Services, "Statistics and Things You Should Know About Long-term Care." http://www.sf-financial.com/htme/statistics.htm

CHAPTER 7

Taking the Mystery Out of Native American Coverage

Teresa Trumbly Lamsam and Dennis McAuliffe, Jr.

Imagine the reader outrage if a newspaper story about African Americans was replete with unwarranted references to chains and whips and other imagery from the tragic slavery period of American history, or if it needlessly referred to spears and other weapons of warfare in black Americans' ancestral homelands. Now imagine that ethnic group's reaction to the media if practically *all* stories about African Americans, regardless of topic, routinely carried those images.

Native Americans are making significant contributions to society today as political leaders, lawyers, doctors, writers, teachers, social workers, entrepreneurs and entertainers; and bold, new exercises of their unique tribal sovereignty are changing the rules by which millions of Americans live, work and play. But in the nation's media, Indians still "circle the wagons," "smoke the peace pipe," "bury the hatchet," "say ugh" and go "on the warpath" and "off the reservation,"[1] which is what else but their "home of the brave."[2]

In the words of a scathing assessment of the media's coverage of ethnic groups, such "cookie cutter, cliché-ridden 19th Century images shove aside complex stories of contemporary people facing the challenges of

[the] real world."[3] The clichés and "war metaphors"[4] also obscure for the average reader an aspect of Native American journalism that Indian readers spot immediately: mainstream journalists' lack of knowledge and seriousness about their subject, a nationwide issue that is growing in consequence, coverage and complexity.

Indian stories are arguably the most inaccurate stories being done in journalism today. There is perhaps no other area of American society in which reporters routinely get their facts wrong—and get away with it. Their editors don't know enough about Indians, either, to notice, correct or chastise, or to demand better. Rare is the Indian tribe that does not complain about the accuracy or one-sidedness of its media coverage. The 600-member watchdog Native American Journalists Association (NAJA) routinely rebukes the media for what it describes as "serious deficiencies in the context and content of news stories involving Native Americans," especially the frequent "stereotypical images of Native populations through [the media's] selection of stories, the way stories are organized and written, and use of derogatory terms and phrases."[5]

In truth, the story of modern Native America affects the majority of Americans, whether they realize it or not; if they've relied on the media for Indian news, it will be news to them. Native American issues are a Gordian knot of old treaties ("the supreme law of the land"), court rulings, federal law, bureaucratic regulations, tribal council resolutions, and state legislative, gubernatorial and public pressure. Most general assignment reporters, who typically are assigned to "go get an Indian story," don't know whether to start untying—or where to cut through. They simply lack training, the type of training routinely required (and expected) of reporters and editors assigned to cover international relations, public policy, political campaigns, the environment, the economy—comparatively less complex stories that the media take far more seriously.

What You Can Do

The Native American Journalists Association maintains that only Native American journalists can correctly cover Native America. According to the NAJA, only Native Americans are culturally sensitive enough and educated in things Indian to fully grasp and thus correctly report the nuances of Native American issues to begin whacking away at that Gordian knot. NAJA shows its partiality for Native reporters in the selection for its annual Phoenix Award for "best coverage of Native Americans by a mainstream newspaper":[6] Rarely has a non-Native reporter won. In 1999, the *Washington Post* formed an Indian beat, for which veteran reporter William Claiborne wrote intelligent, sensitive and enlightening stories unmatched by anyone, and the *New York Times* published an outstanding series on the complexities of tribal sovereignty. Yet, NAJA declined to select a winner that year, saying the mainstream media hadn't done a good enough job to merit recognition.[7]

On the other hand, if NAJA got its wish and only Native Americans were allowed to cover Native Americans, there would be far fewer stories about Native Americans in the media than there are today. There would be practically no stories at all, mirroring the miniscule number of Native reporters in newsrooms. The American Society of Newspaper Editors' 2000 newsroom census counted 292 American Indians at daily newspapers, or 0.52 percent of a newsroom workforce of 56,200. The low number—lower than the percentage of Native Americans in the population at large—is dramatically higher than the previous year, when only 241, or 0.44 percent, American Indian journalists were at work in the newsroom—and that number represented a decline from the previous year. At the same time, minority employment increased a third of a percentage point, 11.85 percent of newsroom employees.[8]

The numbers for Native Americans point to a reality that may not be to NAJA's liking: Non-Indian reporters will write most of the stories about Native Americans, and any improvement in the coverage of Native Americans must come from non-Indian journalists.

Who Cares?

The U.S. Census Bureau estimated in 1998 that about 2.4 million Native Americans live in all 50 states and the District of Columbia. That miniscule number represents less than 1.0 percent of the national population estimate of 272 million Americans. If that were the extent of the American Indian story, then the lack of media attention to tribes—both in column inches and airtime—probably would be justified.

However, the significance of Indians today is not in the number of people, but in the unique legal status that their 550 federally recognized tribes hold: tribal sovereignty. This grants tribes powers of self-government as "domestic, dependent nations" and exempts them, with some exceptions, from the laws and regulations of the states in which their reservations or communities are located.

When tribes flex their tribal sovereignty—and more and more tribes are doing so in ways both significant and maddening to many non-Indians—the ripple effects are felt far beyond the borders of their reservations. They are felt all the way to statehouses, to Capitol Hill, and to the homes of millions of Americans all across the country.

Those 550 federally recognized tribes in villages of Alaskan Natives and in tribal communities and reservations of American Indians occupy land that is under the trust protection of the federal government, and beyond the jurisdiction of the 34 states where they are located—states where 183 million other Americans live, 67 percent of the U.S. population. Indian tribes are located in—and their rule-changing, game-altering tribal sovereignty affects the politics, economies and ways of life of—some of the country's most populous states: California, Texas, New York, Florida, Michigan, Massachusetts, North Carolina, Washington, Wisconsin.

But the appeal of Indian stories extends to more Americans than these 183 million living in these states. There are countless people who consider themselves to be "part Indian," descendants of unknown—or, more likely, imagined—Indians in their family trees. And in a sense, U.S. history, and especially how it has shaped our national- and self-identity, has made all Americans "part Indian," if only at an emotional level.

These millions of people who are affected directly or indirectly by the tribes in their vicinities also are the consumers that keep journalism in business. They travel. They can see the changes in the political and cultural countryside, and they must wonder why the media hasn't noticed—or hasn't progressed to the level of sophistication that tribes themselves obviously have. People who probably had never seen Indians before are now gambling in their casinos, shopping in their stores, sleeping in their hotels and RV parks, sending their children to their day-care centers and their aging parents to their nursing homes, attending their tribally owned community colleges, playing on their golf courses, fishing with their lures and in their water, surfing the Web with their Internet access, eating their pizza, yogurt and buffalo-burgers, wearing their T-shirts and—if some tribes get their way—putting their money in their "offshore" banks.

Millions more Americans also are benefiting from the Indians in their midst in ways they may not realize (especially if they've relied on the media for the news): The water they drink may be clean only because some tribe exerted treaty rights to force a state or local government to decontaminate it; the schools they send their children to may be underwritten by federal dollars that the handful of Indian children in attendance have brought with them; the jobs they hold may exist only because a nearby Indian casino is fueling the local economy; their local and property taxes may be lower because of it, too. In fact, some tribes—the Coeur d'Alenes of Idaho, the Oneidas of both New York and Wisconsin, for example—have become the largest employers of non-Indians in their counties and regions.

By their nature, Indian stories are compelling and dramatic; they are at once evocative of our history and illustrative of the epoch struggle against adversity that made this country great—at the Indians' expense. And the recent, increasingly bold exercise of tribal sovereignty is creating stories even more compelling and controversial than Indian stories of that past.

But the nationwide mainstream media appear not to have noticed the important changes taking place in Indian Country. The media either ignore them or report them the old-fashioned way: as problem people obstructing progress (defined as anything non-Indians want to do); as historical curiosities stripped of any present-day realities; as simplistic embodiments of various and often inaccurate stereotypes (poverty, crime, alcoholism); and, most alarmingly and inaccurately, as existing outside the context and current of mainstream American society and having nothing to offer the larger society but casinos and welfare cases.

Getting the Stories in Indian Country

One of the complaints about coverage of American Indian stories is that mainstream reporters somehow *just get stupid*. And that's a quote. Who said it? Well, at the yearly conference of NAJA, just about everyone. In fact, NAJA has a reward for those journalists who do the best job of "getting stupid." Every year the Columbus Award is given for the most insulting story of the year about Native Americans. Past "winners" have included the *Washington Post* and CBS's "Sixty Minutes."

Unfortunately, criticism alone doesn't seem to be stemming the tide of inaccurate reporting, mythical portrayals, or the astounding lack of Indian stories in the news. So, what goes wrong? Why does the world's most reputable media do such a poor job of reporting on Indian issues? The answer, in part, has to do with problems wrought by history, ignorance and journalistic training.

The good news is that the media industry recognizes a problem and is well on its way to correcting an embarrassing failing. This chapter is another step in that direction. By the end of this reading, you should be full of new insight and convinced that you can *and need to* report these stories.

Keeping It Simple

Remember one of the first axioms your journalism teacher taught you: *Keep it simple, stupid*. Take it to heart. This is one bit of advice that will keep you out of trouble when writing Native American stories. This is not to suggest that you can't handle complexity but rather a suggestion on how to get started and what to do with those assignments that editors are so apt to make at the last minute.

Remember, the failure of American Indian coverage is that accuracy, fairness and objectivity are stuck in the muck and mire of convoluted reporting. Your job is to clean off the complex issues so that your readers can have a fair and accurate picture. To do that, you need to return to the basics of journalism.

For example, here is the typical scenario for coverage of gasoline tax. The stories tell readers that the state is deprived of much-needed revenue and the non-Indian gasoline/convenience stores face unfair competition from tribal-owned stores that can undercut prices because no state gasoline tax is required. The article offers information and statistics gathered from interviews with the state and the non-Indian businesses. Few reporters would dare turn in such a lopsided story, but with Indian issues, it is common.

Even double-checking the statistics only requires basic math: addition, subtraction, multiplication and division. And in some cases, you need only common sense. Take these numbers, for example. A story reports that the state is losing $100 million a year in gasoline tax revenue. By knowing the amount of tax per gallon, a reporter could quickly calculate how many gallons the tribal stores must sell to validate that figure. You would also need to know the number of tribally owned stores in the state. Let's say the number is 25, which would be high for any state. If the tax is 17 cents per gallon, which is the rate in Oklahoma, that means 25 individual tribally owned stores would have to be selling more than 20 million gallons of gasoline per year on average. Next, ask yourself, "Is that a reasonable amount?" It wouldn't take much additional reporting to find out. If you looked into it, you'd find that an average convenience store is doing well to sell 3 million gallons per year—a far cry from 20 million. The numbers don't add up.

The traditional form of news writing and reporting may be criticized for a lack of creativity or for giving away the punch line too soon, but the fact remains that the majority of newspaper and news service stories follow the "inverted pyramid." A reporter who has mastered this form can make judgments on what is important and then present the information clearly and concisely. The result should be "the best obtainable version of the truth," in the words of the *Washington Post*'s Bob Woodward. Dusting off the old questions—who? what? when? where? why? how?—may be your best chance of obtaining the truth for American Indian stories. Traditional journalism will help you (1) find and keep a focus and (2) eliminate bias and stereotypes—yours included.

Finding and Keeping a Focus

Most of the Native American stories you report will be tied to bigger issues within a larger context. Take the popular stories of Indian gaming and taxation. Tribal sovereignty is intrinsic to both gaming and taxation, and neither can be fully understood outside a historical context. Does either sound like a story you can turn around in a day? Yet, in the current method of covering Native issues, it's likely that an editor will ask you to do just that.

The first thing you will have to do is find a focal point—the same thing you would do if your editor went a little crazy one day and told you the paper needed a story on welfare and, oh, by the way, it's for the next edition. If you're sticking to basics, you'll have or find a news hook for the topic. In the example of Indian gasoline taxation, the news hook could be anything from the opening of a new Indian convenience store to an update on the latest "hidden" amendment to a bill or more specific legislation affecting the issue.

Finding a perspective based on news value offers at least two advantages. One is that you complete your assignment without Cliff Notes on American Indian law and without relegating the taxation issue to 15 column inches of news hole or two minutes of airtime. The second advantage is that you have just started covering Native American issues in the same day-to-day fashion you cover everything else: one story at a time, which means you *will* be doing follow-up stories, including in-depth, ongoing research. The challenge will be to write the second story or to convince the editor that the gas tax report is worth more than one hit.

Eliminating Bias and Stereotypes

Along with the news judgments required by the inverted pyramid, traditional journalism principles underscore the need for accuracy and fairness. Asking the following two questions of every story would eliminate at least half of the criticism levied against Native American coverage: Is this accurate? Is this fair? The only problem left would be the lack of coverage. If these two questions had been asked, then an Oklahoma reporter probably wouldn't have referred to the Creek Nation as the *renegade* tribe in a story about Indian tobacco sales. And a headline on a financial story wouldn't have read: "Chiefs Say Ugh!"

As obvious as these mistakes seem, these actual occurrences are common. Other problems of bias and stereotyping are as routine but more insidious in nature. Consider the following quote in a news story taken from a prepared statement of the Oklahoma Petroleum Marketers Association: If Indian tribes "are successful in Oklahoma, it won't be long until this cancer is nationwide."

The quote is accurate. It was lifted right off a prepared statement. The source is saying that American Indians are a cancer spreading to other parts of the country. A fine point, but the same thing. But does that mean the reporter is in the clear? You will have to ask yourself if the inclusion of this quote stands up to the question of fairness. What if the reference was to African Americans instead? You can't just drop a racial stereotype or bias into a news story *because a source said it was so*. Doing so contributes to the perpetuation of the problem.

Take a look at another newspaper story with the same tone. An Ohio attorney representing gasoline sellers in the state was quoted as saying, "In Ohio we've been fortunate in some ways. We have no tribal trust lands. We have no Native American reservations." The reporter then paraphrased him: "But, he said, that does not make Ohio immune to the problem."

The problem here is that not only are these comments racist but could also be inaccurate. The most likely interpretation of this attorney's words is that Ohio is darn lucky not to have any Indians, but the state better watch out because the Indian problem could be spreading! To be fair to the attorney, a reader can't know the intended meaning of his comment without benefit of context or more information. The reporter didn't follow up on the comment by asking, "Hey, are you saying that Ohio is lucky not to have Indians, whom you seem to be referring to as a problem?" From these two examples, readers are treated to images of American Indians as a *cancer*, a *disease*, or a *problem*.

Katherine Spilde, who has a Ph.D. in anthropology and is the director of research for the National Indian Gaming Association, sees these images as being more than impediments to public awareness and understanding:

> [False images] become truly dangerous to the viability of Indian communities when they are used to justify Federal Indian policies. The complicated historical and legal relationship between tribal governments and the federal government is overlooked or concealed when stereotypes and false images dominate contemporary policy decisions. In the 1990's, the image of the "rich Indian" gave voice to an aggressive anti-sovereignty movement in Congress. In short, "Rich Indian" imagery implies that gaming tribes no longer need sovereign rights (such as treaty rights to hunt and fish) in order to be self-sufficient. By insisting that having both gaming and treaty rights constitutes a "surplus," policy makers proposed legislation that would have required tribes to prove, through a process known as "means testing," that they still "deserved" their original treaty rights.[9]

There are three main reasons the media are botching Indian stories: (1) treating Indians only as problem people; (2) consigning them to history (or to the "trash heap of history," in the words of a former president[10]); and (3) not taking Indians seriously.

Reporters, or at least their stories about Indians, constantly manifest these attitudes.

Treating Indians as Problem People. The fairly typical Indian story begins with one or a group of non-Indians complaining about something a local tribe is doing. For example, at the start of each fishing season, stories invariably appear in the Montana media in which local fishermen gripe about a legal requirement imposed by a tribal government: In addition to a state fishing license, fishermen must purchase a tribal fishing permit from the Confederated Salish and Kootenai Tribes if they want to fish on the Flathead Reservation. The tribes have jurisdiction over all water on their reservation, including the southern half of Flathead Lake, one of the prime fishing spots in the Northwest.

These stories tend to lead with the most accessible and most vocal side of the dispute: the non-Indian complainers. Thus, the tribe is cast, simply by story structure, as the "bad guy" or "guilty party" and on the defensive, since any remarks by tribal authorities tend to be comments defending their actions. Since the Salish-Kootenai people are tired of this seasonal issue (and of the complainers and of their messengers, the media), they tend to ignore reporters' queries on this subject, resulting in this unfortunate but near-standard statement in countless Indian stories: "Tribal authorities could not be reached for comment." Thus, we have the one-sided story that treats Indians as problem people.

A more serious example of this flawed approach—and of the kinds of disastrous corners that uninformed reporters can unwittingly write themselves into—was published under the unfortunate headline "Indian Adoption Runs Afoul of Law."[11]

The lead focused on how a non-Indian couple rescued a Native American infant "addicted to methamphetamine from her [Indian] mother's drug use; and [the child] suffered from fetal alcohol syndrome. [But the child] not only survived—she … came to thrive in the [non-Indian couple's] home." Now the Chippewa-Cree Tribe of Montana's Rocky Boy's Reservation, "citing a federal law designed to keep American Indian children in native homes," wanted to remove the child from the home so she could be adopted by a Chippewa-Cree family. "It's going to tear her apart," the non-Indian "father" complained. "She was born into adversity. She overcame drug addiction at way too young of age. She's overcome a tremendous amount of roadblocks to get to where she is at. Why would anybody want to take that kind of success away from a child? It makes no sense."[12]

It makes plenty of sense to the Chippewas and Crees and to other tribes protected by the federal Indian Child Welfare Act, legislated to halt the widespread practice of adoptions, sometimes even thefts of Indian children by well-intentioned non-Indians to "save" them from what they apparently see as a fate worse than death—growing up Indian.

The story contains a multitude of sins, but it is illustrative of what not to do when writing an Indian story: For starters, it begins in the living room of the weepy non-Indian complaining about those heartless, cruel (and, guilty by association with the mother, drunken and drug-addicted) Indians. The lead immediately casts them in the role of "bad guy" and puts the tribe on the defensive. The reporter then failed to balance her story with equally emoting arguments from the other side—Chippewa-Cree tribal authorities. The director of social services on the reservation is paraphrased as saying many people are not familiar with the federal law, and the tribal police chief (who doesn't have any business being in this particular story in the first place because his presence suggests a crime is being committed) is quoted as saying, "Our values that we have as a tribe—the close kinship and the way that we raise our children—is unique, and that is really important." Then the reporter wanders blindly into the minefield of Indian identity questions by allowing her non-Indian subject to speculate—without any comment from the tribe or statement about Chippewa-Cree requirements for tribal membership—that the law shouldn't apply to the girl because she is "only 1/32 Chippewa Cree"—in other words, not really an Indian or not Indian enough.[13]

Consigning Indians to History, or Treating Them as Historical Curiosities.   Search any newspaper's database for American Indian, and chances are museum stories will top your list. These are stories about the Smithsonian's new National Museum of the American Indian or a tribal museum, especially the new multimillion dollar mega-museum built by the casino-rich Mashantucket Pequots in Connecticut. Or they are about a Native American collection in a state or local museum or the controversies surrounding collections, such as repatriation to tribes of Indian remains of the bones they've been storing in boxes in their basements for more than a century.

An issue that has received a lot of column inches and airtime in recent years, the Kennewick Man, falls into this category. A scientist made a much-quoted but apparently premature and ungrounded assertion that Kennewick Man's ancestors were Caucasian, thus calling into question (by some) the legitimacy of Native Americans' aboriginal rights and claims that they were here first. An editor of a newspaper located near Kennewick Man's gravesite in Washington state boasted once that his paper had run more than a thousand stories on the controversy; asked how many stories he had published about live Indians during the same period, he mumbled an inaudible response.

You may think you're writing about Indians when you do a "museum piece." You're not. All you're doing is making them museum pieces, or reinforcing the belief that they already are.

Also included in this category is any Indian story—or put another way, most Indian stories—burdened with the heavy baggage of century-old clichés, references to buffalo, beads, teepees, the advent of the horse, fire, feathers, buckskin leather and other things visibly "Indian" that we saw in the movies, as well as stories about arts and crafts and powwow dancing. Again, think how quickly you'd be out of a job if you applied the same type of writing to other ethnic groups—African Americans, for example. How would your black readership react if the only stories you wrote about them showed them dancing all the time? You absolutely wouldn't do that because you are sensitive about or have become sensitized to the stereotypical and insulting cliché about blacks and rhythmic dancing.

Newspaper pictures of Indians also belong to this category. When was the last time your newspaper ran a photo of an Indian in a three-piece suit and carrying a briefcase? That would be our candidate for the dress of a fairly typical tribal official these days. Here's an example: In 1994, President Clinton hosted a historic gathering of all tribal leaders in the White House. Out of more than 300 who attended wearing business suits, only a handful were dressed in their tribes' traditional clothing, incorrectly called "costumes" by the media—something else to avoid. Guess whose pictures got in the newspapers?

Not Taking Indians Seriously.   Some of the most serious offenses done to Indians by the media can be found in the "not seriously" category: the stupid things that reporters say about them or the knee-jerk reactions they make at the sight of them.

Why clse do so many reporters automatically look for signs of poverty, alcoholism and unemployment on a reservation but appear blind to such sights when they visit and write about other places "off the reservation," if you will. When was the last time you read a story about a federal government decision in Washington, D.C., that routinely mentioned all the stumbling alcoholics in rundown sections of the city? They're there in our nation's capital, just like on Indian reservations, and in greater number. But send a reporter to a reservation to write about a tribal government decision, and you can bet your rent that there will be paragraphs in the story about alcoholism, poverty and unemployment on the reservation, not to mention buffalo, the advent of the horse, Indian wars, "costumes," dancing and beadwork.

By the way, which racial group of Americans has the highest number of alcoholics? It's not Indians; it's the descendants of the people who introduced "firewater" to them. Indians, in fact, are the only group of Americans whose number of alcoholics *decline* each census—but that's another Indian story you've probably never read.

Here's an example of "Reporters Say the Darndest Things": In an otherwise excellent look at the problems of American Indian education and their high dropout rates from school, *Omaha (Nebr.) World Herald* reporters Henry J. Cordes, Lisa Prue and Paul Goodsell first took the reader to "an older time, before the white man washed over the land like a flood," when Indians "learned how to make fire [and] to hunt and gather food."[14]

A few millennia and paragraphs later, we arrive at the nut graph (with emphasis on "nut"): "Symbolically, Indian children need to graduate from school to adulthood holding an eagle feather in one hand and a personal computer in the other."[15]

Okay. Now read the sentence armed with this knowledge, which the reporters obviously didn't have at hand: Eagle feathers, to many Indians, are *religious* objects. Now make a similar statement about this religion: "Jewish children need to graduate from school wearing a yarmulke on their head and holding a personal computer in their hand." Try variations of the sentence with Roman Catholics (rosaries) and Muslims (prayer rugs). You'll never see those sentences in print!

So why are Indians so special? *Because reporters don't take Indians seriously enough to learn even the basics about them.* The only way reporters can be accurate is to be smarter than everyone else. The only way you can inform your readers is to become more informed than they are. Learn the things you need to know about Indians *before* you write about them (not afterward, via the letters to the editors that come in). It would be unheard of and grounds for dismissal—a firing offense—if a reporter covering the White House were found out not knowing the name of the president or if a Pentagon reporter didn't know the difference between the Army, Navy, Air Force and Marines. But reporters covering Indians are not held to the same obvious standards; they can get away with not knowing what they're doing.

Here's an example that shocks (but doesn't surprise) Indians who have heard the story: A Washington, D.C., reporter nominally had been covering Indians for more than five years—the Bureau of Indian Affairs was one of several federal agencies that comprised his beat. One weekend, a group of tribal leaders rallied in Washington to protest budget cuts proposed by a Senate committee. After covering the event, the reporter confided to an Indian friend that he was confused. Talking in a low, confidential, don't-tell-anyone half-whisper, he said, "One thing I don't understand—what do they mean when they talk about 'treaty rights?'"[16]

In a critique of Native American coverage, News Watch said: "Sloppy use of terms—such as calling elected tribal officials 'elders' or referring to Native clothing as 'costumes'—failure to get even the most basic of facts straight and the continuing lack of using Indian sources (or over reliance on a small set of self-appointed Indian spokespersons) send a message to ... readers and viewers of media that contemporary Indian America is not worthy of serious reporting."[17]

Interviewing

Your interviewing, reporting and people skills need expanding if you expect to *connect* within the American Indian communities. Your basic interviewing skills will still serve you well—with a few changes.

- **Allow extra time.** Promptness takes on a whole new meaning in Indian Country. You should still plan to keep your appointment but don't expect your interview to begin promptly. For example, if you have an interview scheduled with a tribal official at 1 p.m., whether on the telephone or in person, don't be surprised if the interview doesn't begin until 2 p.m. Remember, you are working with another culture. The *lateness* is not meant as an insult to you. Also, once your "interview" begins, don't rush into it. Expect to spend some time, sometimes a whole lot of time, "schmoozing" or warming up before delivering that first pitch.
- **Eye contact.** Avoid it. That doesn't mean never look into the eyes of the person you are talking to, but just don't hold eye contact. To do so would show disrespect.
- **Phrasing of questions.** How you structure your questions makes a difference in the response. In your interviews with Native Americans, question-phrasing can make the difference in whether you *keep* the interview. It's a given that you can shelve the Geraldo Rivera approach. Directness will get you nowhere. You *must* show some deference in your questioning, especially when you interview older people, whether the tribal secretary or tribal leader. Open-ended questions are more likely to help you build rapport. Take, for instance, the gaming and housing issues. Save the more direct questions until you've tested the waters.

  The following sets of questions demonstrate the difference between open-ended and direct questions:

  Open: How has gaming revenue been used?
  Direct: How much of the gaming revenue is directed toward tribal social services?

  Open: How are federal housing funds used?
  Direct: What percentage of federal housing funds goes toward administrative costs?

- **Interpreting the responses.** This is when those listening skills come in handy. Don't expect simple responses. You were taught in journalism class that you have to rein in an interviewee who talks too much off subject. That's one lesson you will have to put aside in interviews with Indian people.

  A response to a seemingly simple question may come back in the form of a long story. These stories or anecdotes illustrate a point and are meant as an answer to your question. Your job will be to figure that out. If you don't quite get the meaning, repeat back what you think is the point. In this case, your questions don't signify ignorance so much as your interest and desire to get it right.

- **Attitude adjustment.** Journalists may be unfairly characterized as being somewhat arrogant, but you should know that even a little ego goes a long way in Indian Country. Native Americans don't brag about themselves; it's expected that a friend, colleague or family member will brag for them.

  Reporters make two common mistakes in this area. The first is easy to remedy and so very easy for American Indians to spot: reporters who forget to check their attitudes. In other words, reporters tend to show up at tribal headquarters with an attitude of "I'm the star reporter from the big city. Aren't you lucky." They think that being from a major newspaper somehow matters. Tribal staff usually have an anecdote or two to tell about the big city reporter who thought he/she was doing a favor by being there. The arrogance is either a source of humor or insult. If they've had any dealings with the media, tribal officials and Indian people are used to dealing with journalists who have no knowledge of Indian issues, even the one they're writing a story about. Expect them to treat you, well, like an idiot and talk to you at the most elementary and childish of levels until your questions suggest that, unlike your predecessors in the media, you've actually done your homework.

  The second mistake is not so apparent. Don't expect tribal officials to toot their own horn or even in some cases to defend their actions. For some, this area is not a problem. They know to "sell" their side of a story. But, for a reporter, this is something that will not be readily apparent.

- **Razzing.** Native Americans may be stereotyped as stoic individuals, but their communication practices couldn't be further from that characterization. Indians often communicate using humor. Outsiders might mistake this communication style as a series of put-downs. As a journalist, you may be engaged in this type of talking.

The best advice is that you respond in a similar manner but never try to "outdo" the other individual or that you accept the put-down by self-effacement in a humorous way. In cases where rapport and trust have already been established, you will begin to become comfortable and may even razz back at an equal level. In all cases, you must be aware of the age and status of the individual. If you are interviewing an elder, you should never initiate razzing directed at that person. In other words, don't trade insults, even good-natured ones.

Gathering the News

Sources

Getting to the *right* sources and then gaining some modicum of trust may be the most wearisome part of reporting in Indian Country. You may be fresh out of journalism school or an award-winning veteran reporter, but if the Indian story is virgin territory, you will face the same obstacles.

The first wall a journalist will come up against is usually *sources*. This is where the frustration begins and ends, and more often than not, where the inaccurate, unfair reporting begins. Good intentions won't help you here. But two of the traits that characterize successful foreign correspondents—commitment and tenacity—will. In fact, you should model your reporting forays into Indian Country on foreign correspondents, especially those new to their assignments—treading with the utmost politeness, sensitivity and inquisitiveness on unfamiliar ground whose history, language, culture and politics are foreign to you but that you are determined to master and report accurately.

On your first story out, you get to the sources you can—the ones who appear appropriate to the story. Journalists who are living and reporting outside of their culture don't wait for a story to break before interviewing. Every day is a succession of conversations, just participating in the everyday life of the people around you. Sometimes an "interview" results in a story idea, but more important to the journalist is the network of sources being developed.

The obstacle to building a network of sources for Indian stories appears before you ever leave the newsroom. Indian stories are usually approached as an afterthought or because an event, such as a protest, makes coverage necessary. Native American issues are consigned second-class coverage, which doesn't afford a reporter the luxury of creating a source repertoire. You won't be given the time.

Then, on those occasions when an Indian story is assigned, you will find that people don't want to talk to you. These are also the same people who complain because your newspaper or TV station never covers their stories. Clearly to you, it is a no-win situation.

When you find yourself thinking like this, ask yourself, When was the last time a journalist went after a news story solely because it was for the benefit of sources? Have you heard a reporter say that an education story fizzled because the school board just wasn't into the story idea? Dust off that journalism textbook or get out your notes. Was "source cooperation" listed as criteria for what makes news?

In *News Reporting and Writing,*[18] criteria for what makes a news story are listed as (1) relevance, (2) usefulness, and (3) interest. The first part of this chapter demonstrated that American Indian stories meet all three requirements. And if you've made it into a newsroom, doesn't that demonstrate that you possess some acumen when it comes to news judgment? Don't let your would-be sources tell you otherwise.

If there's a story worth getting, then go after it. Don't back off because tribal officials won't talk to you or give you access to information. But then don't make the mistake that has come to characterize the "bad" reporting on Indian issues. Don't play the game where you "punish" tribal leaders when they won't cooperate. You know the drill: an obligatory "no comment from officials," but these other folks had plenty to say. You get your story by reporting on at least one side of the issue. It's the tribal officials' fault for not getting their view in when they had the chance. News stories of this nature are often associated with lawsuits and disputes between the U.S. government, including states, and American Indian tribes. If you are covering American Indian stories in the same way you go after the rest of the news, your motivation will be to get the story; if you happen to play Good Samaritan in the process, so much the better.

When you do have a story to go after, here are a few of the people you should be talking to:

- **Primary people.** Policy-makers are not likely to make this list, despite being the favorite target of interviews. They make a good choice because they're media savvy: They know how to talk to reporters and are considerate of deadlines. That should be your first clue that you haven't dug deep enough. To get to the primary sources, you're going to have to visit or call tribal offices. Elders may or may not be "officially" part of the bureaucratic structure. In some cases, a tribe has an Elders' Council. But either way, you should consider elders as part of your primary sources.

- **Secondary people.** If they are located in Washington, D.C., or heading an organization such as the Native American Rights Fund, consider them secondary, but still important. At this level, a reporter will find more cooperation and a good bit of information to add context to a story. For example, the National Indian Gaming Association tracks news stories and statistics on Indian gambling and other issues.
- **Documents.** For background, you can find just about anything on paper that you want—if you have the time and money. Viewing incriminating historical documents, most stored in regional warehouses of the National Archives and little of it on microfiche, is too time-consuming for the resources and patience of most newsrooms. And, anything under the authority of the Bureau of Indian Affairs (BIA), you will have difficulty getting to, more than likely because the BIA doesn't know what happened to the documents or because the information was stored in a rat-infested vault. You will have an easier (and cheaper) time locating paper sources through universities, foundations, organizations, and databases that give you access to federal testimony.

Access to Information

Gaining access to information won't be easy and sometimes won't be possible. To help reporters in this area, the Native American Journalists Association recently established a program that provides advice, some of it legal, on gaining access to information held by tribal governments. But a tribal bureaucracy may not be the only hurdle in your race for information.

Most of the anecdotes you hear will be about how tribal governments block access. But some of the most extraordinary cases of information access in Indian Country involve the federal government. A case in point: The newspaper staff of the tribal *Osage Nation News* wanted to send an issue of the paper to the head of every Osage household. The Osage tribal council agreed to the mailing but, in obtaining the membership list for the editor, encountered a surprising obstacle. The Bureau of Indian Affairs claimed the Osage membership list was the property of the federal government. The agency refused to grant the tribe access to the database, which was stored on a BIA computer in the tribal building. That issue of the newspaper, which contained stories about the bureau, was not mailed to the tribal membership. The information flow was successfully dammed.

Reporters first have to determine if the information is tribal or federal. Ask up front. Otherwise, you'll be spinning wheels. If the information comes under federal jurisdiction, you need to file a Freedom of Information Act (FOIA) request—that's a given, even for seemingly trivial information. But reporters who have to file an FOIA request for Indian information can expect to wait until the next millennium.

If you are requesting access to tribal information, you have a few more roadblocks. Indian law is fairly gray in this area in that it hasn't been tested. Tribes have a right to establish their own resolutions or laws regarding freedom of information. You can bang your head on the wall and cite constitutional rights, but you would be better served to take a different approach. Strike up a conversation with someone and ask "how to ask for the information." That way, you cover your cultural bases. Find out what form the information takes—fiscal reports, departmental budgets, demographic data—or whether it even exists. Oftentimes the tribe just hasn't collected the information, especially social data.

The next step is to sit down with a source and talk about the ramifications of the story. Be up front. Show how the information could make a difference to accuracy and fairness. Lay your skepticism aside for a moment. The reluctance could be chalked up to misunderstanding or embarrassment rather than malevolence.

Tribal Public Affairs Offices

Some larger tribes have public affairs offices, and gaining access to information will mean dealing with them. Employees of these offices may be trained to work with the media. Some have been reporters, editors and public relations officers in mainstream jobs, but others have come from outside the media. In other words, you will be up against the typical PR wall.

Michael Dodson, who has worked in tribal public relations for nearly 10 years, says reporters need to pay their dues in American Indian reporting:

"Once a reporter has proved his mettle with fair, accurate reporting on minor stories, maybe even done a favor or two by providing needed publicity for worthy events, sources in Indian Country will be much more likely to grant interviews, open doors, provide information, maybe even come forward with undisclosed information that points the reporter or editor to a major new story."[19]

The advantage of reporting on a tribe with a public affairs office or even a press secretary is that at least someone in the tribal government will answer the telephone or return a reporter's phone message. Reporters working on Indian stories often complain that all telephone lines in Indian Country seem to lead to some black hole in outer space—no one answers the phone, and leaving messages is a one-way street.

But before you get all buddy-buddy with a public affairs officer, don't forget that you still need to view information through your prism of skepticism. Tribal public affairs people also have the job of putting a spin on the news, just like their counterparts in mainstream. Groups of factions within tribes will attempt the same. Careless reporters often find that they have served as a mouthpiece for tribal political factions.

Indian 101

Here are some things you need to know about Indians before you write about them. Officials at the Interior Department and the Bureau of Indian Affairs dealing with those who don't know about Indians (the media and members of Congress and their staffs) call this type of tutorial Indian 101.

When you are assigned an Indian story for the first time, your first phone call should be to the Native American Journalists Association in Minneapolis, Minnesota (612/729-9244). Ask for copies of two publications that NAJA produced with Knight Ridder, *The Wichita Eagle* and the *St. Paul Pioneer Press*; they are "100 Questions, 500 Nations: A Reporter's Guide to Native America" and "Native America: Reporters' Sourcebook."

If you cover Indians regularly, stay in touch with NAJA (its Web address is www.naja.com). NAJA members, who work for the mainstream media and for tribal newspapers, can be immensely helpful to you, not only for guidance but, once you gain their trust and respect, for story ideas and sources as well. Consider going to NAJA's annual conferences, usually held each June near Indian communities around the country. Past conferences have taken place in Bismarck, North Dakota; Bangor, Maine; Tempe, Arizona; and Fort Lauderdale, Florida.

What Is an Indian (and Who Gets to Be One)?

Many Indian people object to being termed a "minority" because they recognize that ethnicity is not the sole source of their "Indianness," their status and lifestyle of "being Indian."

As the federal Office of American Indian Trust says:

> It is important to understand the difference between the ethnological term "Indian" and the political/legal term "Indian." The protections and services provided by the United States for tribal members flow not from an individual's status as an American Indian in an ethnological sense, but because the person is a member of a tribe recognized by the United States, and with which the United States has a special trust relationship. This special trust relationship entails certain legally enforceable obligations and responsibilities.

In other words, being Indian today is not a matter of ethnicity but of membership in a tribe, or to use the prevalent term, being *enrolled* in a tribe. To quote NAJA:

> There are millions of people with Indian ancestry, but that does not make them American Indians in the eyes of tribes or the federal government. The federal government considers someone American Indian if he or she belongs to a federally recognized tribe. Individual tribes have the exclusive right to determine their own membership. Tribal governments formally list their members, who must meet specific criteria for enrollment. Some tribes require a person to trace [a certain percentage] of his or her lineage to the tribe, while others require only proof of descent.[20]

As a reporter, feel free to ask someone who claims to be an Indian if he or she is "enrolled." But avoid the temptation to ask what one author called "the Indian Question:" What percentage of Indian are you? "People [just] don't see how racist it is to ask the Indian Question," the author wrote.

> It's innocuous enough, and posed with the most virtuous of intentions. Some stranger or acquaintance we've never had the slightest curiosity about says he's Indian, and suddenly we're tripping over ourselves to know not just his ethnic background—nothing wrong with that—but the exact percentage or fraction of a certain portion of his racial makeup, commonly referred to as "blood." We've all popped the question: "How much Indian blood do you have?" I've asked. I've never asked a black. I've never asked an Asian. I've

never asked a Hispanic. I've never asked a European. I've never asked any hyphenated American. But I've sure asked an Indian, and I've sure been asked."[21]

Since tribal membership determines whether someone is an Indian, don't just refer to the people you write about as "Indian." There's an argument, on a political-correctness level, about whether to use the term *Native American* or *American Indian*. How about just using the correct tribal name, such as Cherokee, Choctaw, Seminole, or Lenape? He or she is an Osage, Blackfeet, Crow, Cheyenne or Lakota. (Lakota Sioux, by the way, is redundant.) The term *American Indian* just makes things more convenient and "lumpable" for the government and the rest of us.

Now that tribes determine who is a member, and since Indians are officially only those people who are members of tribes, here is something an Indian is not: part Indian. Please keep your copy, as well as your mind, free of that annoying description. Someone either is or is not an Indian and, under the proper "political/legal term *Indian*," no one is "part." On the other hand, in the commonly accepted but imprecise "ethnological term *Indian*," just about every Indian is "part." Few of the 2.4 million Americans who identified themselves as Indians on the census are in fact "full-bloods." Unfortunately, many more people think Indians have to be full-bloods than there are actual full-bloods.

In the period when forced assimilation was the official policy of the U.S. government toward Native Americans, the Bureau of Indian Affairs imposed a 25 percent blood-quantum requirement on most tribes. Since there is no longer a standard by which tribes can accept individuals as members, there is no longer a "standard" look to Indians. You will find, if (or, we hope, as) you tour Indian Country, that not all Indian people—in fact, many do not—look like the Indians you saw in the movies in terms of their hair, eye and skin colors. On the other hand, those Indian actors were mostly Italians. Please try to avoid the statement, "You don't look Indian."

And yes, Indians are citizens of the United States, and they can vote (though few do—a story you might consider writing one day).

And contrary to popular belief, they do pay taxes. Tribes, not individual Indians, are tax-exempt. There are some exceptions, however:

Native Americans employed on reservations do not pay state income taxes. American Indians living on trust land are free from local and state property taxes. Generally, state sales taxes are not levied on Indian transactions made on reservations. Indians do not pay federal income taxes on money earned from trust lands, such as fees received for grazing rights and oil drilling.[22]

What Is a Tribe?

There's only one answer to this question, and it is not one that also could apply to barbershop quartets or other cultural groups. A tribe is a government, pure and simple, and nothing else.

Since tribes are governments, the answer to the question How many governors are at work in the United States? is always 550 short, in a sense—they are the leaders of the distinct and unique governments of the 550 distinct and unique Indian tribes in this country.

Tribes enjoy the unique legal status of tribal sovereignty. Few stories put Indian issues in the context of tribal sovereignty, or try to define it, much less tell readers its significance. According to News Watch, "This lack of context adds to the sense of 'otherness,' that somehow Indians are looking for special treatment above the law."[23]

No other aboriginal groups in the world have tribal sovereignty, which grants tribes powers of self-government as "domestic, dependent nations" and exempts them, with some exceptions, from the laws and regulations of the states in which their reservations or communities are located. "Tribal governing powers ... are defined by a mosaic of federal law—constitutional, statutory, and administrative—and in great measure by judicial decisions of the United States Supreme Court," dating back to the 1820s.[24]

As NAJA puts it, "There is nothing more important to Indian governments and people than sovereignty."[25] They take it very seriously, to the depths of their souls. For the most part, only Indian people can correctly answer this question, because non-Indian schools don't teach it: How many sovereign powers constitute the U.S. system of government? The answer is three: federal, state *and tribal*.

Like the federal government and states, tribes have sovereign immunity—the right "to define the terms upon which it can be sued"[26]— and maintain jurisdiction over its reservation or tribal land. This gets complicated, because so many reservations were opened to non-Indian settlement and land ownership under the General Allotment, or Dawes, Act of 1887. The Dawes Act also abolished many reservations (only one of the 39 tribes in Oklahoma, for example, technically still has a reservation), leaving those tribes with tribal communities and some tribally owned land to govern. Indians are the minority on many of their reservations today; much, if not most, land within reservation boundaries is owned by non-Indians. Generally speaking, tribes do not have jurisdiction over non-Indians and cannot try non-Indians in tribal courts.

What Do the Media Miss in Casino Stories?

Casino stories, the low-hanging fruit of Native American journalism, typically give the impression that individual Indians are getting rich, but neglect to say that federal law (the Indian Gaming Regulatory Act) restricts the way tribes can spend their money: Their gambling wealth must fund educational, health, welfare, economic development and other social programs, even road-building and garbage collection on reservations before individual tribal members can share in the profits. Of the more than 220 tribes that operate casinos, only about 50 have received permission from the Secretary of Interior to make per-capita payments from casino profits to their members.[27]

Chances are, if you write about Indians, the lure of the easy and obvious casino story will be irresistible. If you're working on a casino story, call the National Indian Gaming Association or the National Indian Gaming Commission (one's an interest group, the other a government agency) in Washington, D.C., for help in learning, then making sense of some of the complexities surrounding Indian casinos. For example, what the differences are between Class I, II and III gambling and for what type a tribe is required to secure a "compact" with a state government—essentially getting a state's permission—despite the tribe's sovereignty.

The media demonstrated how little they know about tribal sovereignty and Indian casinos when the National Football League rejected a bid by the casino-wealthy Mashantucket Pequot Tribe of Connecticut to buy the New England Patriots professional football team a few years ago. The NFL dismissed the tribe as a "gambling interest," thus unsuitable (and undesirable) to do business with the NFL. But the tribe, which is a government with sovereign powers, is no more a gambling interest than any state with a lottery (all but two of the 50) that the NFL allows to build stadiums and otherwise subsidize its teams. That was a potentially good story that no one ever read—one of countless in Indian Country that go unnoticed.

If Nothing Else, Walk away with This

The truth is, as the *Post*'s William Claiborne demonstrated with his file of top-notch Indian stories, you don't have to be an Indian to write a good Indian story; neither do you have to be an academically recognized expert in the minutiae of Indian issues. You just have to be a good reporter. It's as simple as that. It's also as complicated as that, as even a cursory look at some of "the good, the bad and the ugly" of Native American journalism indicates.

Some do's and don'ts of reporting on Indian Country include:[28]

- Do get to know the community you are covering; become a familiar face.
- Do subscribe to at least one national Indian newspaper.
- Do include tribal college presidents and professors in your source list.
- Do make native issues a regular news beat.
- Do consider your reporting role vital to native peoples' futures.
- Don't rely on the tribal newspaper as a primary source of information.
- Don't use the same American Indian as the primary source for every story.
- Don't underestimate interest in native-related subjects.
- Don't let tribal politics prevent you from writing an accurate story.
- Don't forget to include tribal elders' perspectives.

Something strange happens to ordinarily good reporters and editors when they're doing an Indian story. For reasons that remain guesses, mysteries, even conspiracies for tribes and others interested in improving coverage of Indians, the instant mainstream journalists type *Native American* into their computer, they forget the tenets of their profession, the basics of good journalism, all those ABCs of the 5Ws that they learned in the very first class of their Reporting 101 course in college. Most of all, they forget to talk to both sides of the story.

Put another way, if you're writing a story about Indians, talk to the Indians, please—and lead with them. That sounds pretty obvious, but it's amazing how many otherwise good journalists fail to do that, resulting in one-sided or lopsided coverage of the side complaining about something those darn Indians are doing. And, most important, be aware of the stereotypes you are bringing to the story. You may not know it, but if you've ever watched a John Wayne western or "The Lone Ranger" on television, you are afflicted with what Walter Lippmann called "pictures in our heads"[29]—the disease of racial stereotypes. Once you've got it, you can't get rid of it—you can only transmit it. Indian stereotypes are lurking just inside your fingertips and are ready to spring onto the keyboard and into your copy the moment you let your guard down.

Resources

Internet

http://www.naja.com/   Native American Journalists Association

http://www.nativeculture.com/lisamitten/aila.html   American Indian Library Association

http://www.hanksville.org/NAresources/indices/NAetext.html   Index of Native American Electronic Text Resources on the Internet

http://muse.jhu.edu/journals/aiq/   American Indian Quarterly

http://www.indians.org/tribes/tribes.html   American Indian Tribal Directory. Helps locate federally recognized tribes by tribe, by state and by city/state.

Books and Article

Baylor, T. 1996. "Media Framing of Movement Protest: The Case of American Indian Protest." *Social Science Journal*, 33:241-255.

Brooks, Brian S., George Kennedy, Daryl R. Moen, and Don Ranly. 1992. *News Reporting and Writing*, 4th ed. New York: St. Martin's Press.

McAuliffe, Dennis, Jr. 1999. *Bloodland: A Family Story of Oil, Greed and Murder on the Osage Reservation*. San Francisco, Calif.: Council Oak Books.

Notes

1. Cited in Center for Integration and Improvement of Journalism, San Francisco State University, "Native Americans: Cliches, Ancient Images Dominate Coverage," in *News Watch: A Critical Look at Coverage of People of Color—A Unity '94 Project* (San Francisco: Author, 1994), 12, 48.

2. Cited in Center for Integration and Improvement of Journalism, San Francisco State University, "News Coverage of Native Americans in the

New York Times and *Los Angeles Times* May 1997-May 1998" in a report on a study by NewsWatch Project (San Francisco: Author, 1998).

3. Center for Integration and Improvement of Journalism, "Native Americans" (1994), 48.

4. Center for Integration and Improvement of Journalism, "News Coverage of Native Americans" (1998).

5. "Native American Youth Pipeline Into the Media Project," Report from the Native American Journalists Association to the W.K. Kellogg Foundation (1999), 5.

6. Ibid.

7. *The Unity News*, student publication of Unity '99, Official Conference Edition, No. 4, 10 July 1999.

8. American Society of Newspaper Editors, "ASNE's 2000 Newsroom Census," 12 April 2000.

9. Katherine Spilde, interview with Teresa Lamsam, October 2000.

10. Former movie actor and U.S. president Ronald Reagan said the Soviet Union and its political philosophy of communism belonged on the "trash heap of history."

11. Lorie Hutson of Lee Montana Newspapers, "Indian Adoption Runs Afoul of Law," *The Missoulian*, 18 October 1999.

12. Ibid. All quotes in paragraph.

13. Ibid.

14. Henry J. Cordes, Lisa Prue and Paul Goodsell, "The Future for American Indians Seems Bleak as Youth Fall Behind and Drop Out," *The Omaha World Herald*, 13 February 2000.

15. Ibid.

16. Dennis McAuliffe, Jr., "The Media and Misunderstanding of Native American Sovereignty," a lecture for The Center for the Rocky Mountain West, 25 February 1999.

17. Center for Integration and Improvement of Journalism, "Native Americans" (1994), 48.

18. Brian S. Brooks, George Kennedy, Daryl R. Moen, and Don Ranly, *News Reporting and Writing,* 4th ed. (New York: St. Martin's Press, 1992).

19. Michael Dodson, interview with Teresa Lamsam, October 2000.

20. Native American Journalists Association, Knight Ridder, *The Wichita Eagle* and the *St. Paul Pioneer Press, 100 Questions, 500 Nations: A Reporter's Guide to Native America* (1998), 6.

21. Dennis McAuliffe, Jr., *Bloodland: A Family Story of Oil, Greed and Murder on the Osage Reservation* (San Francisco: Council Oak Books, 1999), 174.

22. Native American Journalists Association, 9.

23. Center for Integration and Improvement of Journalism, "News Coverage of Native Americans" (1998).

24. James J. Lopach, Margery Hunter Brown, and Richmond L. Clow, *Tribal Government Today: Politics on Montana Indian Reservations,* rev. ed. (Niwot, Colo.: University Press of Colorado, 1990), 13-14.

25. Native American Journalists Association, 9.

26. Ibid.

27. Ibid., 11.

28. The list was compiled by Jodie Rave, an Indian affairs reporter for the *Lincoln (Neb.) Journal Star* and other Lee Enterprises newspapers. She is a Mandan-Hidatsa Indian from the Fort Berthold Reservation in North Dakota.

29. Clint C. Wilson II and Felix Gutierrez, *Race, Multiculturalism, and the Media: From Mass to Class Communication*, 2nd ed. (Thousand Oaks, Calif.: Sage Publications, 1995), 43.

CHAPTER 8

Covering Religion

Judith M. Buddenbaum

Once upon a time, not too many years ago, religion was considered a moribund beat to be shunned by talented journalists. Old attitudes die hard, but today the reality is quite different from that of just 15 or 20 years ago. Religion is no longer an "orphan beat." Now, says former *Aurora (Ill.) Beacon News* religion editor Marcia Z. Nelson, "It's one child in a large, competitive family of beats."

The importance today of that "child" in the "family of beats" can best be illustrated by media response to the events of September 11, 2001. As a shocked and grieving nation sought explanations for the attacks that destroyed the World Trade Center and damaged the Pentagon, reporters at news outlets around the nation scrambled. It proved difficult to produce meaningful stories that would explain Islam as a religion and as a political force as well as ones that would counteract the stereotype of the Muslim terrorist and lessen the danger of retaliation against Muslim Americans.

As the events of September 11 suggest, reporters from all beats may find themselves covering news stories with a religious dimension. This

---

Some material in this chapter is from Judith Buddenbaum, *Reporting News about Religion: An Introduction for Journalists* (Ames: Iowa State University Press, 1998). Used with permission.

chapter is designed to help both religion specialists and those working other beats provide sensitive, accurate coverage of stories with a religious dimension. It also offers tips on using religion reporting as a way to provide news for and about diverse groups within a community.

Why the Media Cover Religion

The mass media cover religion because they have to. But they also cover religion because people want it. They need it. Covering it, and covering it well, is good journalism. And it's good business.

Faced with declining levels of trust and challenged by competition from new media, including the Internet, traditional news media are increasingly seeking ways to reconnect with the public. One way to do that, they have found, is to give people what they want. And people do want religion news.

According to a 1988 national survey led by Stewart M. Hoover, people ranked religion news fifth in importance and sixth in readership among nine kinds of specialty news—behind education, which ranked first on both counts, but well ahead of sports, which the public ranked last in importance and only eighth in readership.[1]

But it's more than just giving people what they say they want. Journalists themselves have become increasingly aware that religion is an important force in society. Religion is, says the *Toledo Blade*'s Rebekah Scott, "a thread woven through all discourse and motivation of action, public and private." Religion shapes people and, through them, culture. Because it is an enduring force in society, news stories are incomplete and potentially misleading unless they take religion into account.

But religion is not monolithic.

According to data released in 2002 by the Glenmary Research Center, most people in the United States identify themselves as Christian,[2] but the 2001 *Yearbook of American and Canadian Churches* lists at least 200 different Christian churches, denominations and sects.[3] Although there are still more Jews than Muslims in the United States, the number of Muslims in America is on the increase.

No one knows for sure how many religions there are. J. Gordon Melton, editor of *The Encyclopedia of American Religion*, identified more than 1200 religions in the United States that have one congregation with at least 2000 members, several smaller congregations, or that draw members from more than one state.[4] By counting even smaller groups, including those brought together by mail or Internet, others find at least twice as many. Although few religions place gender, race, ethnicity or other demographic limits on membership, there are real demographic and cultural differences among them. By covering religion, reporters necessarily cover other kinds of diversity. In some cases, cultivating sources within religious communities can be the only way to gain access to certain immigrant or ethnic communities. Because many health care facilities and social service agencies are sponsored by or affiliated with a religion, religion reporting can also provide insight into the problems of those with special needs.

Because religion is so much a part of many people's lives, covering the beliefs, holidays and holy days, religiously inspired lifestyles and practices of racial and ethnic minorities, gays and lesbians, and people with disabilities can make the unfamiliar understandable and, therefore, less threatening. But good religion coverage is more than just a way to offset the historical tendency of the media to concentrate on activities and interests of white, middle- and upper-class males.

Each religion has its own beliefs and those beliefs influence people's attitudes, opinions and political behaviors. Those attitudes, opinions and behaviors have consequences that extend to believers and nonbelievers alike. While other factors play a role, religion is involved in conflicts around the world: in Northern Ireland, in Bosnia, in the Middle East, in Malaysia, and in India and Pakistan.

And the same thing is true on the domestic front. Within the United States, religiously inspired battles over civil rights, equal rights, affirmative action, immigration, school curricula, television and the movies, welfare, contraception and abortion, environmental protection, homosexuality, and school prayer are evidence of what sociologist James Davison Hunter describes as a "culture war."

Although the culture war is often presented as one between religious people and the forces of modernity/secularity, more often the culture war is between those with different religious understandings. What is at stake is, as Hunter explained, "competing non-negotiable claims about how public life ought to be ordered" that "emerge out of our ultimate beliefs and commitments, our most cherished sense of what is right, true, and good."[5]

Those ultimate beliefs are, at core, religious. Therefore, coverage of competing claims in politics, business, science and medicine, education, entertainment and even sports necessarily requires covering the religious dimension. Especially in cases where problems seem insoluble, coverage that ignores the religion angle will, at best, be incomplete. At worst, it can be misleading or even false.

Good religion reporting, then, is one way to fulfill the Hutchins Commission's challenge to provide "a representative picture of the constituent groups of society"—of minorities.[6] Sensitive attention to the beliefs that underlie private behaviors such as decisions about lifestyles and public concerns about social problems helps tell "the truth about an event" by placing problems "in a context which gives them meaning."

Trends in Religion News Coverage

Although religion has always been a part of the news, the media have changed the way they cover religion in response both to audience demands and to increased public awareness of the importance of religion in people's lives and as a cultural force.

Until recently, most newspapers had a traditional church page on Friday or Saturday; until shortly after World War II, many also set aside space on Monday for brief reports of sermons. To fill that space, religion reporters concentrated on easy-to-write local stories about people and local events—stories about "bingo and bean suppers" and of the "grinding and clanking of ecclesiastical machinery," as veteran Associated Press (AP) religion writer George Cornell described them.

According to studies conducted by Kenneth D. Nordin[7] and by Debra L. Mason,[8] in the larger cities those stories occasionally came from Catholic parishes or Jewish synagogues, but stories about immigrant or African-American congregations were rare. Almost all of the attention went to the large, mainline Protestant churches attended by the middle and upper classes. Few stories had much relevance to those outside a particular faith community. There were, however, exceptions.

As early as 1980, each week Ed Briggs produced a traditional church page and a half-page roundup column devoted to religion news from around the world for the *Richmond (Va.) Times-Dispatch*. But he also wrote some in-depth features and hard news stories that were quite long and complex, particularly by the standard of the day. Those stories sometimes ran in the main news section and, on occasion, the front page. "Richmonders Watching Religious Shows at $2\frac{1}{2}$ Times National Rate," the March 22, 1982, story he and Thomas R. Morris produced, remains one of the most thorough early examinations of the audience for religious television. As survey-based research, methodologically it compares favorably with and is much more readable than similar studies of the electronic church that appear in the academic and scholarly literature.

While depth and variety were the exception just 20 years ago, today they are quite common. According to Bill Broadway, religion page writer-editor for the *Washington Post*, "Religion news has moved beyond denominational reports and simple events coverage to include lifestyle explorations of all forms of personal spirituality." And that spirituality is not just the faith of white, middle- and upper-class Protestants. It is the faith of religious, ethnic and racial minorities as well as the quest for purpose, meaning and values by those who do not consider themselves religious.

As a way of signaling this broader emphasis, the name for space set aside for religion news began to change. The "church page" with its exclusively Christian connotation became a "religion page," but even that seemed narrow. By 1990 many papers created religion sections with names such as "Religion and Ethics" or "Faith and Values."

Stories in those sections explore both the private face of religion—its role in people's everyday lives—and its public face—the interplay among religion, politics and culture as it affects both believers and nonbelievers. There are stories about issues, trends, theology, values and ethics, and about faith, spirituality, good works, programs, policies, holidays and holy days, people and events. All may be reported from a variety of perspectives—those of the religious institutions, their clergy, lay members, outside observers and of secular institutions. The stories often cut across many religions and draw on numerous sources.

To tell the stories, reporters frequently abandon the inverted pyramid in favor of more literary styles. As stories have become more complex and more innovative, they also have become longer. In the 1980s, a newspaper story running 20 column inches was very long. A decade later, religion reporters routinely produced weekly stories that, with graphics, filled an entire page and often spilled over to a second.

Since 1994, when *The Dallas Morning News* began publishing a six-page section, the paper has been the leader in providing in-depth coverage of religion news. To produce that kind of coverage on a weekly basis, the paper employs a religion editor, an assistant editor, religion writers, and support personnel, including researchers and graphic artists.

The results of that kind of commitment of resources have been rewarding. According to Bob Mong, who as managing editor was instrumental in expanding coverage, the religion section has created more excitement than any other project he has launched during his career. Almost every year since the section was started, it has won the Schachern Award, given annually by the Religion Newswriters Association to outstanding religion sections in general circulation print media.

While few papers can match the resources *The Dallas Morning News*, with its weekday circulation of 500,000 and a Sunday circulation half again as large, commits to the religion beat, the trend at other papers has generally been toward expanded religion news coverage. Since 1985, the average amount of space set aside for religion news has increased by at least one full page. The number of full-time religion reporters at newspapers has nearly doubled; the number of papers with more than one full-time religion reporter has more than quadrupled.

Public Criticism of Religion News Coverage

Now that the media are devoting more resources to religion news, many stories about religion are excellent. The worst are probably no worse than poorly done stories from other beats. However, complaints about news coverage of religion abound.

Hoover's 1988 study, which found that people generally rank religion news much higher in importance and readership than news about sports, revealed a very different picture when it comes to reader satisfaction. Sports, which people ranked last in importance, moved up to first place for satisfaction with coverage. Religion fell from fifth place for importance to last place in reader satisfaction.

In 1994 the 65 top leaders who responded to my mail survey of all Christian churches listed in the *Yearbook of American and Canadian Churches* gave the mass media an average grade of D for their coverage of religion. Only two leaders awarded religion news coverage a grade of B; there were 13 C's, 33 D's and 15 F's.[9]

While clergy from all denominations said reporters miss or ignore important stories and sensationalize or mangle others, those from conservative Protestant churches were much more likely than other clergy to believe the media are biased against religion. They described journalists as a-religious at best, openly hostile to religion at worst. Mass media, they said, work to undermine religion and religious values.

Catholic clergy also sometimes complained about what they perceived as unfair and sensationalized coverage of their church and its problems, but they were less inclined to attribute negative coverage to outright bias among journalists or to their lack of religious faith. Like the clergy from the moderate to liberal "mainline" or "old-line" Protestant churches, they were much more concerned about missing stories and shallow coverage that produce an incomplete and sometimes misleading picture of religion and religious people.

Although there are no similar studies of leaders from non-Christian faiths, the available evidence suggests that rabbis generally share the concerns of mainline Protestant leaders. Muslims and members of alternative or new religions more often detect a kind of bias that favors the Judeo-Christian religious tradition to the detriment of their own faith.

Across all religious traditions, lay members' criticisms of religion news parallel those of their leaders. And they often act accordingly. Conservative Protestants are often loath to believe there are any Christian journalists, even in cases where reporters for the local paper are members of their own congregations. Because they have heard so often that the media are part of a secular humanist plot to destroy religion, they are the most likely of all religious people to avoid both television news and newspapers entirely or to turn off the TV or drop their subscriptions in response to even a single story they consider offensive. Members of other faith communities are less likely to respond so strongly to one or a few stories they consider poorly done or offensive. They will, however, seek out alternative news sources if they feel the traditional mass media are not giving them enough of the kinds of news they want to make watching or reading worth the time and money.

Leaders and laity alike, regardless of their own religious beliefs, generally complain that journalists fail to take religion seriously, treat it as a joke, or fail to show its beneficial effects. Those with no religion more often complain that the media take it too seriously. Like Muslims and members of alternative religions, they see a Judeo-Christian bias that marginalizes and delegitimizes their own understanding. In their opinion, the media accept at face value and perpetuate meaningless claims about the existence of a god. For example, Don Barker, director of public relations for the Freedom from Religion Foundation, asks why the media routinely quote people who, having survived a disaster, attribute their good fortune to God without asking why a supposedly all-powerful god would let others who also claim to believe in him perish in the same disaster.

Understanding the Criticisms

Some of the criticisms leveled against the way news media treat religion are overblown. Others have more merit. However, all are regularly repeated and promoted through books such as Marvin Olasky's *The Prodigal Press: The Anti-Christian Bias of the American Press*, which is often cited by conservative Christians as proof of media bias against religion.[10] Therefore, even criticisms that are little more than repeated myths must be taken seriously.

The most commonly heard complaint is that journalists are out of touch with their audience and biased against religion because they are an irreligious lot who could not possibly understand or report accurately and sensitively on matters of faith. That complaint is, at best, a half-truth.

Stories of cynical reporters and hard-bitten editors who reject out of hand any story even touching on religion are a part of the folklore of journalism. So are tales of those who think religion is, in the words of CBS News senior political producer Brian Healy, news only if it "enters the world of party politics, pageantry or pedophilia."

In support of the image of the irreligious journalist, critics most often cite a survey in the 1980s conducted by Robert Lichter, Stanley Rothman, and Linda Lichter, in which half the respondents reported no religious affiliation and 86 percent said they "never" attended worship services.[11] But in citing those figures, the critics ignore widely available results that present a very different picture.

In contrast to the Lichter, Rothman and Lichter study, which included only journalists working for elite media located in the northeastern United States, data from a survey of a random sample of all journalists collected by David Weaver and G. Cleveland Wilhoit for their book, *The American Journalist,* indicate that only about one-fourth of all journalists considered religion "unimportant."[12] Levels of "religiosity" are even higher if one considers only those journalists whose main responsibility is for religion news. In surveys that I conducted in 1980 and 1985 and that Debra L. Mason, Guido Stempel III and I conducted in 1995, only about 10 percent of all religion reporters said they did not identify with any religion.[13] Four out of five respondents called themselves "Christian." Another 10 percent identified with non-Christian religions such as Judaism, Islam, Buddhism, Baha'i and New Age. Moreover, of those who identified with a religion, about two-thirds said they are "somewhat" or "very" active in their religion. Only about 10 percent reported no activity. Therefore, it is hard to see how problems associated with covering religion news can be caused by reporters who are a-religious and anti-religion. Even if one were to agree with the critics that a religious person should cover religion news, hiring only religious people would not solve the problem. The religion of the reporter would necessarily differ from that of many, if not most, audience members. The key to good coverage really is whether the reporter has sufficient knowledge to understand religion in all its infinite varieties, the temperament to approach all religions with an open yet questioning mind, and the talent to cover it in ways that are both factually accurate and meaningful to believers and nonbelievers alike. Both having a religion and not ascribing to one represent attitudes toward the subject that may or may not have some unfortunate effects on coverage. In some cases the belief or nonbelief of the reporter can produce bias. But in either case it is not likely to be a bias against religion *per se*. Far more common, and perhaps more pernicious, is the bias that creeps in as a result of easy acceptance of cultural norms and overreliance on craft traditions.

As Mark Silk, a former newspaper reporter who now heads the Center for the Study of Religion in Public Life at Trinity College in Hartford, Connecticut, pointed out in his 1995 book *Unsecular Media: Making News of Religion in America,* journalists use a few common "topois" or themes to frame stories about religion. Those themes generally support conventional notions of what a religion is and what it means to be religious. Because America's religious heritage is Judeo-Christian and most Americans are and always have been Christian, those themes tend to favor Christianity and, to a lesser extent, Judaism. Other religions are more often treated as false and/or dangerous, especially when the tendency to filter religion through Judeo-Christian norms coincides with an equally strong tendency to understand other nations in terms of American self-interest or to marginalize and delegitimize racial, ethnic and other minorities at home.

Those tendencies show up most clearly in coverage of Islam. In news from the Middle East, references to "Arab," "Muslim," "Jew" and "Israeli" are used so interchangeably that it is often difficult to tell who is at odds with whom; it is even more impossible to understand the roots of the conflict because the stories rarely contain any meaningful information about religious or national interests. Yet when conflict produces bloodshed, it is almost always "Muslim terrorists" versus Israelis "defending their homeland," as the noted Middle-Eastern scholar, Edward W. Said, documented in his 1997 book *Covering Islam: How the Media and the Experts Determine How We See the Rest of the World.*

Although there are, as Said also notes, Muslim terrorists, the two words have been linked so often in news from the Middle East that the image of Islam as a dangerous religion carries over into domestic news. The bombing in Oklahoma City was quickly attributed to Muslim terrorists. Initial stories focused on the supposed link between Islam and fanaticism. But within a few weeks, sensitive stories, such as one Julia Lieblich wrote for Newhouse News Service about the fears of retaliation sweeping Muslim communities, began to get wide play.

That pattern repeated itself after September 11. Initially many stories with a religion angle quite appropriately sought to examine links between the hijackers' religious beliefs and terrorism. As in the case of the Oklahoma City bombing, that kind of story continues to appear, especially in the news section of daily newspapers. But just as occurred in the wake of the Oklahoma City bombing, stories that put the events in broader perspective and that put a more human face on Muslim Americans and their religion very quickly began to appear on television and in newspapers around the country.

For the September 15, 2001, edition of the Twin Falls, Idaho, *Times-News*, religion editor Denise Turner managed to pull together a package of locally written and news service stories examining reactions to the attacks on the World Trade Center and the Pentagon from a variety of religious perspectives. Within a week, newspapers around the country began producing sections like the one in the Northwest edition of the *Arkansas Democrat Gazette.* In the lead story on the front page of the September 22 religion section, Nancy Caver told of Arkansas Muslims' appreciation for the United States and their horrified reaction to the attacks. A second story, by Christie Storm, tackled misconceptions about Islam. A prominently placed kicker accompanying that story quoted Jonathan E. Brockopp, co-chairman of an American Academy of Religion study of Islam, as saying: "I would liken [Osama bin Laden] to those who would bomb abortion clinics in the name of Christianity. Most Christians would be embarrassed [to claim them]. It's the same with bin Laden."

Those kinds of stories have undoubtedly helped reduce the danger of reprisals against American Muslims and others of Middle-Eastern descent. But like the features about Ramadan, which have become as much a staple on religion pages as the obligatory coverage of Christmas and Easter, they have not been able to overcome completely the stereotype of the fanatical Muslim terrorist.

The tendency to dehumanize and delegitimize by omitting necessary religious and political context that continues to link Muslim and terrorist, particularly in stories from the Middle East, also shows up in accounts of conflicts between Muslims and Hindus and Hindus and Christians in India and Pakistan, and to a lesser extent in reports of ongoing battles between Catholics and Protestants in Northern Ireland. It also occurs in news stories about religions in the United States.

Conservative Christians often complain loudly that they are victims of the same kind of stereotyping. To some extent that is true. The *Washington Post* once sent a science reporter to cover a trial concerning challenges by conservative Protestants to the teaching of evolution in public schools. The reporter brought back a story with stereotypical references to fundamentalist ministers wearing polyester suits. More recently the same paper had to apologize for insensitively referring to conservative Protestants as "largely poor, uneducated and easy to command."

As is true for Muslims, conservative Protestants have been unfairly victimized by shorthand labels such as "fundamentalist." At the same time, journalists have more often labeled them simply as "Christian." One effect of the constant repetition of that correct, yet imprecise, label has been to marginalize Catholics, more-moderate to liberal mainline Protestants, and those who are not Christian.

That kind of marginalization shows up in story framing and sourcing. Because conservative Protestants have been so politically active in recent years, journalists must cover them and the issues they care about. In doing so, however, they often accept the conservative position at face value. Consider, for example, the lead to this March 1997 story about a proposed religious freedom amendment to the U.S. Constitution:

Ellen Pearson was shocked when a principal barred her 9-year-old daughter from reading her Bible during 90-minute bus trips to and from a Dumfries, Va., school.

The ban was required by laws that mandate the separation of church and state, the principal said.

The case and others like it show that Americans need a constitutional amendment to protect them from judges and officials who mistakenly believe the Constitution requires them to stamp out all public religious expression, Rep. Ernest Istook, R-Okla., said Monday.[14]

The anecdote used as the lead is almost certainly true, but leading with it invites the casual reader to mistake the principal's misunderstanding of the law for the law itself. That understanding works to the advantage of conservative Protestants, who have been the most ardent supporters of prayer and Bible readings in public schools, and to the disadvantage of others.

Although that AP story also included quotes from religious leaders who oppose such an amendment, many such stories do not. In too many stories about debates over prayer in school, the teaching of evolution versus creationism, parental authority, abortion and gay rights, one side is presented by clergy or other spokespersons given the "Christian" label and the other by spokespersons from the American Civil Liberties Union, People for the American Way or Planned Parenthood.

Juxtaposing the views of just a single religious source with those of a secular one creates the illusion of conflict between "good religious people" and "bad secular ones." It also shuts many Christian and non-Christian voices out of the debate. Lost in the process is the diversity of opinion both within and across religions.

The problems of shorthand labels and inadequate sourcing are most severe when hard news stories play to public fears about unconventional religions. In Waco, Texas, reporters turned to public officials, the police, the Federal Bureau of Investigation and the Bureau of Alcohol, Tobacco and Firearms for information about the Branch Davidians. Their characterization of David Koresh as a "cult leader," the Branch Davidian religion as a "fundamentalist" and "terrorist" organization and its members as "hostages" inflamed public opinion in ways that made the fiery outcome almost inevitable.

"Too often we listen to the loudest voices, not the most discerning ones," says John W. Smith, religion editor for the *Reading (Pa.) Eagle-Times*. The tendency to go to the most visible and vocal sources for story angles and evidence tends to police the boundaries between "acceptable" and "unacceptable" religion. Missing until too late was any attempt on the part of the media or the government to understand the Branch Davidians as an alternative religion, protected by the First Amendment.

Partly the problem with coverage of the Branch Davidians, as with much religion reporting, is structural. Most newspapers operate on a beat system. While many journalists are personally religious, few, other than those who cover religion full time, know much about religions other than their own. Some don't even know much about the one they personally profess. Most of those who cover religion at smaller papers and those from other beats who suddenly find themselves covering a religion story like Waco have never taken even a single course in comparative religion or the sociology of religion. For them, the learning curve can be steep. Most of the egregious examples of missed and mangled religion stories come from inexperienced religion reporters or from journalists working other beats.

Although many top religion specialists today have studied both religion and journalism at the undergraduate or graduate level, even specialists make their fair share of mistakes. With more than 2000 religions in the United States, the potential for misunderstanding and misinterpretation is immense.

But if part of the problem can be traced to journalists themselves, to the system in which they work and the cultural and craft assumptions they bring to their work, at least part of the problem must be traced to the audience. Although it is convenient to speak of an audience for religion news, in reality there are two rather distinct audiences. Many of the complaints about religion news stem from their very different views of what religion news is and what it should be.

Surveys dating back to 1980 consistently indicate that the first, and probably largest, audience is made up primarily of older women who are relatively conservative Christians. Members of this audience generally prefer a kind of "religious news" that supports their own religious beliefs. Because they often misinterpret "coverage of" as "support for," they tend to prefer features that tell of people of faith and dislike harder, issue-oriented news stories and stories about unconventional religions.

The second audience tends to be younger and religiously more diverse. It includes many mainline Protestants, people from non-Christian religions and those with no particular religious convictions. It also includes more men and more people of relatively high socioeconomic status than does the first audience. In contrast to that first audience, this second audience does not want "religious news." Instead, it is quite comfortable with and may even demand news with a harder edge: substantive stories about issues, problems, and trends, as well as stories about religious traditions other than their own.

Meeting the Challenge

Serving both audiences simultaneously is probably the greatest challenge facing those who cover religion. The first audience tends to be the most vocal with its complaints. Members of that audience are also the ones most likely to drop their newspaper subscriptions or turn off televisions in response to even a single story that offends them. The second audience also complains when stories are missed or mangled, but they rarely quit reading or watching because of what they perceive as bad coverage.

Because of their reaction to coverage that offends them, catering to the first audience sometimes seems the easy solution. But the easy solution probably is not the best. While those in the second audience are less likely to drop subscriptions or quit watching in response to a single story, they will turn to other information sources if, over a period of time, they feel they are not getting enough of the kind of information that serves their needs. Because the demographics of that second audience suggest that it is really the core audience for news, serving it is also important.

Fortunately, for all their differences, these two audiences do like some of the same kinds of news (see Table 8.1). Therefore, there are ways to put together packages of information that will appeal to both audiences as well as to combine elements that appeal to the different audiences into the same story.

Both audiences are interested in local news, including news of local people. They also like opinions, commentary and advice columns. Those shared interests suggest ways to reach both groups and entice each one to pay attention to stories they might otherwise overlook. Complex regional, national or international stories can be given a local angle. A sidebar story about a person with expertise or insight can give hard news stories greater appeal by putting a human face on the subject. Personality profiles and personal experience stories can add depth and invite understanding, as can stories or invited columns in which people with diverse perspectives share their thoughts.

Good religion sections provide just that kind of complex mixing of story types. Good stories combine elements that broaden their appeal.

TABLE 8.1.   NEWS PREFERENCES OF THE AUDIENCES FOR RELIGION NEWS

Subject preference	First audience	Second audience
Religion news		
Church positions/politics		yes
Doctrine and practices (Judeo-Christian)	yes	
Doctrine and practices (other religions)		yes
Ecumenism and cooperation	yes	yes
Ethical issues	yes	
Faith experiences	yes	
International religion news		yes
Local congregations/one-time events	yes	
Missionary activity	yes	
National denominations/groups	yes	yes
Ongoing projects and programs	yes	
Opinion and commentary	yes	yes
Religion and politics		yes
Religious issues	yes	yes
Social issues		yes
Surveys and trends		yes
General news		
Accidents and disasters	yes	
Advice columns		yes
Arts and entertainment		yes
Business and the economy		yes
Editorial page		yes
Education news	yes	yes
Environmental news		yes
International news		yes
Lifestyle		yes
Local government	yes	yes
National news		yes
Science news		yes
Sports		yes
Weather	yes	yes

The pages reproduced in this chapter illustrate both. They also illustrate ways in which religion news can provide a window into the world of various subcultures without making the attention given them come across as "time out for diversity."

At *The Dallas Morning News*, the first page of the religion section typically carries substantive hard news or news features, which often are continued on page 3. As in the pages reproduced in Figures 8.1 and 8.2, there may also be a roundup of shorter, more-local stories on page 1, but those stories plus a schedule of events and holidays usually appear on page 2. Pages 4 and 5 are usually a mixture of locally written columns, letters from readers similar to those found on editorial pages, and some pickups from news services that did not make it into other sections of the paper. Reviews of music, books, plays, movies, television programs and art exhibits, stories about religious artists and performers and a

SPIRITUALITY · VALUES

Religion

Saturday, August 14, 1999 · The Dallas Morning News · www.dallasnews.com · Section G

KEEPING UP

Preparing for Y2K

Bach in Rockwall

EYES ON CLINTON

FACE TO FACE

J. Neaul Haynes

INSIDE

Violence Against Jews

AS WE FORGIVE OUR DEBTORS

Movement to relieve the Third World's financial burdens is rolling like a juggernaut

By Deborah Kovach Caldwell
Staff Writer of The Dallas Morning News

New Bible is by and for black women

Local pastors contribute to first project of its kind

By Kimberly Winston
Special Contributor to The Dallas Morning News

Praise between Sundays

A&M student brings weeknight service to home parish

By Berta Delgado
Staff Writer of The Dallas Morning News

FARMERS BRANCH — It's Tuesday evening, just days before the start of the school year, and Brian Murawski and his friends are in church, singing.

Brian Murawski (left), Casey Moser (in the back) and Patrick Dougherty lead a praise service at Mary Immaculate Catholic Church in Farmers Branch.

Figure 8.1 Page 1 of the religion section in the August 14, 1999, **The Dallas Morning News**.

Project looks at the Bible through black women's eyes

Continued from Page 1G.

lishing is dominated by niche marketing for everyone from Latina brides and new moms to golfers, has no one published a Bible just for African-American women?

"Because most blacks who had the power to do it did not have the resources," Ms. Weatherspoon said.

Enter Melvin Banks II, the owner and publisher of Nia Publishing, the six-person operation in Atlanta that is responsible for the new Bible.

As a 27-year-old single businessman, Mr. Banks acknowledges that he is an unlikely proponent of a Bible for African-American women. His two previous books were for African-American children — The Children of Color Story Book Bible, published with Thomas Nelson, which has reached 100,000 in print since it appeared in October 1998, and The Children of Color Holy Bible, published with World Bible Publishing, which has hit a quarter-million copies since its 1993 debut.

But he was drawn to the project by what he saw as a dearth of products for people of color.

"We really believe that to be Christlike means to be more inclusive," said Mr. Banks, who belongs to a nondenominational church. "We believe that God is an inclusive God and there has to be an effort made."

For a long time it seemed clear that Mr. Banks would have to be the one to make it. Several major Christian publishing houses turned down the Women of Color Study Bible, saying it conflicted with projects already under way. But once the book was nearly complete — and had gotten the interest of mass merchant Wal-Mart — World Bible Publishing agreed to take part in publishing it.

The Women of Color Study Bible is expected to appear in bookstores this fall, and a conference for its readers is planned in Dallas next spring.

Contributors' notes focus on women who they say were probably black because of where they were born and lived. Among them are Esther, Ruth, Naomi, Miriam, Martha and Phoebe. Such women are often shouldered to the sidelines — much like women in general and African-American women especially, contributors say — by a scriptural mention or two.

But for this Bible, contributors were asked to research the women, think about them, pray about them — and then write about what they might have to say to modern African-American women.

"Women of color are not so neglected in the Scriptures, and many times they have leadership roles," said the Rev. Jacquetta Chambers of McMillan United

The Rev. Janette Koty of St. Paul United Methodist Church in Dallas believes that the Women of Color Study Bible will remind African-American women that they are not an "afterthought but a definite part of God's plan."

Methodist Church in Fort Worth. She contributed essays on Candace, queen of Ethiopia, and Jochebed, the mother of Moses.

Ms. Chambers holds that women of color especially need to read about prominent women because they too often put the needs of others — family, husbands and children — before their own.

She hopes the Women of Color Study Bible will encourage African-American women — especially younger ones — to step forward and claim more leadership roles.

"If our voices are lost in supporting others we will never be the woman who commanded the space shuttle or the CEO of Hewlett-Packard," she said.

While some ethnic-specific organizations, publications and celebrations have lately been criticized as divisive, contributors to this Bible hope its narrow, race-based focus will help its readers find strength and self-esteem.

"This Bible, I think, will be used to reinforce what we as a people already know is true," said the Rev.

Claudette Sims, a Houston minister and a contributor. "That we should continue to put our trust in God and understand that we are not alone. It will encourage us, inspire us to keep on keeping on."

For Mr. Banks, producing the Bible — a two-year process — was a crucible.

"I learned that you can believe that the Lord has put you through something, that you have put your greatest challenge, and yet there will be a tougher challenge around the corner and you still have to

The Rev. Katherine Davis of First United Methodist Church in Arlington, who contributed to the new study Bible, calls the project refreshing and liberating.

meet it," he said, recounting nearly missed deadlines, the abdication of the first editor, the depletion of finances. There were many times he thought about giving up.

"But we got through it," he continued. "I am still holding off my sigh of relief, but I know it is coming in the end."

And it could be a very big ride, too. Phyllis Tickle, religion editor emeritus of Publishers Weekly, a magazine that tracks trends and sales, said Mr. Banks' Bible could become a runaway seller.

She points to the phenomenal success of Zondervan's Women's Devotional Bible, a two-volume title that has sold 2.9 million copies, and the recent publishing successes of African-American spiritual leaders such as Bishop T.D. Jakes of Dallas and Iyanla Van Zant.

"Anything that offers a female touch to religion is going to sell, and anything that offers an African-American female slant doubly so," Ms. Tickle said.

"If this Bible doesn't sell, I'll eat one with ketchup on it."

Kimberly Winston is a free lance writer in Northern California.

Jubilee 2000 building support among churches, celebrities

Continued from Page 1G.

"All of a sudden people are paying attention," said Carole Collins, national coordinator of Jubilee 2000/USA in Washington. "We're reaching the end of one millennium and the beginning of another, and we're thinking about righting wrong relationships."

The movement draws its name from the biblical Book of Leviticus, which describes a Year of Jubilee every 50 years. During the year, social inequalities are rectified: Slaves are freed, land is returned to original owners and debts are canceled.

Jubilee 2000 scored its biggest publicity coup in June during a meeting in Cologne, Germany, of the leaders of the world's industrial-ized countries. There, 50,000 supporters created a human chain, demanding that wealthy countries "break the chain of debt." People also created human chains around the Treasury Building in Washington, the Federal Building in Louisville, Ky., and the Bush America building in San Francisco and on bridges across the Thames River in London.

During the Cologne meeting, the coalition presented a 17-million-signature petition to leaders of the G7 — the Group of Seven wealthiest nations.

When it was over, President Clinton announced that the G7 would cancel $27 billion in debt — a major victory, though not a big enough step, according to Jubilee 2000 organizers.

Some people are wary of the movement.

Robert Snyder, a former missionary to Rwanda and a biology professor at Greenville College in Illinois,

wrote an essay critical of Jubilee 2000 that appeared last month in The Christian Century, a magazine aimed primarily at the mainline Protestant audience embracing the cause.

"If we are going to forgive debt, let us not fool ourselves into thinking that we can outsmart the cunning men and women who are experienced at manipulating the international community for their own benefit," Dr. Snyder wrote. "These leaders ... will empty our pockets while they throw a few crumbs to the poor."

During an interview, Dr. Snyder said he teaches courses on international development and often reminds students of the role that the West has played in destabilizing poor countries.

But Jubilee 2000 supporters need to realize that people in developing countries are "grown-ups," Dr. Snyder said. Corruption in these countries is rampant at every level, he said, and that is an internal spiritual problem that only those citizens can fix.

"I have talked to so many Africans who are as discouraged and heartsick about their countries," he said.

They want the West to hold debt relief over the heads of their corrupt leaders as a way of making their governments change, Dr. Snyder said.

He chalked up what he calls Jubilee 2000's "bandwagon effect" to guilt.

"We constantly are bombarded by scenes of hungry kids, and we feel a little bit helpless," he said. "So this is something we feel we can do."

And so the movement rolls on.

A bill pending before Congress would allow poor nations that meet certain criteria to forgo paying their debts.

Last month, the Treasury Department hosted an all-day conference with Jubilee 2000 organizers and international finance officials. Such a meeting would have been unimaginable two years ago.

Then there is the move into pop culture.

"Jubilee 2000 has managed to put a relatively arcane issue ... on the negotiating table throughout the world. It's one of the most effective global lobbying campaigns I have ever seen."

— Anthony Gaeta, a spokesman for the World Bank

This summer, Jubilee 2000 set up literature tables at most of the 27 Lilith Fair concerts around the country. The group also had a table at the Woodstock concert in New York last month.

In July, Church World Service, a relief and development agency, mailed 1,200 lapel chains attached to glossy brochures to religious leaders, opinion makers and journalists. The brochure included a postcard to send to Mr. Clinton, urging him to expand debt relief.

Next month, the issue is back on the agenda of the Beltway movers and shakers, when the World Bank and International Monetary Fund — two of the major lenders to poor nations — hold their annual meetings.

"Jubilee 2000 has managed to put a relatively arcane issue ... on the negotiating table throughout the world," said Anthony Gaeta, a spokesman for the World Bank "It's one of the most effective global lobbying campaigns I have ever seen."

Indeed, some observers view the seal of Jubilee 2000 as a sign of millennium fever.

"I see it as the other side of the coin from the Y2K problem," said Lee Quinby, an associate of the Center for Millennial Studies at Boston University and a humanities professor at Rochester Institute of Technology. "There's this intensifying anxiety on one hand, so we have the doom-drenched voices that everything is going amok.

"And we have the polar opposite in this intensity about this millennial hope: With the sweep of a pen we write off debt," she said. "It's completely utopian and the opposite of the doomsday view."

She described the lapel pins, gigantic petitions and demonstrations as the "Disney-fication" of an important issue.

So matter how they've accomplished it, however, Jubilee 2000 organizers have succeeded in making people care about an obscure topic.

According to the group's literature, more than 50 countries have unpayable debt, owed primarily to Japan, the United States, Britain, Canada, France, Germany and Italy

In the poorest countries, the debt burden is 93 percent of income. In Zambia, every citizen now owes the country's creditors $760, which is more than twice the average annual income.

The United Nations Development Programme estimates that if money were diverted into programs to eradicate AIDS, malaria and malnutrition, for example, the lives of 7 million children could be saved within a year.

Experts say many factors have combined to cause the debt problem, including irresponsible creditor countries and corrupt dictators who borrowed money, then spent lavishly on themselves.

"The result, experts say, is that the governments of impoverished countries are servicing their debts by taking out new loans.

The World Bank took a preliminary stab at addressing the problem in 1996, when it unveiled its program for heavily indebted Poor Countries. Under the program, countries that consistently meet rigorous economic criteria over three years are given debt relief. But by the end of 2000, only six countries — among them, Bolivia and Uganda — will get debt relief.

Jubilee 2000 supporters say the amount of relief is too small anyway. They estimate that it would cost each American about $7.50 to cancel the debts owed directly to the United States by the world's poorest countries.

Few people disagree that helping the developing world with debt is a noble cause.

Jeffrey Sachs, the Harvard University economist who helped re-

structure Russia's economy, served as economic adviser to Jubilee 2000. In a recent essay he suggested that by not facing the reality of the poorest nations' bankruptcy, the World Bank and International Monetary Fund "have invented a perpetual motion machine for endless missions to these hapless countries."

That must stop, he wrote, particularly because in the past three years, stock market wealth of the rich countries grew by more than $3 trillion, 50 times the debt owed by the 41 poorest countries.

Even as the World Bank once considered the richness of Jubilee 2000 leaders, everyone seems to have gotten on board.

"Jubilee 2000 has done a tremendous job in building an international political consensus for expanded debt relief. There's no doubt about it," said Carolyn Reynolds, a World Bank spokeswoman who acts as a liaison between the bank and relief and development groups. "But now they have to go back and work with those same governments to get financing. The trick is: where is the money going to come from?"

The bank, owned by 180 countries, finances its work by selling bonds on the capital markets and by donations from wealthier governments.

"Now we're getting onto another level of debate," Ms. Reynolds said. "It's been an incredible learning experience for the bank. Civil society has brought real-life experience into the discussion about the impact on poor people.

"They've had good ideas," she said. "And they've helped shape the political consensus."

round-up of television and radio programs that are specifically religious or tackle religion-related subjects appear on page 6.

The lead story on the front page of the August 14, 1999, religion section edited by Diane Connolly blends religion with international, business and economic issues. It is the kind of issue-oriented story that usually has greatest appeal for the second audience. However, by using a feature lead, award-winning religion writer Deborah Kovach Caldwell increases the story's appeal. The chances that members of the first audience will also read the story are further enhanced by using artwork and by surrounding it with excellent stories whose primary appeal would ordinarily be to the first audience: the "Keeping Up" roundup column, the story about a new Bible for African-American women, and one about two young men's efforts to start a Catholic praise service of the kind common in conservative Protestant churches.

In the lead story, Caldwell uses multiple religious and secular sources to give depth and balance to her report on Jubilee 2000. Most Dallas area residents are Christian, so few readers would have noticed if she had left out any reference to other religions. However, Caldwell carefully notes, just after the lead, that the movement includes Jews and Muslims. She then tucks in a paragraph explaining the biblical basis for forgiving or reducing Third World countries' debts before offering a variety of religious and secular opinions about the movement. Because the movement is controversial, those opinions both support and oppose the initiative, but Caldwell doesn't allow any one source to frame the debate or get the last word. To eliminate the illusion of unfair instant rebuttals, she uses background information and explanatory details to separate the differing opinions before ending with a quote from a secular source who acknowledges both the diversity of opinion and the value of religious input on such an important but potentially divisive issue.

In "New Bible," Kimberly Winston, a prize-winning religion reporter who free-lances for a number of papers, gives a national story a local angle by concentrating on women from the Dallas area who were instrumental in producing the Bible. The story helps readers understand the depth of African Americans' faith and the special challenges they face. The color pictures on page 3 of three women, two of whom wrote essays for the Bible, put a human face on the story; the use of multiple sources and the inclusion of information about other similar publishing efforts add depth and perspective.

In "Praise," staff writer Berta Delgado uses a feature lead to set the scene. She then allows quotes from hymns, from those who organized the worship services and others who attend it tell the story. Along the way, she tucks in enough information about similar services at other churches and about the contemporary Christian music scene to put what otherwise could be a simple "people and event" story into broader perspective.

In covering religion news, newspapers like *The Dallas Morning News* obviously have the advantage. Not only can they commit more resources to in-depth coverage, but they also can draw on the multiplicity of religions within their circulation area for story ideas and for sources. In big cities there are religious organizations catering to different racial and ethnic groups and congregations using different languages in their worship services. There are also ones with ministries to, for, or by homosexuals and the differently abled.

While only a handful of very large papers can match *The Dallas Morning* News in devoting resources to covering religion, any paper can find creative ways to produce the same kind of thoughtful mix of stories the Dallas paper provides for its weekly religion section.

At papers such as the *Reading (Pa.) Eagle-Times*, where John W. Smith divides his time between duties as religion editor and copy editor, all reporters have been deputized to find religion stories that they may offer first to Smith for use in the three-page weekly religion section or "sell" to the news or feature editors for use in other sections. At other papers, such as the *Greeley (Colo.) Tribune,* religion reporter Anne Cumming writes one long story each week but supplements it with others from the wire services, which she sometimes localizes.

For papers without a religion reporter, using stories from wire services, news syndicates, and from the more specialized Religion News Service can provide excellent coverage, especially if some stories are localized. A combination of wire-service stories and some locally written enterprise ones can provide even better coverage.

Even if there is no space set aside especially for religion news, there still can be room for good religion reporting. Of the stories from the August 14, 1999, *The Dallas Morning News*, for example, "Jubilee 2000" could run appropriately in the news section of any paper. "New Bible" might run in a section devoted to book reviews or arts and entertainment. Both that story and "Praise" could also run in feature or lifestyle sections.

Diversity can be introduced by defining the local community more broadly to include nearby towns, by using some pick-ups from news services, and by incorporating information from census and survey data or quotes from experts to localize national stories or to put local ones in broader perspective.

All of those techniques can be seen in the November 1, 2001, religion section of the Logan, Utah, *Herald Journal*. In that edition, religion editor Cindy Yurth combined local "people and event" stories of Latter-day Saints with a locally written one about a Vietnam veteran's efforts to build a Buddhist meditation center in nearby Park Valley. She also included two news service stories about Islam, one of which reported both the theological and the racial diversity of American Muslims.

Guidelines for Covering Religion

Because many people care so deeply about religion and because religions have such enormous potential effects on members and nonmembers alike, people want and deserve good religion reporting. As a first step to providing good coverage, journalists must decide religion is important, learn something about the subject, find stories about religion, make a strong case to their editors for their importance, and then cover the stories well.

But because religion is connected to everything, news of religion occurs on all beats. Therefore, responsibility for improving religion news rests with both specialists and nonspecialists. To cover religion news well, both specialists and nonspecialists need to:

1. **Think broadly**. Religion news isn't just about the clergy and it isn't just about local congregations and events. Those are important because they help create a representative picture of a community, but that kind of story isn't enough. Almost everything can affect religious people and organizations; people and organizations get involved in almost everything.

    Whenever issues seem intractable and passions run high, there's a good bet religion is involved. But it often works its influence "behind the scene," through the encouragement and organization that goes on in places of worship, in other religion-related organizations and through religious media. It shows up in social and political movements and in the individual decisions people make about how to conduct their lives. Therefore, religion news is also about politics and law, business, taxes and economics, science and medicine, education, lifestyles, arts, entertainment and sports.

Providing in-depth coverage, along with the more routine stories that have long been associated with the religion page, is crucial. Good religion reporting means recognizing differences in audience interests and then providing something for everyone: a variety of story types and stories about different religions written in ways that address the sensitivities of each of the two audiences for religion news.

Finding stories that go beyond the routine and that will satisfy the information needs of both audiences requires casting a wide net: reading about religion in religious and secular publications, visiting large churches and small ones, checking with agencies affiliated with religions and the bookstores and other businesses that cater to religious people, being on the lookout for evidences of religious involvement at meetings and hearings and, most of all, talking to everyone to learn about their beliefs, values, and ethics and those of their friends and acquaintances.

2. **Honor the First Amendment.** Because many people complain when the media cover stories about people or groups they find offensive, reporters must constantly remind themselves, and be prepared to remind their audiences, that the First Amendment protects all religions—not just those that fall comfortably within the Judeo-Christian tradition. The First Amendment also protects those who choose not to accept any religion.

Journalists need to remember that religions come in all shapes and sizes. Some, like Judaism, Christianity and Islam, worship a single, transcendent god. Some have many gods; others may be more akin to philosophical debating societies. But whether or not everyone accepts each of them as "real religion," they are religion if they shape people's values and opinions and help them find meaning and purpose in life.

The correctness of religious viewpoints is a matter of faith. Religious beliefs cannot really be proved true or false, but the conventional practice of providing multiple perspectives within a story can make one viewpoint seem correct. Giving one side the "first word" sets the framing for a story; giving someone the "last word" can seem like an instant rebuttal. Therefore, it sometimes can be better to present diverse viewpoints by grouping together several shorter stories, each giving one perspective.

Honoring the First Amendment requires treating all religions with respect, but it does not mean that journalists should avoid asking hard questions about religion. Nor does it mean that investigative reporting is inappropriate on the religion beat. It simply means that reporters working for the mass media must resist all temptations to practice "religious journalism." Religious journalism promotes or defends religion or a particular religion. It is an honorable profession, but it belongs in religious media or in clearly labeled personal opinion columns. The goal for reporters who work for the mass media should be "religion journalism"— an accurate, fair account of what is going on in the world of religion.

Practicing religion journalism does not mean that reporters should avoid putting religion into their stories. Explaining theology or quoting religious texts is a necessary part of providing the background that helps readers understand the rationale for other people's beliefs and judge those beliefs for themselves. Including that kind of information is simply providing evidence the same way reporters from other beats might quote from other kinds of documentary sources. It becomes religious journalism only when journalists substitute their own beliefs or their own choice of proof texts for those of their sources.

3. **Show. Don't tell.** Religious journalism can appropriately tell people how things are, why they are that way, how they should be and how to make them that way. Religion journalism gives people the information they need in order to understand and reach their own conclusions.

Showing requires providing facts, background information and context, details and descriptions. The goal is to help people find answers to their questions without providing the answers for them. Personality profiles and personal experience stories can show without telling by putting a human face on complex issues or demystifying beliefs that may strike many people as strange.

Showing also means letting people speak for themselves so others can draw their own conclusions about them and their causes. In some cases, this may require abandoning the traditional "balanced story" with its penchant for instant rebuttals in favor of separate, parallel stories devoted to different religious perspectives. In others, it may require refusing to accept or use the story angle or the labels one religious source offers when those angles or labels could provide an incomplete or misleading picture of another group.

4. **Watch the language.** Good religion reporting requires using words carefully. Words inform, but they can also mislead, anger and ostracize.

Like everything else, religion has its own jargon. But in religion, the same word often has several meanings. Journalists must be sensitive to those different meanings in order to understand what their sources are really saying. Because of those different meanings, good reporting requires defining words carefully. However, even with careful definition, words that categorize people and their religions can cause problems.

Words such as *liberal, fundamentalist, charismatic, cult, sect, catholic* or *evangelical* are all perfectly good labels, but carelessly used they can invite misunderstanding. Good reporters avoid imposing labels as much as possible. When they must use them, they try to use the most precise one possible: *Independent Baptist* for *fundamentalist* or *Unitarian* for *liberal*, for example. Good reporters also take steps to make sure they don't let their sources appropriate favorable labels, such as *Christian*, for themselves or impose unfavorable ones, like *fundamentalist* or *cult*, on others.

5. **Strive for balance.** Journalists are trained to think objectively. They should not take sides or inject themselves into a dispute. Instead, they should give equal, accurate, fair coverage to all sides. That kind of objectivity is important in religion coverage, but it often doesn't go far enough.

In religion reporting, it is particularly important to use spokespersons who are equivalent to present different viewpoints. That is, if one side is presented as religious, it is important, whenever possible, to seek out and then air views from religious people on the other side. If one side also requires giving the views of secular sources, balance requires looking for and then reporting similarly secular viewpoints for the other side.

But because there are so many religions, balance also requires giving appropriate attention to a multiplicity of religious perspectives. It isn't enough to seek out only the most easily identified and most readily available spokespersons. Neither is it appropriate to limit the debate by reporting only viewpoints from the most generally accepted religions. Truly balanced coverage requires bringing minority religious voices into the debate.

However, this requirement to cover a multiplicity of voices raises other problems that also need to be considered in order to provide appropriately balanced coverage. Too much emphasis on minority viewpoints may create a false impression of their strength or, in some cases, the importance of their opinions; too little can make minority religions and potentially important minority perspectives inappropriately invisible. Similarly, too much attention to the views of religious institutions and religious leaders invites ignoring the effect of official doctrine, policy and practices on lay members and on others who are not affiliated with a particular religion. Too much attention to the views of average church members and/or outsiders to the faith may make it appear as if proper beliefs and practices should be decided by majority vote or that nonbelievers should have veto power over religious beliefs, practices and policies.

Balance requires taking seriously the needs of the various audiences. Therefore, journalists must look at more than just the way they cover individual stories. In order to provide a representative picture of religion, over time there should be balance among subjects, religions, kinds of stories and writing styles. Some stories should be hard news and others softer features. Some of each type should show the public face of religion—issues, trends, activities and organizations that have or could have effects at the individual or societal level. Others should show the more private face of religion—its role in people's everyday lives.

Resources

Internet

http://www.religionwriters.com   Religion Newswriters Association. Religion-
     Link.

Books

Buddenbaum, Judith M. 1998. *Reporting News about Religion: An Introduc-
     tion for Journalists*. Ames: Iowa State University Press.
Buddenbaum, Judith M., and Debra L. Mason, eds. 1999. *Readings on Religion
     as News*. Ames: Iowa State University Press.
Eck, Diana L. 2002. *On Common Ground: World Religions in America*. Cam-
     bridge, Mass.: Harvard University Press.
Haddad, Yvonne Yazbeck, and Jane Idleman Smith. 1994. *Muslim Communi-
     ties in North America*. Albany: New York University Press.

Lindner, Eileen, ed. Annual. *Yearbook of American and Canadian Churches.* New York: National Council of Churches.

Miller, Timothy, ed. 1995. *America's Alternative Religions.* Albany: State University of New York Press.

Morrelale, Don, ed. 1998. *The Complete Guide to Buddhist America.* Boston: Shambhala.

Payne, Wardell J., ed. 1995. *Directory of African American Religious Bodies.* Washington, D.C.: Howard University School of Divinity.

Religion Newswriters Association. 2002. *A Guide to Religion Reporting in the Secular Media: Frequently Asked Questions.* Westerville, Ohio: Religion Newswriters Association.

Singer, David, ed. Annual. *American Jewish Yearbook.* New York: American Jewish Community.

Weber, Paul J., and W. Landes Jones, eds. 1994. *U.S. Religious Interest Groups: Institutional Profiles.* Westport, Conn.: Greenwood Press.

Wellman, James K., Jr. 1999. "Religion out of the Closet: Public Religion and Homosexuality." In *The Power of Religious Publics: Staking Claims in American Society*, ed. William H. Swatos, Jr., and James K. Wellman, Jr., 131-152. Westport, Conn.: Greenwood Publishing Group.

Williams, Raymond Brady. 1988. *Religions of Immigrants from India and Pakistan: New Threads in the American Tapestry.* New York: Cambridge University Press.

Notes

1. Stewart M. Hoover, Barbara M. Hanley and Mark Radelfinger, *The RNS-Lily Study of Religion Reporting and Readership in the Daily Press* (Philadelphia: School of Communications and Theater, Temple University, 1989); Stewart M. Hoover, Shalani Venturelli and Douglas Wagner, *Religion in Public Discourse: The Role of the Media* (Boulder: School of Journalism and Mass Communication, University of Colorado, 1994).

2. Glenmary Research Center: http://www.glenmary.org/grc. Data will be published as *Religious Congregations and Membership in the United States: 2000.*

3. Eileen Lindner, ed., *Yearbook of American and Canadian Churches* (New York: National Council of Churches, 2001).

4. J. Gordon Melton, ed., *The Encyclopedia of American Religion* (Detroit, Mich.: Gale Research, 1983).

5. James Davison Hunter, "Before the Shooting Begins," *Columbia Journalism Review* July/August(1993):29-32.

6. Commission on Freedom of the Press, *A Free and Responsible Press: A General Report on Mass Communications: Newspapers, Radio, Motion*

Pictures, Magazines, and Books, ed. Robert D. Leigh (Chicago: University of Chicago Press, 1947).

7. Kenneth D. Nordin, "Consensus Religion: National Newspaper Coverage of Religious Life in America, 1849-1960," (Ph.D. diss., Ohio University, 1975).

8. Debra L. Mason, "God in the News Ghetto: A Study of Religion News from 1944 to 1989" (Ph.D. diss., Ohio University, 1995).

9. Judith M. Buddenbaum, "Reflections on Culture Wars: Churches, Communication Content, and Consequences" in *Religion and Prime Time Television*, ed. Michael Suman (Westport, Conn.: Praeger, 1997), 47-60; Judith M. Buddenbaum, "Christian Perspectives on Mass Media" in *Religion and Popular Culture: Studies on the Interaction of Worldviews,* ed. Daniel L. Stout and Judith M. Buddenbaum (Ames: Iowa State University Press, 2001), 81-94.

10. Marvin Olasky, *The Prodigal Press: The Anti-Christian Bias of the American Press* (Wheaton, Ill.: Crossway Books, 1988).

11. Robert Lichter, Stanley Rothman, and Linda Lichter, *The Media Elite* (New York: Adler & Adler, 1986).

12. David Weaver and G. Cleveland Wilhoit, *The American Journalist* (Mahwah, N.J.: Lawrence Erlbaum Associates, 1996).

13. Judith M. Buddenbaum, "Religion in the News: Factors Associated with the Selection of Religion News from an International News Service" (Ph.D. diss., Indiana University, 1984); Judith M. Buddenbaum, "The Religion Beat at Daily Newspapers," *Newspaper Research Journal* 9(4)1988:57-70; Judith M. Buddenbaum, Debra L. Mason, and Guido Stempel III, unpublished data, Religion Newswriters Association, Westerville, Ohio, 1995.

14. Quoted in Judith M. Buddenbaum, *Reporting News about Religion: An Introduction for Journalists* (Ames: Iowa State University Press, 1998).

CHAPTER 9

The Changing Faces of Advertising

Minority Images and the Media

Cynthia M. Frisby

I am an invisible man. No, I am not a spook like those who haunted Edgar Allen Poe; nor am I one of your Hollywood movie ectoplasm. I am a man of substance, of flesh and bone, fiber and liquids—and I might even be said to possess a mind. Like the bodiless heads you see sometimes in circus sideshows, it is as though I have been surrounded by mirrors of hard, distorting glass. When they approach me they see only my surroundings, themselves, or figments of their imagination—indeed, everything and anything except me.

> —Ralph Ellison, *Invisible Man*, 1952

Abercrombie & Fitch recently created a line of graphic T-shirts adorned with Asian caricatures. The prints on the T-shirts contained such slogans as "Two Wongs can make it white" or "Get your Buddha on the floor," partnered with stereotypical portrayals of Asian laundrymen wearing rice paddy straw hats and Asian women standing passively in the background. Other shirts featured slant-eyed Asian subservient restaurant workers and the phrases "Love you long time" or "Eat in or wok out."

After thousands of Asian-American university students and the Organization of Chinese Americans made public outcries against the advertising campaign, Abercrombie & Fitch was forced to recall the T-shirts. The company also issued a public apology that stated that the "intent" of the marketing campaign was "to be funny." As Abercrombie & Fitch quickly found out, racial stereotypes, ethnic targeting and disrespecting a religion are not funny.

Thomas Lennox, the company's senior public relations official, said: "It's not, and never has been, our intention to offend anyone. These graphic T-shirts were designed with the sole purpose of adding humor and levity to our fashion line" (www.petitiononline.com/BCAF/petition.html; modelminority.com/media/abercrombie.htm).

Lessons about ethnic stereotypes appear to be hard for advertisers to learn. The 2002 controversy is almost a replay of a more than 30-year-old incident involving another ethnic group. Beginning in the late 1960s, the Frito-Lay company began a widely successful campaign that employed the Frito Bandito, a grizzled, gold-toothed Bandito cartoon character who stole Fritos from anyone he could find. The Hispanic community protested the commercials' negative personification of a Hispanic character. Frito-Lay responded first by cleaning up the image of the Frito Bandito, removing his beard and replacing his scowl with a smile. By 1971, Frito-Lay had dropped the popular character.

An opposite and also controversial approach has been employed by Benetton, an Italian clothing manufacturer, since 1984. Unlike the previous examples, Benetton has used stereotypes to "put forward" ideas about racism, sexism, human rights, animal rights, the environment and a host of other major issues of our time (www.benetton.com). Advertisements have involved a black horse mounting a white one; the naked buttocks of an AIDS carrier tattooed with "HIV Positive;" a black baby and a white baby facing each other, sitting on their potties, smiling; a priest and a nun in a sensual kiss; an empty electric chair; and child laborers, each under the age of 12. Each of these ads included Benetton's slogan, "The United Colors of Benetton," in a green box in the corner.

According to the Benetton website, the strategy of the advertising campaign is "to 'communicate' to consumers rather than to sell to them. All over the world Benetton stands for multiculturalism, world peace, racial harmony, a progressive approach toward serious social issues and colorful sportswear" (www.benetton.com/press/). The Benetton home page has a large collection of news stories on such topics as whale hunting, ozone layer depletion, land mines and North Korean girls being sold into marriage.

Reactions to Benetton's controversial advertisements have varied widely. To many, they are offensive and tasteless. Take an ad that ran in 1989, for example. The image was that of a black man and a white man handcuffed to each other. For many people, the image in the ad implied tension between separate races. Critics felt that the ad communicated the idea that humans are "chained" to each other against their wishes.

A second Benetton ad in 1989 included an image of a black woman breast-feeding a white baby. This image suggested to critics that Benetton was stereotyping the African-American woman by suggesting her position in society is a wet nurse or mammy.

The portrayal of women in advertising is often controversial. Critics argue that women are still predominantly cast as homemakers, sex objects or nurturing mothers. So, is Benetton wrong in disseminating such images? Or is the company simply trying to get people to look beyond the color of people's skin and see the "content of their character"? What makes some people so angry about Benetton's ads?

Abercrombie & Fitch, Frito-Lay and Benetton are all outliers, in different ways, in their approaches to minorities. But the controversies they stimulated are symptomatic of the continuing changes through the years in how minorities are treated (or ignored) in mainstream advertising.

In this chapter, we explore the history of these changing patterns of advertising and conclude with suggestions for advertisers who want to reach the growing market of minority consumers. This chapter focuses largely on the treatment of African Americans, the topic that has generated the most media research.

What Is Prejudice and How Does It Affect Us?

Prejudice is a negative attitude directed toward people simply because they are members of a social group. A person who is prejudiced toward some group tends to ignore the individual qualities of its members and prejudges them based on this negative evaluation. Stereotypes are often associated with prejudice because we as humans naturally categorize other people, and we develop beliefs about the personalities, abilities, and motives of those within the categories. The social beliefs that we hold are stereotypes—fixed ways of thinking about people that do not allow for individual variation. Negative stereotypes can form the basis for later prejudicial feelings and actions. Thus, even though Abercrombie & Fitch, Frito-Lay and Benetton may not have intended to offend or perpetuate stereotypes, the ads are controversial because critics believe such images can encourage rigid and unflattering views of the ethnic group in question.

Many ethnic cultures have powerful stereotypes associated with them. Members of Native American groups are assumed to be heavy drinkers, Asians to be excellent students, African Americans to be subservient, Mexicans to be bandits and Hispanics to be drug dealers. Marketers have used ethnic stereotyping in the past as a way to connote certain product attributes. Research suggests that the interpretation of images can also be biased by racial stereotypes (Duncan 1976). The images used in the Benetton ads clearly show us how racial stereotypes can distort images. Thus, instead of seeing a "woman" breast feeding a baby, some see the image of a BLACK woman and interpret that image as "nanny," "caretaker" or "subservient slave."

Gerbner and his colleagues (1986) analyzed television's portrayal of American life and found it to provide a misleading stereotype of many social groups. Historically, one of the most negative stereotypes depicted on television and in movies has been that of gay men and lesbians. Even before the AIDS epidemic, gay characters appearing in Hollywood films and television programs were often ridiculed and depicted as being physically weak.

It can be argued that it is the *manner* in which advertising and news is reported that distorts our view of reality. In real life, negative events generally occur less frequently than positive or neutral events. Minority group members receive less press attention than those in the majority group. Thus, when a news account includes a minority group member and it is coupled with a negative event, these two bits of information may command greater attention because of the fact that they both occur relatively infrequently.

Historically, blacks have been viewed as lazy and dependent slaves, or even carefree minstrels. American Indians have similarly been characterized as an uncivilized and lazy people who cannot take care of their own welfare (Trimble 1988). These blatantly negative stereotypes based on white racial superiority, coupled with opposition to racial equality, have been termed old-fashioned racism (Jordan 1968; McConahay 1986).

Old-fashioned racism may explain why some, if not most, people were outraged by the images portrayed in the Frito-Lay, Benetton and

Abercrombie & Fitch advertising campaigns. We often forget that people tend to perceive members of ethnic groups as acting similarly, and stereotypes simply reinforce that. People may say casually, "Well, you know men, they are all alike" or "African Americans were outraged at the O.J. Simpson verdict." This tendency to see others within a given ethnic group as being more alike than they really are is one of the consequences of prejudice and lack of experience. These stereotypes are strengthened by biased information processing and by unrepresentative media portrayals that make the stereotype difficult to change.

The Magnitude of the Problem

In the United States, African Americans, Hispanic Americans, Asian Americans and the elderly are important market segments because these subcultures account for more than $500 billion in purchasing power (Edmonson, 1985; Reese, 1997). The growing importance of minority groups to advertising has stimulated a number of studies since the 1960s that focus on minority portrayals. In the 2000 U.S. census, the African-American subculture represented 12 percent of the U.S. population. Research also shows that along with the impressive buying power, the African-American population is increasing in size faster than the general population and is rising in socioeconomic status (Edmonson 1985; Reese 1997; Thompson 1997). The size and buying power of the African-American population make it an attractive target market for advertisers.

Despite the attractiveness of this segment to advertisers, critics feel that the increase in the number of African-American portrayals in the media is largely due to placement of these images in "all-black" media vehicles (i.e., *Jet*, *Essence*, Black Entertainment Television, etc.). Research shows that, historically speaking, African Americans have been underrepresented in mainstream advertising. Wilkes and Valencia (1989), for example, found that from an advertising perspective, African-American images are more likely to appear in minor or background roles.

The infrequency, or shall we say the lack of utilization, of African-American models in mainstream media may reflect society's reticence to accept blacks into the mainstream culture. Negative stereotypical pictures of minorities or the exclusion of minorities from visibility in mainstream media has been a topic of debate and major controversy for more than a century. During the late 1800s and throughout the mid-1900s,

African Americans were negatively portrayed in print, radio, television and movies. Black children were shown as dirty, animal-like, savage children. "Pickaninnies" were often targets of comic violence. Then, when emancipation threatened the comforts of the South and African Americans were competing with whites for jobs, the media responded with a new image: aggressive, vicious and immature. The pickaninny, sambo and coon images were all depicted during this time in advertisements, comic books, postcards and greeting cards, cartoons, minstrel shows and vaudeville.

The first stereotypes of African Americans were connected to slavery and life on the plantation (Kern-Foxworth 1994). Slaves were often depicted as being content with being enslaved. The uncle, the mammy and the pickanniny were stereotypical characters who seemed to enjoy life on the Southern plantation. When shown with whites, many of the black characters were standing in the background in a bent-down position. Closer inspection of the advertisements shows that most African-American images of slaves depicted a smaller person (in relative size) than that of the white image. This image found in many ads during this time period seems to communicate that the slave understood (and may even have appreciated) his role in society and accepted this role and second-class status.

The labeling of black children as pickaninnies was commonplace until the 1930s. The pickanniny, usually a young boy, was often depicted with a grin and was always eager to bite into a big slice of watermelon.

Blacks were often used to sell products through images in ads that portrayed blacks as servants and caretakers or as Uncle Toms or Aunt Jemima's. Following the abolishment of slavery, blacks were used extensively in ads because they reinforced the stereotype of the docile servant who was always ready to serve (Kern-Foxworth 1994).

The activism and civil rights movement of the 1960s led to a transformation of the traditional stereotypes. Advertisers adapted the blatant portrayals of African Americans to changing times. Aunt Jemima lost weight, and black children lost their strong attachment to watermelon.

Are African Americans Gaining Equal Representation in Advertising?

More and more advertisers have begun to turn to minority agencies for expertise in reaching minorities. In the past, many advertisers lumped

African Americans together as a single market segment, but research provided evidence of an emerging and desirable African-American middle-class demographic. In 1980, *Black Enterprise* coined the term *buppie* to describe college-educated African Americans who live in suburban areas and hold upscale tastes in fashion, food and lifestyles. By the 1990s, nearly 32 million African Americans were in this category. They have an estimated purchasing power of between $300 and $889 billion (Woods 1995).

Elements of this buppie culture were incorporated into several successful ad campaigns. For example, commercial jingles based on rap and hip-hop music along with images that are considered to be "hip," "cool" and "phat" can be found in most ad campaigns. Budweiser used familiar slang in its "Whazzup" campaign, Jell-O used Bill Cosby in the 1980s, Pepsi incorporated music legend Michael Jackson, and the ever popular Michael Jordan has pitched everything from shoes to batteries to car mufflers.

Research suggests that one influence on white consumer response to ethnic images in ads is source credibility. The effectiveness of source credibility on the persuasive influence of an advertising message is central and important in any discussion of images in media and advertising. Source credibility, and not the color of one's skin, it could be argued, is the most important characteristic in advertising. For journalists and advertisers, credibility can be enhanced when the consumer/reader likes the endorser/source, when there is perceived similarity and when the source is attractive and trustworthy (Mellot 1983).

Increased Portrayals

The underutilization of black models in advertising was documented in a 1992 report entitled *Invisible People,* issued by the New York City Department of Consumer Affairs. Researchers reviewed more than 11,000 ads in 27 different national magazines and found that over 95 percent of the models were white. The research also showed that most of the blacks in the ads appeared in group shots, again proving the claim that black models appear in background roles. The researchers found that when used, black women were usually light skinned and had long, wavy hair.

In a study of portrayals of blacks in magazine and television commercials, Zinkhan et al. (1990) found an upward trend in portrayals of African-American characters and actors in both magazine and television advertisements. This trend was later confirmed by studies that showed African Americans accounted for approximately 25 percent of characters or actors in advertisements (Bowen and Schmid 1997; Wilkes and Valencia 1989). However, some researchers believe that the increase in the number of portrayals is not as promising as it appears. "The large number of appearances of African Americans in minor and background roles and the converse—their relative infrequency of appearance in major roles—suggest an unwelcome tokenism" (Taylor et al. 1995), a finding that seems to contradict earlier research.

"It's easy for an advertiser to simply add minority models to diffuse criticism; and, if one were to simply count the number of times minorities appear in advertisements, the increase could be viewed as progress" (Bowen and Schmid 1997, 144). While research continues to discover that the number of African-American portrayals in the media is on the rise (Zinkhan et al. 1990), actual portrayals of African Americans in advertisements still appear to be clouded by controversy.

According to Bowen and Schmid (1997), "For those black models pictured in mainstream advertising, the roles are often limited or demeaning" (p. 134). Minority group actors and models receive less space and airtime in major media than do members of the majority group. There are few advertisements in mainstream advertising in which minorities appear alone, and when minorities do appear, "they are outnumbered by whites" (p. 144).

Not Quite There: Light- versus Dark-Skinned Images

Advertisers commonly use light-skinned black models to cater to a diverse consumer population. Using light-skinned black models in advertising may have roots from when the mulatto population began growing during slavery. Mulattos are mixed, with African and Caucasian blood, and often have lighter skin, straighter hair and perhaps lighter eyes than a "nonmixed black" in America. With society now demanding more diversity in media, advertisers seem to rely on black models with some kind of European physical feature to advertise mainstream products. Take Revlon cosmetics, for example. In the early 1990s, Revlon began a campaign using actress Halle Berry. Berry, the daughter of a white mother and a black father, was the first African-American model for Revlon. For many black women, however, Berry was not a true representation of the African-American female. Frisby (2000) found that black women felt that the inclusion of Berry in the Revlon ad was just the advertiser's way of using a "safe" black image in their ad. One woman said, "I'm looking at the model and saying, that's not me. She doesn't even look like me" (Frisby 2000, 7).

The advertisers for Pantene, a hair product, realized that to diversify their target market they must use different races. One Pantene advertisement shows a black woman with long flowing hair using the product. Do white consumers see the black model and assume that Pantene works only on "black" hair? On the other side, do black women who do not have long straight hair think that Pantene works only for the "good" hair? With several mainstream products using black models with European features it is believed that the self-esteem of dark-skinned black women, in particular, is bound to suffer from exposure to light-skinned women in ads (Russell 1992).

Keenan (1996) found that blacks in advertisements had lighter complexions and more Caucasian features than those in news editorial photographs. Keenan also discovered that black women in ads were lighter than black men. Leslie (1995) investigated the changing image of blacks in advertisements and found significant differences in the aesthetic qualities of the models used in ads. Leslie found that many of the models used in the ads were fair skinned and had European features. So while research reveals an increase in the use of black models and black products, the trend seems to suggest that their facial appearance and features tend to be more "Caucasian-like." In sum, most of the studies on African-American portrayals in mainstream media support the idea that, while representations of blacks have increased, most of the African Americans shown had typical Eurotypic (white and/or Caucasian) facial types or hair.

What You Need to Know About African-American Consumers

Mainstream media attract minorities. According to a report conducted by Mediamark Research (1995), many of the major media (magazines such as *Cosmopolitan* and *Time*) attract at least 10 to 15 percent of the ethnic population. Broadcast television programs also attract African Americans, Hispanics and Asian Americans. Market research reveals that ethnic minority groups are regular consumers of many popular mainstream media. What many companies and advertising agencies don't seem to realize is that they do not have to use minority media to reach minorities.

According to Bowen and Schmid (1997):

> For advertisers to assume that minorities do not (attend to) mainstream (media) is naïve, and from a marketing standpoint, economic suicide given the size and financial resources of many minorities. If minorities do not ignore mainstream media, why should advertisers? (P. 142)
>
> Minorities read mainstream magazines and buy mainstream products. It's time they receive mainstream treatment. (P. 144)

Research shows that, with respect to attracting minorities, many broadcast programs can have a cross-cultural appeal. Soap operas have an ethnic audience rating of 21.6 percent. Evening news shows garner a rating among African Americans of about 15 percent. Prime-time serials like "Beverly Hills 90210," "Dawson's Creek," "The Practice," "Ally McBeal" and "Friends," to name a few, have been found to reach up to 34 percent of the ethnic audiences in the United States (Mediamark Research 1995). In addition, market data on broadcast audiences reveal that compared with Caucasians and other segments, African Americans watch television more than any other group between 7:30 p.m. and 2:00 a.m. Yet there remain few advertisements with African Americans in prime-time, mainstream media.

It has been suggested that Caucasian reaction to ethnic images and motivation to purchase an advertised product may be driven by other factors—factors that do not necessarily relate to ethnicity. Much of the research in the area of mainstream advertising and how whites and blacks respond to advertising stimuli was conducted in the late to mid-1960s, a time in which our society as a whole was overcoming controversies and problems in civil rights (refer to Barban 1964, 1969; Bush et al. 1974; Pitts et al. 1989). Have things changed since the 1960s? Have people become more tolerant for and accepting of cultural differences?

Advertisers in the mid-1960s were hesitant about including blacks in advertisements. A lot has happened, however, since the 1960s. Forces such as desegregation and affirmative action have cut across cultures to create similarities and cultural changes. The few studies conducted on the impact of ethnic images on attitudes suggest that young Caucasian adults might be more tolerant of the use of African-American images used in advertisements (refer to Frisby 1999). This suggests that perhaps attitudes and feelings about blacks in ads have become more positive.

Consumer Reactions to Images in the Ads

Published studies have measured both white and black consumers' reactions to black models featured in ads. The studies have been conducted using different media and different products. They have measured both attitudes and sales figures. The researchers usually create identical ads—one version with white models and another with black models. Ads are shown to groups of consumers who are asked how they "feel" about the ad. These attitude scores are then compared to determine how consumers respond toward the models.

The studies have used TV ads, newspaper, magazine, radio and even sales promotion materials. The general conclusion is that white consumers do not respond negatively to black models in ads. This finding has led many researchers to conclude that advertisers should use more black models in their ads. Advertisers could aim the same messages at both black and white audiences rather than create expensive separate campaigns for two market segments. If black models are more effective in reaching black consumers and at the same time do not affect appeal to whites, clearly the use of black models in a single campaign would appear to be highly desirable.

Unlike in earlier shows that presented blacks in stereotyped roles, most television roles created for African Americans now tend to depict them as middle- to upper-class individuals who also happen to be black (e.g., "The Cosby Show"). Some blacks object to this portrayal, arguing that this portrayal is not "real-life" either, and believe that black consumers can be reached in ways other than over-utilization of "black media."

Future research should explore whether using black models to advertise black products in "all-black" media creates a new stereotype or heuristic cue for consumers—a stereotype that communicates that African-American models are only able to sell to other African Americans. While this may be true of some products (e.g., hair relaxer), it is certainly not true of most of the products that blacks use and consume (e.g., contact lenses, hand soap, toothpaste, detergent). Future research might attempt to discover whether people have developed schemata or conceptualized images and scripts about endorsers and their associations with products.

Purchase intent, as prior research suggests, is not influenced by ethnicity; it is more a function of the product being advertised. Given the widespread use of physically attractive images to sell or influence product-liking, images do not seem to affect consumers as much as knowing how well the product features match with aspects or features of one's self-identity.

To make improvements in the portrayal of African-American images, it is argued, enhancements are needed not in the number of portrayals but in how and when the images are portrayed. Advertisers and advertisements need to begin to show African-American images in major roles, particularly in major media.

Black Female Consumer Responses to Idealized Images

Every day, at any moment, images of beauty, particularly images in advertisements and television commercials, confront women of all colors. According to Richins (1991), women see unrealistically attractive idealized images in advertising and either consciously or subconsciously engage in self-evaluation. These images, Richins argues, "engender comparison and in so doing create self-doubt and dissatisfaction" (p. 72). Do these images, for example, create self-doubt and dissatisfaction for women from different ethnic backgrounds?

Using the theory of social comparison, Frisby (2000) looked at the impact of exposure to advertisements including thin, physically attractive Caucasian and African-American models on the self-evaluations of African-American women exhibiting varying levels of self-reported body esteem. Frisby discovered that exposure to idealized images of Caucasian models was not related to lower self-evaluations, regardless of level of body esteem. (Research has yet to uncover how African-American women respond to images of attractive African-American women.) The study demonstrates that African-American women are not affected by exposure to advertising with images of physically attractive Caucasian women, supporting the idea that African-American women have a more positive body image than do white women and, no matter what the size, are relatively unaffected by exposure to idealized images in traditional print media. These data are consistent with research that found African-American women are able to buffer self-esteem when exposed to idealized images in ads (e.g., Botta 2000; Milkie 1999, 2001). Results obtained from the Frisby (2000) study seem to suggest that similarity or ethnicity of the idealized image may have an impact.

Toward More Accurate Minority Images in Advertisements

A 1998 television commercial for fast-food chain Taco Bell illustrates how marketers (intentionally or not) use ethnic and racial stereotypes to craft promotional communications. A Florida-based Hispanic civil-rights activist campaigned against Taco Bell's popular Spanish-speaking Chihuahua ad campaign. The critic found the ad demeaning. However, Hispanics did not support the outcry and as a result, the ad resulted in a major increase in product sales for Taco Bell (http://www.eonline.com/News/Items/0,1,2664,00.html).

More Inclusive Advertising

Reaching the African-American market is an easy task, but marketers face a real hurdle in communicating with sensitivity to and understanding of people in this market. In some ways, the greatest weapon we have for solving racial problems in advertising and media is knowledge. Some suggestions on how to craft more inclusive and successful advertising:

1. *Know the facts about the target market and the ethnic group you are trying to communicate with.* It's always a hot topic of debate, but how much do we really know about one another and about racial issues? How much of what we think or feel about members of different ethnic groups is positive and how much of what we think or believe is stereotypical or based on some media representation? As we learn more and more about a person, stereotypes fade away.
2. *Recognize your own biases.* For coverage of ethnic groups and stereotypes to improve, we must be in tune with our own attitudes toward members of a racial group.
3. *Interact with members of ethnic groups in settings where everyone has roughly equal social status.* The interaction in this instance be-

tween members of different groups should be one-on-one and should be maintained over time. College and work environments often provide these opportunities.

4. *Realize the need for better media coverage of racial issues and more-accurate representation of minorities.* Whether we are looking at news coverage or inclusion in advertising, what we should agree on is a need for a greater understanding of others and greater sensitivity to their needs. Instead of showing blacks as victims, welfare dependents, athletes, entertainers, rappers, musicians, comedians and/or criminals, why not focus on the middle-class, everyday average consumer?

5. *Strive for integration into mainstream media.* Segregation is still a pervasive, if subtle, problem. This is not an argument for our society to become "color blind" or to ask people to think less or focus less on one's skin color, but to focus on other variables that bind us together as consumers. For example, instead of placing black ads only in black media, advertisers might begin to focus on shared demographics in audiences and place commercials for common or global products in mainstream media.

6. *Encourage dialogue and focus group discussions with your audience.* Sometimes those of us who are unfamiliar with others may hold misconceptions and ask questions that seem politically incorrect and/or rude. For advertisers and journalists, the first thing we should consider is what our thoughts are about certain groups. That is, when we think of group X, we think: ... This exercise is helpful for all demographic groups.

Race and cultural diversity issues have become a pervasive concern not just for media practitioners but also for our society. In today's multicultural environment, we find more demands for change. This may explain the changes in minority representations in commercials. The advertising industry discovered the increased buying power of middle-class blacks and responded to it.

Media practitioners should treat individuals within a demographic group with sensitivity while not holding them up as typical representations of or the spokespersons for, the entire group. We should strive for balance. We should strive for equity in portrayals. We should strive to write stories and ads that portray a range of lifestyles within a particular ethnic group. We should strive to appreciate differences within groups and be sure that we accurately communicate differences in our content.

Resources

Internet

http://www.nabj.org/   National Association of Black Journalists
http://www.tbwt.com/   Black World Today
http://www.mediachannel.org/atissue/womensmedia/   African Women's Media Center (AWMC)
http://www.asanet.org/sections/rgcbiblio.html   Race, Gender, and Class Bibliography

Journals

Journal of Black Studies. Publisher: Sage Publications, Inc.
Gravity. An African-American journal of politics, art and culture. C. Brown, 1994. Former title: *Meanderings*
The Network Journal. Black professional and small business news. Brooklyn, N.Y.: Jackson and Jackson Management Plus, 1995

Books and Articles

Kern-Foxworth, M. 1994. *Aunt Jemima Uncle Ben, and Rastus: Blacks in Advertising, Yesterday, Today, and Tomorrow*. Westport, Conn.: Greenwood Press.
"Media Campaign Reaches Multi-cultural Populations." http://www.allied-media.com/Publications/african_american_publications.htm
Woods, Gail Baker. 1995. *Advertising and Marketing to the New Majority*. Belmont, Calif.: Wadsworth.
Woods, Keith. "'NIGGER': A Case Study in Using a Racial Epithet." The Poynter Institute for Media Studies. http://www.poynter.org/research/me/me_ec1195a.htm

References

Barban, A. 1964. "Negro and White Response to Advertising Stimuli." *Journal of Marketing Research* 1(Nov.):53-56.
Barban, A. 1969. "The Dilemma of Integrated Advertising." *Journal of Business* 42(Oct.):477-496.
Botta, R.A. 2000. "The Mirror of Television: A Comparison of Black and White Adolescents' Body Inage." *Journal of Communication* 50(3):144-159.

Bowen, L., and J. Schmid. 1997. "Minority Presence and Portrayal in Mainstream Magazine Advertising: An Update." *Journalism and Mass Communication Quarterly* 1(Spring):134-146.

"Boycott Abercrombie & Fitch web site" www.petitiononline.com/BCAF/petition.html; modelminority.com/media/abercrombie.htm

Bush, R., R.F. Gwinner, and P.J. Solomon. 1974. "White Consumer Sales Response to Black Models." *Journal of Marketing* 38(Apr.):25-29.

Duncan, B.L. 1976. "Differential Social Perception and Attribution of Intergroup Violence: Testing the Lower Limits of Stereotyping of Blacks." *Journal of Personality and Social Psychology* 34:590-598.

Edmonson, B. 1985. "Black Markets." *American Demographics* November 20.

Frisby, C.M. 2000. "Black like me: Effects of Idealized Images on African American Women's Perceptions of Body and Self-esteem." Paper presented to the Association of Education in Journalism and Mass Communication, August 2000.

Frisby, C.M. 1999. "Beyond the Looking Glass: Thoughts and Feelings of African American Images in Advertisements by Caucasian Consumers." Paper presented to the Association of Education in Journalism and Mass Communication, August 1999.

Gerbner, G., L. Gross, M. Morgan, and N. Signorielli. 1986. "Living with Television: The Dynamics of the Cultivation Process." In *Perspectives on Media Effects,* ed. J. Bryant and D. Zillman, 17-40. Hillsdale N.J.: Erlbaum.

Jordan, W.D. 1968. *White over Black: American Attitudes Toward the Negro, 1550-1812.* Chapel Hill, N.C.: University of North Carolina Press.

Keenan, K.L. 1996. "Skin Tones and Physical Features of Blacks in Magazine Advertisements." *Journalism and Mass Communication Quarterly* 73(4):905-912.

Kern-Foxworth, M. 1994. *Aunt Jemima, Uncle Ben, and Rastus: Blacks in Advertising Yesterday, Today, and Tomorrow.* Westport, Conn.: Greenwood Press.

Leslie, M. 1995. "Slow Fade to ?: Advertising in Ebony Magazine, 1957-1989." *Journalism and Mass Communication Quarterly* 72(2):

McConahay, J.B. 1986. "Modern Racism, Ambivalence, and the Modern Racism Scale." In *Prejudice, Discrimination, and Racism: Theory and Research*, ed. S.L. Gaertner and J. Dovidio. New York: Academic Press.

Mediamark Research, Inc. Spring 1995. Television Audiences Report. New York: Mediamark Research, Inc.

Mellott, D.W. 1983. *Fundamentals of Consumer Behavior.* Tulsa, Okla.: Pennwell Publishing.

Milkie, M.A. 2001. "The Impact of Pervasive Beauty Images on Black and White Girls' Self-Concepts." In *Sociological Odyssey: Contemporary Readings in Sociology*, ed. Peter Adler and Patricia Adler, 123-131. Belmont, Calif.: Wadsworth.

Milkie, M.A. 1999. "Social Comparisons, Reflected Appraisals and Mass Media: The Impact of Pervasive Beauty Images on Black and White Girls' Self-concepts." *Social Psychology Quarterly* 62:190-210.

New York City Department of Consumer Affairs. 1992. "Race Bias Seen in Magazine Ads" in the report *Invisible People.*

Pitts, R.E., D.J. Whalen, R. O'Keefe, and V. Murray. 1989. "Black and White Response to Culturally Targeted Television Commercials: A Values-based Approach." *Psychology and Marketing* 6(Winter):311-328.

Reese, S. 1997. "When Whites Aren't a Mass Market." *American Demographics* (March):51-54.

Richins, M.L. 1991. "Social Comparison and the Idealized Images of Advertising." *Journal of Consumer Research* 18:71-83.

Russell, K., M. Wilson, and R.E. Hall. 1992. *The Color Complex: The Politics of Skin Color Among African Americans.* New York: Anchor Books.

Taylor, C.R., J.Y. Lee, and B.B. Stern. 1995. "Portrayals of African, Hispanic, and Asian Americans in Magazine Advertising." *American Behavioral Scientist* 3(Feb.): 608-621.

Thompson, F. 1997. "Blacks Spending Potential up 54 Percent Since 1990." *Montgomery Advertiser*, May 9, p. 1.

Trimble, J.E. 1988. "Stereotypical Images, American Indians, and Prejudice." In *Eliminating Racism: Profiles in Controversy,* ed. P.A. Katz and D.A. Taylor, 181-202. New York: Plenium Press.

Wilkes, R.E., and H. Valencia. 1989. "Hispanics and Blacks in Television Commercials." *Journal of Advertising* 18(Winter):19.

Woods, G. Baker. 1995. *Advertising and Marketing to the New Majority.* Belmont, Calif.: Wadsworth Publishing Company.

Zinkhan, G., Q. Qualls, and A. Biswas. 1990. "The Use of Blacks in Analysis of Blacks in Magazines and Television Advertising, 1946–1986." *Journalism Quarterly* 67:547-553.

CHAPTER 10

People with Disabilities

Elizabeth Wissner-Gross, with contributions by
Alexander Wissner-Gross

A frail-looking man, hunched over a cane, approached a set of subway doors just as they were closing. A young New Yorker jumped out of her seat on the train to help hold the automatic doors, so the man could clear the entry safely. As the doors slammed shut behind him, the man (aboard safely) turned angrily to the responsive passenger and said, "You didn't think I could do it myself? Why don't you mind your own business?"

Although most people probably would not consider the alert passenger wrong to have offered assistance, two lessons can be learned from this incident. The first is that *people with disabilities differ as much from each other as people without disabilities or people with minimal disabilities.* No single response is necessarily correct, and no single standard of dealing with disabled people—in writing or in person—is universally appreciated. People have different needs, sensibilities, expectations, approaches and styles. *Considerate to one person might be construed as an intrusion to another.* (At the same time, it should be noted that certain insensitive responses are definitely incorrect and inconsiderate.)

Writers and editors need to be sensitive to the individuals about whom they are writing—not just the disabilities of the individuals. To do this, avoid generalizing about people with a shared disability. Avoid making assumptions about individuals' abilities and especially restrictions based on visible physical differences.

The second lesson might be that *caring, responsive individuals do make occasional inadvertent mistakes in their treatment of others.* This kind of well-intended error, however, is obviously better than erring in the opposite direction and apathetically letting a frail person be crushed by automatic subway doors or the equivalent. Whereas a journalist should not second-guess an interview subject or be presumptuous (read *restrictive*) about the subject's abilities, thoughtfulness and consideration are better than apathy. Thorough research and preparation help promote this thoughtfulness. Good journalists should familiarize themselves in advance with any specific disability experienced by the interview subject, time permitting, assuming the journalist knows of the disability in advance.

Guidelines for Journalists Covering People with Disabilities

The Meaning of Disabled

Before focusing on how to familiarize oneself with particular disabilities, one should first understand what is meant by *disabled.* What constitutes a disability? Definitions vary widely. A disabling factor for one person might seem like a minor discomfort for another. The best journalistic definition of *disability* is probably *obstacle* or *hardship.* A person who faces an obstacle or hardship is disabled. Thus, a person who manages to overcome an obstacle or hardship may not view himself or herself as disabled.

This broad definition embraces some of the traditionally known *handicaps,* including blindness, deafness, absence of limbs, malfunctioning organs and muscles, as well as other less obvious handicaps, including debilitating diseases, heart irregularities, or even weight problems, height disadvantages, skin disorders, psychological disorders and learning problems. Disabilities vary in degree and response.

Understanding a Particular Disability

In familiarizing oneself with a disability, the main question to ask is, "What are the obstacles for people with this disability?" Although obstacles are found to exist, the journalist should never assume that the obstacles are impossible to overcome or that a person with a disability has not already overcome the obstacles or compensated for the obstacles in some other way.

Do not go into an interview assuming, for example, that a blind person is not well read, that a wheelchair user is not athletic or strong, that a deaf person has not been to an opera, or that a person with a severe speech impediment is not articulate or even brilliant.

A writer who has no experience with a particular disability should ask a second question: "What famous, successful people have had this disability and continued to achieve despite this disability?" Keep some of the most classic examples in mind. Beethoven composed some of his best music while he was deaf. Stephen Hawking articulated some of physics' most difficult concepts using a computer to pronounce the words for him. Franklin D. Roosevelt remained a strong leader from his wheelchair. Leonardo da Vinci is believed to have had dyslexia. The powerful Napoleon was unusually short in stature. Use these famous examples to remind yourself that people who have not already overcome disabilities have potential to overcome them.

At the same time, do not go to an interview *expecting* your interview subject to have conquered all, or even any, obstacles. Although many people overcome or compensate for disabilities, do not assume that everyone can compensate equally, and do not look down on those who cannot. Remember that disabilities vary in degree, and people vary in their abilities, inclinations, access to a support network, and drive to overcome their disabilities.

Some people are better equipped to face obstacles and hardships. For example, a person in top physical shape with few physical obstacles is more likely to recover faster and better from a physical accident than a person with additional obstacles. Sometimes combating an obstacle is a matter of economics. A wealthier person may have more opportunities to seek the best treatment, to hire the best support staff, or to purchase more costly therapeutic supplies or enabling apparatus.

Staying Focused on the Story

In covering people with disabilities, writers' and editors' most common egregious offense is to make the disability the story itself. This error often appears right from the lead.

Journalists should heed this simple but vital rule: *Remember that disabled people are people first.* Although this may sound obvious, major news outlets violate this rule constantly.

Savvy journalists who know not to describe people on first reference by ethnicity, race, or appearance if such traits are not the focal point of the story sometimes inappropriately detail people's visible disabilities on first reference ("John Smith, who is blind" or "Jane Smith, who is a paraplegic"). Unsophisticated editors may claim that such labels add "flavor" or important description to the lead or nut paragraph when, in fact, such description steals the focus of the piece. The focus then turns to the disability, as if this obstacle is the most important element of the piece and/or person covered.

While obstacles may play a significant role in a person's life, no lead should mention the obstacle unless the story is specifically about that obstacle or the method that the person used to overcome the impediment. In any case, never mention the obstacle before the person's name in the lead ("Blind John Smith" or "Alcoholic Jane Smith"), as if the obstacle is part of the person's name. Persons should not be described by the obstacles they face unless the obstacles are meant to be the focus of the story. Nor should journalists assume that obstacles automatically become the focus of the story when the subject of the story is disabled. On first reference and in the lead, the person should be described in context and in relation to the story.

If the disability is relevant to the story, the disability should be introduced into the piece when the context calls for such a reference (when the disability becomes relevant to the story). Otherwise, a mere gratuitous mention of the disability sidetracks the story and detracts from the piece.

If the disability has no correlation to the piece, the journalist should not mention the disability at all. Many descriptive facts are withheld from articles—not out of censorship, but because they are irrelevant and do not fit. To include certain information reveals writer bias and can remove objectivity from journalism.

In an interview about plans for a new wing at the local library, for example, a physical description of the research librarian would probably be irrelevant to the story. If the librarian was a 30-year-old woman with crooked teeth who weighed more than 250 pounds and had a nervous laugh, such description might not find its way past most trained editors. Likewise, if the woman had a hearing impairment or used a wheelchair, the medical obstacles should not generally find their way into the piece. If the art librarian was blind and the lack of vision impacted the job, a writer could justify inclusion of the impediment in the article. Even if the assignment were to write a profile piece about a new librarian, the journalist should be very wary about including description that details disabilities or suggests that the new librarian will be unable to do the job, based on the journalist's perceived notions of the librarian's disabilities.

Journalists can help themselves by remembering that, as a general, sobering rule, *everyone is disabled to some extent*. Bodies are imperfect. Nobody has ever lived forever—which means that everyone dies of some malfunction—at least so far in our history. Some people inherit or are beset with significantly more severe disabilities than others. Some face numerous small obstacles and setbacks. Some people go through life seemingly obstacle-free for longer periods of time than others do. Some people are born with obstacles that constantly threaten their lives or make them uncomfortable physically or socially. But nobody so far has inhabited the perfect machine that works forever.

In keeping with that line of thought, journalists should not be pointing to or commenting on every visible disability. Obviously the people most vulnerable to media scrutiny in this regard are those with the most visible disabilities. In contrast, a person with a heart disease is not described typically as "a heart patient" unless the person specifically tells the reporter that he or she has a heart problem. Likewise, people with diabetes, high blood pressure, vertigo or other less obvious but potentially disabling conditions and disabilities are often treated with more dignity by the media. Some journalists erroneously think that because they spot a physical disorder or disability, they must dutifully report it to the public—as if not disclosing it would be the equivalent of concealing or censoring information and depriving the public of its right to know.

Novices should note that professional journalists never report *everything* that they see. One could not possibly report everything due to time and space limitations. Nor would journalists want to. Good journalists make good decisions in deciding what is newsworthy and what is not. Disabilities should not be assumed to be newsworthy. They are only newsworthy inasmuch as they have relevance to what is happening in a particular news story.

Granted, there are some disabilities that are so unusual that they become news stories in themselves. In a story about overcoming obstacles, it is appropriate, even desirable, to mention a person's obstacles or disabilities in the lead or nut paragraph. The majority of stories that refer to disabled people, however, do not fall into this category.

Arranging an Interview

When arranging a meeting with someone that you know to have severe disabilities (disabilities that might prohibit the individual's access to otherwise commonly accessible locations) you should probably ask the person to recommend a meeting place that is comfortable. Depending upon the disability, different places are comfortable. A person who is unusually short, for example, and considers his or her height to be a disability might prefer to stay away from meeting places where automatic doors respond to weight or height, or where restroom toilets are prohibitively high, information counters are uninvitingly high, or seating is limited to high stools at counters. Likewise, if the interview subject is unusually overweight, a supposedly cozy booth in a restaurant might make an uncomfortable meeting site.

For an interview subject who uses a wheelchair, a reporter can phone a potential meeting place in advance to inquire about ramps and wheelchair accessibility. A few simple phone calls can positively impact the flow, the tone, and the productivity of the interview. At the same time, the reporter should be able to be flexible, understanding that even the most elaborate, detailed arrangements do not always work out (elevators malfunction, location accommodations are not always as described or envisioned, seating may not be as private as represented, etc.) and last minute changes may be necessary.

A smart reporter should ask for a suggested meeting site, since the interviewee is more likely to know of a more conducive setting.

Interpreting a Disability

After interviewing someone with a disability, do not pretend to your readers (or listeners or viewers) that you thoroughly understand how it feels to face your subject's obstacles on a daily basis. You do not—unless you live with identical obstacles, and no two people do.

After interviewing many people with a common or similar disability, a journalist may draw some conclusions and discuss similarities. Again, do not presume to fully comprehend how it feels to live with the disability, lest you belittle the struggle of the people working to overcome some of their obstacles. Instead, quote the disabled people you have interviewed, using their language wherever possible to describe their situation.

Disabilities

Blindness

Representatives of advocacy organizations for blind people say that blind people are among the most misunderstood people by society and the media. Journalists, when speaking with blind people, often shout or speak inappropriately loudly, as if trying to compensate through sound for a blind person's lack of vision. The representatives point out that such shouting is not only rude but generally unnecessary, since blind people are more dependent on hearing and tend to develop their other senses more than do sighted people.

In comedy films, blind people tend to be the targets of more jokes than people with other disabilities. Advocacy organization representatives point out that in most comedy or suspense films in which a blind character appears, the blind person drives a car or truck before the end of the film. The audience laughs or screams depending on the context, and the blindness is used as a cheap shot to manipulate the audience and guarantee an emotional response from the audience. Likewise, blindness is among the disabilities most commonly depicted in cartoons—whether political cartoons or animated films for children. Advocacy organizations argue that society, taking a cue from journalists, filmmakers and cartoon artists, tends to be insensitive to blind people. They explain that blindness is an increasing problem despite the inventions of glasses, contact lenses, and laser surgery. More people than ever are blind, largely because people live longer and more babies with initial birth defects survive.

Advocacy groups explain that definitions of blindness may vary by degree and cause. Some people are born blind. Others become blind as a result of illness, aging, or accidents. Regardless of the cause, blindness should not be referred to flippantly in journalism (as in "Are you blind or something?" or constant references to "the blind leading the blind" or "blind dates"). Likewise, it is inappropriate to generalize about people who are blind. Avoid referring to blind people as *the blind,* for example, unless making reference to a specific group that uses that wording in its title.

Preparation for interviews with blind people should not be very different from preparation for other interviews. The exception is when the interview requires that the subject refer to printed documents or any written material. Depending on the context of the interview, you might want to ask the interviewee in advance if he or she is familiar with the documents in question. Never assume that a blind person is unfamiliar with printed materials.

As a courtesy (as you would probably do with a sighted person as well), you might advise the person in advance to familiarize himself or herself with any documents that are likely to be discussed. Many materials are available on tape or can be made available on tape with advance notice. Also with advance notice, materials can be available in large print (for people with sight impairments who are not completely blind), readers can be hired, or Braille copies may be obtained. As a rule, advance notice about documents is a courtesy that can help the journalist interview a more informed subject.

Deafness

Interviewing someone with a hearing impairment poses different obstacles for the interviewer. The interviewer needs to find out in advance how the interviewee communicates. Is a sign-language translator required? Does the interview subject lip-read? Would printed resources be helpful?

If a sign-language translator is required, the journalist or news publication should cover the cost. Never assume that a deaf interview subject has round-the-clock access to a translator or that the interviewee should finance the service. You might ask the interview subject, however, to recommend an appropriate translator if such service is required.

With the prevalence of computer use in society, the Internet now provides a comfortable "setting" for interviews. The Internet offers an easy way to "chat" with a deaf person, if the interview does not require an in-person meeting. Even if the interview does require an in-person meeting, typing into a computer can be useful and cost efficient in the absence of a translator or when lip-reading fails.

When speaking with an inexperienced lip-reader, avoid colloquialisms as much as possible. Be conscious of moving your lips. Exaggerate the movements slightly—Americans are known for speaking without moving their lips. Consciously change this stiffness when speaking with a lip-reader, if possible. Speak directly. Make sure you have eye contact when you speak, or what you say will not be seen. Slow the pace of your speech slightly. Avoid inserting unnecessary "habit" words and phrases if you can. (Some common ones: *like, really, uh, actually, for sure.*) Although many lip-readers are familiar with the more common habit words, regional habit words and unfamiliar expressions may take time to untangle, for no valuable purpose. Such usages frustrate both interviewer and interviewee and waste time.

Bring paper to an interview in case you want to write some words that seem otherwise incommunicable or difficult to communicate. Do not be embarrassed to jot down words. Try to print all words neatly, so the person you are interviewing can read your writing easily and does not face the double humiliation of not being able to hear you or read your handwriting.

If necessary, do not be afraid to gesture or pantomime more than usual where appropriate, if that facilitates comprehension of a word.

Do not shout if the interview subject is completely deaf. Shouting does not help a deaf person to lip-read more easily. If the hearing impairment is partial, shouting might help, but if the person is completely deaf, exaggerating lip movements is more helpful—as long as the movements do not become so extreme that they become unrecognizable. Many deaf people not only lip-read but also speak as clearly as those with full hearing ability. Remember, for example, that a person born with full hearing ability who learned to speak as a child and later became deaf does not lose the ability to speak. *Never assume that the deaf person you interview is unable to speak.*

However, tape recording an interview with a deaf person who speaks may be insensitive, depending on context. Taking notes or typing into a computer may be more helpful if you need to play back what was said during the interview, particularly if you want the interviewee to double-check what was said.

Do not refer to people as *the deaf*, since deafness involves a wide range of people. *The deaf* tends to lead to generalizations. Deaf people may be completely deaf from birth, be hard of hearing because of old age, or have severe hearing impairment as a result of a disease or accident. Do not assume that all deaf people you come in contact with were deaf from birth or that they have never heard music, speech, or other sounds. Do not assume that they are less educated or have not seen movies, read books, or participated in other cultural or educational activities as a result of their deafness.

Mental and Psychological Disabilities

Can a disease or a condition constitute a disability? Any condition an individual experiences that seems to pose an obstacle may be considered a disability, whether recognized as such or not. Paranoia, whether it seems justified to the journalist or not, can be disabling. Fears and phobias can be disabling. Fear of public speaking, vertigo, claustrophobia, and fear of flying, for example, can be disabling. Superstitions can be disabling. Extreme self-consciousness can be disabling as well.

When interviewing someone with a so-called mental disorder, find out as much as possible about the situation in advance. If writing about a person with a specific known disorder, find out the actual name of the condition. Do not mention it in the story unless it specifically pertains to the story or is necessary to establish the credibility of the person quoted.

Do not assume that the interview subject is dangerous, crazy, or unintelligent. Do not act as if you are embarrassed to be talking with the person in front of other people. Do not act patronizing. Always treat the interviewee with dignity, as you would any other person you interview.

For years, writers sloppily grouped together people with a wide range of brain-related problems, referring to them all as *retarded* or *mental*, undermining what these people had to say. Physical brain-related disorders still commonly get lumped together with emotional difficulties by unsophisticated writers and society.

The stereotyping problem is not unique to journalists. Many so-called educators make the same mistake of lumping together people with unrelated conditions. Children with a variety of learning disabilities and disorders are assigned to the same class in some schools. Whereas all of these students may have completely different impediments and needs, schools commonly assign them to one teacher who is then expected to meet all needs at the same time. In some of these classrooms, the only common element is dysfunctional students. In such a classroom, it is common, for example, to see a combination that includes children with attention deficit disorder, children reacting emotionally to dysfunctional family histories, retarded children, battered children, children with dyslexia, children with hearing loss, and juvenile delinquents.

When journalists incorrectly classify a wide range of disabilities into a single heading, the writers lose credibility among their readers (and listeners and viewers) and demean the people about whom they write. Never assume that the fact that a person behaves differently in some way indicates that the person is not intelligent. A speech impediment, an unusual phobia, a loss of memory and many other psychological or brain-related disabilities may be entirely unrelated to intelligence.

Illnesses and Conditions

Certain diseases may cause visible symptoms, scars, or conditions: slurred speech, memory loss, physical twitches, facial paralysis, etc. Although some of these symptoms may strike the reporter as unusual or even bizarre, do not mention these features in the piece unless it relates specifically to the story. Some of these symptoms may be temporary. Bell's palsy, for example, causes temporary facial paralysis, but by the time a magazine piece is written, the paralysis may be gone completely. Other conditions may be longer term, as in some paralyses associated with strokes, but writers still should not include descriptions of such conditions in a piece unless it ties into the story directly.

This rule may be excepted if a photo is required or TV footage is required to accompany the piece. The reporter might feel obligated to help the audience interpret the condition that is being photographed. If a person appears to be winking, for example, because of an eye injury or disease, a caption or voice-over should probably explain.

As a rule, photojournalists and photo editors need to be sensitive to photo subjects with disabilities. Although candid photography is generally preferred in journalism, extra sensitivity and care is required in photographing people with visible disabilities, particularly nonpublic figures in photos that accompany stories that are not focused on disabilities or health. Nothing is gained by photographing a "cheap shot" of someone with an upset stomach or a severe back pain that precludes the individual from standing straight, or a tooth that just chipped, if these conditions do not relate to the story being written.

In contrast, in a piece about war crimes, photographs of people with missing body parts, people in pain, or bloodied bodies may be entirely relevant. In a piece about dentistry or street fights, chipped teeth could be justified in a photograph. But in pieces unrelated to physical or medical conditions, when photographers know they are assigned to photograph someone with a physical disability, some advance warning or notice would be considered courteous.

Terms to Avoid.   Editors need to watch out for writing that labels people who experience illnesses and conditions as becoming intricately linked to those diseases and conditions. Eliminate usage that classifies a person as *an anorexic, a manic, a dyslexic, an alcoholic, a leper, an epileptic, a bulimic, a schizophrenic,* or *a lunatic.* Instead, opt for language that indicates that the person "has struggled with anorexia," "has experienced manic depression," "has mild dyslexia," or "has been struggling with an alcohol problem," etc.

Regardless of what self-help organizations say to their own members or about their own members as part of the help process, journalists are not at liberty to impose labels on people. If Alcoholics Anonymous wants to call its members *alcoholics,* for example, that does not give journalists the same "insider" license to label AA members individually or as a group as alcoholics.

Another rule should be noted here: *Objective journalists are necessarily outsiders and must behave like outsiders in their writing and editing (except in first-person accounts).* Even if a writer is a member of a self-help organization and is experiencing the same or similar condition or disease as the subject about whom he or she is writing, when writing about another person, journalists should not use labels used by insiders.

When writing about a person who happens to be battling a disease, do not label the person a *patient.* A person who undergoes cancer treatment, for example, should not be labeled a *cancer patient* in articles unrelated to the person's health. Nor should a person who undergoes heart surgery be labeled a *heart patient* in articles unrelated to the person's surgery or health. If the particular health obstacle is not relevant to the story, no mention of the condition should be made within the story. Examples of inappropriate usage include "The mayor, a prostate cancer patient, spoke about the crime problem in the surrounding suburbs" and "The company vice president, who underwent heart bypass surgery five years ago, outlined the new fall fashion line." In both cases, the medical condition only serves to tarnish the image or the power of the speaker, reminding the reader of the speaker's vulnerability for no reason. Medical conditions are best omitted when they bear no relevance to a particular story.

Journalists should not assume, however, that medical conditions must be banned or censored completely from the news. Many medical conditions—particularly when public figures experience medical obstacles—are considered newsworthy and should be covered by the media. Examples include Princess Diana's bulimia, President Ford's stroke during the 2000 Republican convention, and Darryl Strawberry's bouts with cancer. When reporting on a baseball game, however, Darryl Strawberry should not be referred to as "cancer patient Darryl Strawberry." Likewise, when discussing British history or the Royal Family, journalists should not write "bulimic Princess Diana," as if *bulimic* were part of her title. Nor should they write "Princess Diana, who was known to have had bouts with bulimia," unless the article is specifically about eating disorders or about the psychological condition of Princess Diana. Nor should an article label the former president "stroke patient Gerald Ford" or refer to "former President Gerald Ford, who suffered a stroke" unless Ford's health or the health of other leaders is a specific focus of the article.

In articles where diseases and conditions are deemed relevant, writers should avoid using the word *suffering* unless the person described is actually in pain or somehow suffering. Do not write, for example, "the unidentified man was suffering from amnesia" if he was not in fact suffering. Instead, write that he was "experiencing amnesia," if that is what he was doing. Do not write that someone was "suffering from lack of attention" or even that someone is "suffering from cancer" if they are resting comfortably or beginning to heal or are in remission. People who are in pain (suffering from hunger, suffering from burns) can legitimately be described as *suffering*. The term should not be used flippantly.

Also, watch the usage of *complained of*, as in "He complained of heart failure." Journalists should not portray people judgmentally as complainers. Better usage would be "He experienced heart failure," "He suspected heart failure," or "He suffered from chest pain."

In writing about people who experience diseases, avoid labeling them as *victims*. Whereas it is incorrect to label someone "a cancer patient," it can be worse to label the person "a cancer victim." Victim implies that any struggle is over and the labeled person is a "loser."

Also avoid using *afflicted* as a noun, as in "The doctor treated the *afflicted* with care," or as an adjective before a noun, as in "The *afflicted* man received treatment." Instead, when using the word *afflicted*, try to use it as an active verb, as in "The virus *afflicted* three children at the camp." Less preferred, but acceptable is *afflicted* as a passive verb, as in "Three children were *afflicted* by the virus."

The words *fits* and *spells* also should be avoided. The preferred usage is *seizures* in reference to epilepsy. *Fits* is the most offensive and implies an immature tantrum or emotional outburst rather than a legitimate medical condition, as in "fits of anger," "fits of rage," or "emotional fit." People commonly refer to *heart attacks* and *asthma attacks* in everyday speech. In articles discussing health, it is better to be specific. Specify "clogged artery" or "heart murmur" or "irregular heartbeat" where possible.

Personal Appearance

Journalists should not necessarily classify people who are unusually short or tall or who are unusually heavy or light as disabled. If a person does not consider his or her difference to be an obstacle or to be disabling, a journalist should not be quick to impose the label *disabled*.

It is important to point out a helpful principle of journalistic philosophy: *We are all different*. Aside from identical twins, triplets, quadruplets, etc., we all have different appearances. There is no "normal" appearance. To suggest that there is a normal way of looking introduces a writer's bias, suggesting that whatever the writer is accustomed to is normal and less familiar appearances are abnormal. Writers need to be very careful in describing people in terms of height, weight, health condition, sociability, posture, gait, and so on.

In many cases, subjective descriptions of people's appearances should be avoided completely. A fashion story obviously requires such description. A news story in which police are seeking a suspect or a missing person also generally requires a description. In such a case, however, the description must be a defining description to be useful. A defining description is one that provides enough information for a reader or listener to reasonably be able to identify the missing person or possible suspects, based on the traits provided. An example of this would be: "The suspect was described as a white male with bright red hair, with a quarter-inch dimple on his chin, a purple heart-shaped tattoo on his right hand, who walked with a limp." Using this description, a reader likely could recognize the person described.

Inadequate descriptions only insult people or cause readers or listeners to look at other people suspiciously, thus creating bias. Here are some examples of inadequate descriptions: "The suspect was described as a black male, about 5-foot-11, wearing jeans." "The suspect was an overweight white woman with curly black hair and brown eyes." In the first example, the description encourages readers and listeners to look at black men suspiciously and accusingly, without providing information useful enough to help identify the suspect. In the second example, the audience is encouraged to look accusingly at white overweight women, again without being helpful.

When a writer is unable to provide enough information to offer a defining description, a scant description should probably be excluded from the piece until more information is known. This is particularly true when describing people with disabilities. To write that a suspect has "blue eyes and walks with a cane" merely makes readers suspicious of people who walk with canes. Likewise, to write, "John Smith, whose face was scarred with pockmarks and acne, produced the highly acclaimed show" sounds unkind and does not add to the story. Nor is it helpful to write, "Jane Smith, who limped to the podium eagerly, despite her sagging posture and prosthetic leg, had only accolades for the mayor." Both examples gratuitously point out vulnerabilities and inexcusably offend, without adding interesting "flavor."

Most articles are not about fashion, missing people, or suspects on the loose. In news stories on other topics, descriptions of people's disabilities may be hard to justify. As a rule, *avoid descriptions of people in news stories unless the description somehow contributes to the focus of the story or some significant point within the story.* If so, make sure that the description is objective, not subjective. When writing about people with specific vulnerabilities, disabilities, or obvious sensitivities, be extra sensitive about incorporation of description.

Sources of Information for the Journalist

Advocacy organizations for people with different disabilities are generally eager to offer advice and share their observations about coverage of disabled people. Public relations departments of such organizations generally answer questions and specific concerns about meeting with people within their area of specialty. Many organizations' public relations department officers will provide names of experts so that journalists can make contact with informed medical doctors, scientists, psychologists, and social workers.

Use a local phone directory or the Internet to find the names of national advocacy organizations—most major disabilities have corresponding advocacy organizations. Larger organizations include the American Foundation for the Blind, National Association of the Deaf, and Little People of America. Lesser-known disabilities generally have advocacy organizations as well. Also search the Internet for chat groups and "online communities" of people with specific disabilities. Often you can find willing interview subjects online.

For a more thorough treatment of this and other subjects relating to bias in reporting on disabilities, I recommend Chapter 8, "Bias Based on Appearances and Disabilities," in *Unbiased: Editing in a Diverse Society.* (See "Resources" below.)

Conclusion

In approaching stories about people with disabilities, journalists need to maintain journalistic sensitivity to ensure lack of bias. As a rule, *disabilities should not be mentioned in a piece unless the disabilities directly pertain to the piece.* Disabilities are not inherently newsworthy topics to be mentioned in most pieces, nor do descriptions of private citizens' disabilities necessarily add flavor to a piece. Disabilities merit mentioning in pieces about health, overcoming obstacles, and safety. Visible disabilities may add valuable description when combined with other visual trait information in pieces about missing persons and criminal suspects on the loose. When writing pieces with other focuses, however, journalists should be wary about what disability information to include.

Understand that disabled people are as different from each other as are so-called able-bodied people. Treat each article subject as an individual. Also understand that nobody has a body that functions perfectly indefinitely, that everyone has malfunctions and disabilities, and that everyone faces obstacles during life. This should help put into perspective coverage of those who are visibly disabled. Remember that a condition that disables one person may not disable another, and that ability to surmount an obstacle often depends on an individual's circumstances.

Resources

Internet

http://www.afb.org/   American Foundation for the Blind website
http://www.nad.org/   National Association of the Deaf website

http://www.lpaonline.org/lpa.html   Little People of America website

http://www.schoolnet.ca/aboriginal/disabl12/   "A Way With Words: Guidelines and Appropriate Terminology for the Portrayal of Persons with Disabilities"

http://www.mcil.org/mcil/log/1104log.htm   *The Memphis Center for Independent Living Journal:* A Guide to Writing About People with Disabilities, 2001.

http://www.communitygateway.org/faq/writing_guidelines.htm   Massachusetts Community Gateway: "Guidelines for Reporting and Writing About People with Disabilities"

http://nadc.ucla.edu/Communic.html   National Arts and Disability Center

http://www.culturalaffairs.org/iac/info/info18.htm   Iowa Arts Council. Suggestions for communicating, working with and writing about people with disabilities.

http://www.rtcil.org/public.htm   University of Kansas: "Guidelines for Reporting and Writing About People with Disabilities" brochure

Books

Miller, N., and C. Sammons, C. 1999. *Everybody's Different.* Baltimore, Md.: Paul H. Brookes Publishing Company.

Schwartz, Marilyn. 1995. *Guidelines for Bias-free Writing.* University Bloomington: Indiana University Press.

Wissner-Gross, Elizabeth. 1999. *Unbiased: Editing in a Diverse Society.* Ames: Iowa State University Press.

CHAPTER 11

From a Troubled Past to a Confused Present

The Need for Better Coverage of Asian Americans

Fritz Cropp

In *All-American: How to Cover Asian America*, the Asian American Journalists Association (AAJA 2000, 32) noted that "in the American Press, Asians are covered poorly or not at all." This chapter is dedicated to understanding why that has been true and will provide journalists with suggestions for doing a better job.

The History Isn't Pretty

William Wong, author of *The Yellow Journalist*, noted that American race relations often have been cast as black versus white and that people of Asian descent have received relatively little attention. Yet history reflects that racism has been aimed squarely at Asians in America for more than a century and a half. Helen Zia, author of *Asian American Dreams: The Emergence of an American,* said, "The real story of Asian Americans is inextricably bound to several of the driving forces of

American History—the westward expansion to the Pacific and beyond, the growing nation's unquenchable need for cheap labor, the patriotic fervor of a young country in the throes of defining itself, and the ways in which race and racism were used to advance those ends" (Zia 2002, 24-25).

The following paragraphs highlight the historic treatment of some Asian groups in the United States by society and by journalists.

Exclusionary Practices

There was a thriving Chinatown in Mexico City in the 1600s, well before the 13 colonies declared their independence. There are records of Asian Americans in what is now U.S. territory as early as the 1500s. Some of the earliest settlers were from the Philippines. "From 1565 to 1815, during the lucrative Spanish galleon trade between Manila and Mexico, sailors in the Philippines were conscripted into service aboard Spanish ships. A number of these seamen jumped ship for freedom, establishing a settlement on the coast of Louisiana; today, their descendants live in Louisiana" (Zia 2000, 23-24).

It was during the Gold Rush in the mid-1800s that large numbers of immigrants from Asia began to arrive in the United States. The first large influx was from China. In 1848, the year gold was discovered in California, there were fewer than 100 Chinese living in the state. By 1860, more than 40,000 Chinese men had left their homeland for "Gold Mountain," their name for America. Most were bearing high-interest loans for their passage (Wong and Chan 1998).

Life in America was hardly easy. Zia (2000, 26) reported:

> Initially, the Chinese were welcomed to San Francisco, and some even participated in California's statehood ceremonies in 1850. The reception quickly turned cold, however, as new laws and taxes singled out the Chinese. A foreign-miners tax targeted the Chinese, but not Europeans. The tax gave way to complete prohibition of Chinese from mining. Laws forbade Chinese to testify in court, even in their own defense. Special zoning ordinances were selectively enforced against the Chinese. Hair-cutting ordinances forced Chinese to cut off the braids, or queues, that the emperor required as proof of loyalty—ironically making it harder for workers to return to China.

Even as African-American men were given the right to vote following the conclusion of the Civil War, citizenship was specifically denied to the Chinese.

The 1850s were marked by violence against Chinese that resulted in the loss of hundreds of lives. The Central Pacific Railroad provided temporary refuge from the violence. With the goal of a transcontinental railroad within sight, the Central Pacific hired as many as 12,000 Chinese workers to hasten its completion—an estimated 90 percent of the work force. Working under rugged conditions, an estimated 10 percent of Chinese workers died during this period. Chinese workers were paid 60 cents for every dollar paid to white workers. (Even an attempt at a strike failed when Charles Crocker, superintendent of construction for the Central Construction, cut off the strikers' food supply.)

> When the transcontinental railroad was completed in 1869, Chinese workers were barred from the celebrations. The speeches congratulated European immigrant workers for their labor, but never mentioned the Chinese. Instead, the Chinese men were summarily fired and forced to walk the long distance back to San Francisco—forbidden to ride on the railroad they built. (Zia 2000, 27)

Throughout the next decade, Chinese were met with violence in American cities. In Tacoma, Washington, hundreds of Chinese were herded onto boats and set adrift in the Pacific, presumably to their deaths. In Denver, mobs burned the homes and businesses of Chinese. The fervor of anti-Chinese "Yellow Peril" culminated in 1882 with the passage of the Chinese Exclusion Act, the first legislation ever passed by Congress that specifically targeted a group based on race.

Factories in the Fields

Although America was closed for Chinese, the need for low-cost labor made it impractical for the gates to be closed for all other Asian nations. Thus, the late 1880s saw an influx of immigration from Japan, India, Korea and the Philippines. By 1934, there were nearly 500,000 people from Asia—primarily laborers—living in the United States.

In *Factories in the Fields*, Carey McWilliams documented the decades-long saga of migrant workers in California, from the Spanish land grant purchases through the 1930s. Originally published in 1939, the book provides an historical perspective of the systematic exploitation of ethnic groups as migrant workers to support California's agricultural system.

Although they were not necessarily singled out by California's landowners, circumstance and prejudice made Asians most often available. "The established pattern has been somewhat as follows: to bring in successive minority groups; to exploit them until the advantages of exploitation have been exhausted; to expel them in favor of more readily exploitable material. In this manner the Chinese, the Japanese, the Filipinos and the Mexicans have, as it were, been run through the hopper" (McWilliams 1939, 305-306).

Internment

When the Japanese bombed Pearl Harbor on December 7, 1941, the United States predictably entered World War II against Japan—but allied with China and the Philippines. This changed the face of race relations in the United States. "Japan was part of the 'Axis of Evil' at the time," said William Wong (2002). Using Census Bureau information, the Federal Bureau of Investigation (FBI) compiled a list of all Japanese Americans living on the West Coast. On the day war was declared, hundreds were arrested by the FBI. Bank accounts were frozen, Japanese American soldiers were reclassified to menial duties, and those working in local, state or federal government offices were fired (Zia 2000, 41).

President Franklin D. Roosevelt had previously ordered a report analyzing the loyalty of Japanese Americans. The report concluded that Japanese Americans posed no security threat. Delos Emmons, Lieutenant General in charge of Hawaii, concluded that Japanese on the islands had nothing to do with the attack on Pearl Harbor. J. Edgar Hoover, the director of the FBI, recommended against a mass evacuation of Japanese Americans. But Lieutenant John DeWitt (1943, 34), head of the Western Defense Command, concluded:

> The Japanese race is an enemy race and while many second and third generation Japanese born on United States soil, possessed of United States citizenship, have become "Americanized," the racial strains are undiluted. … Along the vital Pacific Coast, over 112,000 potential enemies of Japanese extraction are at large today. … The very fact that no sabotage has taken place to date is disturbing and confirming indication that such action will be taken.

With the American public already fiercely aligned against Japan, Japanese Americans were vilified by editorials in prominent outlets such as the *Los Angeles Times* and *Time* magazine. On February 19, 1942, President Roosevelt signed Executive Order 9066, which authorized the evacuation and internment of Japanese Americans. All people of Japanese descent living in the United States, regardless of their citizenship or contribution to American society, were given 10 days to pack their personal effects. Then, they were sent to one of 10 internment camps, where they were stripped of the rights afforded to all other people living in the country at the time.

Until the conclusion of World War II in 1944, Japanese Americans lived in the villages created by the U.S. government. They were forced to sign statements disavowing allegiance to the Emperor of Japan. For Nisei (second-generation Japanese Americans born in the United States), there was nothing to disavow. But signing the documents was tricky for most, since U.S. citizenship was not an option and disavowing allegiance to Japan would leave them stateless.

More than 23,000 Nisei joined the U.S. military, most in the segregated and highly decorated 442nd Nisei Regimental Combat Team. Zia (2000, 43) noted that, like the Chinese Americans who built the railroad, these soldiers were not included in historical accounts:

> Ironically, near the end of the war in Europe, the Japanese American GI's of the 442nd broke through the German defensive "Gothic Line" in northern Italy, and were among the first to liberate the Nazi concentration camp in Dachau, Germany. However, the U.S. military commanders decided it would be bad public relations if Jewish prisoners were freed by Japanese American soldiers whose families were imprisoned in American concentration camps.

For the next two decades, Asian Americans persevered. With GI bills, some Japanese Americans attended college, but Chinese Americans worried that they, too, would be interned as the United States braced itself against Communism. The landmark 1954 *Brown v. Board of Education* Supreme Court decision, generally associated with the rights of African Americans, also was important to Asian-Americans. "A contingent of Asian Americans from Hawaii joined the Reverend Martin Luther King, Jr., in Selma, Alabama, bringing him the lei he wore during the march" (Zia, 2000, 45). This marked the first time Asian Americans felt comfortable exercising their rights as citizens, and it inspired a wave of civic consciousness and involvement among Asian Americans.

Four Decades of Growth

Equal rights legislation passed in the 1960s changed the legal landscape and opened the gates for millions of people from Asia to enter the United States. New laws included the Immigration Act of 1965, which opened the door to immigration from all countries by abolishing discrimination based on national origin. People from Asia had been excluded from immigration quotas for 40 years. The Immigration Act, which took effect in 1968, used three criteria to evaluate whether aliens could be admitted as immigrants:

1. The possession of occupational skills needed in the U.S. labor market (occupational immigration)
2. Their close relationships to those already here (family reunification)
3. Their vulnerability to political and religious persecution

A limit of 20,000 immigrants from each country was established. However, unmarried children under 21 years of age, spouses and fiancés were among the exemptions, which meant each country could actually send more than 20,000 immigrants to the United States each year.

One major effect of the new immigration law was a shift in the major source of immigrants from European to non-European countries. In 1960, Europeans constituted approximately 80 percent of total immigrants to the United States. Since the passage of the Immigration Act, the percentage of European immigrants has decreased steadily. By 1984, immigrants from European countries were only 18 percent of the total. The top 10 source countries all were Asian (Arnold et al. 1987). Between 1980 and 1988, Asians made up between 40 and 47 percent of all immigrants to the United States (Min 1995).

The effect of the 1965 Immigration Act has been dramatic. Min (1995) noted that the large increase in numbers of immigrants from Asia came as a surprise to U.S. officials:

> U.S. policy makers in the late 1960s and early 1970s never expected this phenomenal increase in immigration from Asian countries. At that time, because only a small number of Asian Americans were U.S. citizens, a relatively small number of Asians immigrated as relatives of U.S. citizens. However, many Asian immigrants have become naturalized since the mid-1970s and have invited their spouses, children, parents and brothers/sisters with their own families to join them in the United States.

Prompted by the economic recession of the 1970s, the Immigration Act was altered in 1976 to reduce the number of occupational immigrants. From that point, more than 90 percent of immigrants from Asia have entered the United States under different family reunification categories. The Immigration Act of 1990, which further revised the 1965

Immigration Act, increased the number of employment-based immigrants. But it did not reduce the number of family reunification immigrants. Thus, through 2000, millions of immigrants from Asia have entered the United States. In recent years, source countries have become more varied (Table 11.1).

Min (1995, 14) characterized immigrants from Asia as "economic migrants, seeking a better standard of living," noting that between 1965 and 1987, among Asian countries only Japan had a level of economic development comparable to the United States. He also indicated that since 1988, as South Korea's economic climate improved, there had been a significant decline in the number of immigrants from South Korea.

Refugees

The aftermath of the Vietnam War also had a substantial effect on the number of immigrants from Asia. After the fall of Saigon, some 135,000 government officials, military personnel and U.S. government personnel—primarily Vietnamese and Hmong—were moved to safety, relocated to military bases in California, Florida, Texas and Arkansas and then resettled in communities around the United States (Zia 2000). A second wave of refugees came as "boat people," who set sail on the South China Sea to seek refuge from political persecution and turmoil in Vietnam. Those who survived the trek ended up in refugee camps in Thailand, Indonesia, Malaysia and the Philippines. A third wave came from Cambodia and Laos after Vietnam attacked Cambodia in 1978 (Zia 2000).

To address the refugee crisis, Congress passed the Indochina Migration and Refugee Assistance Act of 1975 and later the Refugee Act of 1980. In addition, the Amerasian Homecoming Act of 1987 opened the borders for about 100,000 children (the offspring of American GIs) and their Southeast Asian mothers. All told, more than 1 million Southeast Asians came to America after 1975—nearly doubling the Asian-American population in the United States (Zia 2000).

Demographics in 2000

It may be impossible to underestimate the combined effect on American culture of the immigration and migration of people from Asia to the United States. In the 1980s and 1990s, Asian Americans began to achieve numbers unparalleled by other groups. Consider

TABLE 11.1. CHANGES IN ASIAN AND PACIFIC ISLANDER AMERICAN POPULATION, 1970–2000

	1970[a]	1980	% Increase 1970–1980	1990	% Increase 1980–1990	2000[b]	% Increase 1990–2000
Total U.S. Population	203,211,926	226,545,805	11.4	248,709,873	9.8	281,421,906	13.2
Asian Pacific Islander population	1,438,562	3,550,439	146.8	7,273,662	104.8	12,773,242	75.6
Asian Pacific Americans as % of total population	0.7	1.5		2.9		4.6	
Chinese	436,062	806,040	84.8	1,645,472	104.1	2,432,585	47.8
Japanese	591,290	700,974	18.5	847,562	20.9	796,700	-6.0
Filipino	343,060	774,652	125.8	1,460,770	88.6	1,850,314	26.7
Korean	69,155	354,593	412.9	798,849	125.3	1,076,872	34.8
Asian Indian		361,531		815,447	125.6	1,678,765	105.8
Vietnamese		261,729		614,547	134.8	1,122,528	82.6

Sources: U.S. Census Bureau 1973, Table 140; 1983, Table 62; 1993a, Table3; 2000, QT-P5, QT-P7.

[a]In the 1970 census, Asian Indians were classified into a white category and Vietnamese Americans were not tabulated separately. Since 1980, the census has classified Asian and Pacific Islander Americans into one racial category.

[b]In the 2000 census, Asian Americans were separate from Native Hawaiians and other Pacific Islanders. Asian Americans were further classified into three subcategories: Asian alone, Asian in combination and Asian alone or in combination. So were Native Hawaiian and other Pacific Islander Americans. This table puts together the categories Asian alone or in combination, and Pacific Islander alone or in combination.

these observations in *American Demographics* magazine ("Diversity in America" 2002):

- The number of Asian Americans grew 48 percent between 1990 and 2000.
- By 2007, the number of Asian Americans is expected to grow an additional 27 percent, a faster rate than other groups.
- The two largest groups of Asian Americans are from China and from the Philippines.
- Between 1990 and 2000, the number of Asian Indians grew 106 percent to 1.9 million, making it the fastest growing subgroup.
- Asian-American households make more money than any other ethnic group and are overrepresented in the top income brackets. A large share of Asian-American households (21.9 percent) earn $100,000 or more annually.
- Most Asian Americans report that they speak English "very well" or "well."
- Forty-four percent of Asian-American adults hold a bachelor's degree or higher. This is 20 points above the national average and well above the rate of any other racial or ethnic group.
- Eighty-one percent of Asian Americans live with two or more people, most in married-couple families with children present.
- Many Asian Americans live in California. In fact, seven of the top 10 Asian metropolitan areas are in California (Table 11.2). However, the growth of the Asian population in Chicago is expected to

TABLE 11.2. TOP 10 ASIAN METROPOLITAN AREAS IN 2000

Metropolitan area	Total population	Asian population (%)
1. San Jose, CA PMSA[a]	1,682,585	25.6
2. San Francisco, CA PMSA	1,731,183	22.7
3. San Francisco-Oakland-San Jose, CA CMSA[b]	7,039,362	18.4
4. Oakland, CA PMSA	2,392,557	16.7
5. Orange County, CA PMSA	2,846,289	13.6
6. Los Angeles-Long Beach, CA PMSA	9,519,338	11.9
7. Middlesex-Somerset-Hunterdon County, NJ PMSA	1,169,641	11.2
8. Los Angeles-Riverside-Orange County, CA CMSA	16,373,645	10.4
9. Seattle-Bellevue-Everett, WA PMSA	2,414,616	9.4
10. New York, NY PMSA	9,314,235	9.1

Source: "Diversity in America: Asians" 2002.

[a]PMSA = Primary Metropolitan Statistical Area.

[b]CMSA = Consolidated Metropolitan Statistical Area.

top traditionally highly populated cities such as San Francisco and San Diego.

Such figures should be taken with caution, however. It is important to note that Asian Americans tend to live in expensive cities, where the above-average salaries must also cover an above-average cost of living. And it should be noted, it is extremely difficult to assess who is being counted:

> The Census Bureau defines "Asian" as people who have origins in any of the original peoples of the Far East, Southeast Asia or the Indian subcontinent. This includes people who indicated their races as Asian Indian, Chinese, Filipino, Korean, Japanese, Vietnamese or "other Asian," as well as people who wrote in entries such as Burmese Hmong, Pakistani or Thai. It also includes some people of Hispanic origin, who may be of any race. ("Diversity in America" 2002, 16)

And although for the first time in 2000 the Census Bureau allowed people to identify themselves with more than one race, only about 2 percent of the population did so. This leaves unanswered questions about offspring of Asian Americans and non–Asian Americans. Table 11.3 indicates the subgroups reflected in the 2000 U.S. census.

What is clear is that Asian Americans have become a dominant force in American culture. In certain cities, they represent a significant percentage of the population. With overall population growth expected to continue, along with education and income levels, the Asian-American population is important. The Selig Center for Economic Growth at the University of Georgia projects that in 2007, Asian Americans will spend $454.9 billion, a 287 percent increase over 1990. By comparison, the Selig Center estimates that the buying power of the general U.S. population will grow 131 percent over the same period (Humphreys 2002).

Also clear is that grouping all Asians together is a matter of statistical and linguistic simplicity but not a reflection of cultural reality. As Ronald Takaki, author of *Strangers from a Different Shore: A History of Asian Americans*, said, "There are no Asians in Asia." People tend to align themselves with their country, not their continent. He also noted that the distinction "Asian American" is discriminatory: "This broader identity was forged in the crucible of racial discrimination and exclu-

TABLE 11.3. ANALYSIS OF ASIAN AMERICANS

Asian subgroups	Population of subgroup, alone or in any combination*
Chinese	2,734,841
Filipino	2,364,815
Asian Indian	1,899,599
Korean	1,228,427
Vietnamese	1,223,736
Japanese	1,148,932
Other Asian, not specified	369,430
Cambodian	206,052
Pakistani	204,309
Laotian	198,203
Hmong	186,310
Thai	150,283
Taiwanese	144,795
Indonesian	63,073
Bangladeshi	57,412
Sri Lankan	24,587
Malaysian	18,566
Burmese	16,720
Okinawan	10,599
Nepalese	9,399
Singaporean	2,394
Bhutanese	212
Indo Chinese	199
Iwo Jiman	78
Maldivian	51

Source: U.S. Census Bureau. Census 2000 data.

*According to Census 2000 data, this category may reflect more than the total population of each subgroup because people identifying with several Asian groups were counted several times.

sion: their national origins did not matter as much as its race" (Takaki 1998, 502).

Implications for Journalists

How should journalists prepare themselves to cover groups with no unifying demographic or pyschographic variable?

Journalism has been among the institutions struggling to keep pace with the steady change in American society. The American Society of Newspaper Editors (ASNE) figures quoted in Chapter 1 of this book indicate that although Asian Americans now compose 4.2 percent of the

American population, only 2.35 percent of the reporters, editors and producers in newsrooms are Asian Americans. While these journalists may be more sensitive to understanding the many cultures that compose the broad category Asian American, they fall into individual categories themselves. Their colleagues, mostly educated in America, are handicapped by the fact that most American education tends to concentrate little on Asia.

The Asian American Journalism Association noted that coverage of Americans has tended to fall into five broad categories. Asian Americans are "eternal foreigners," the "model minority," "honorary whites," "from nowhere in particular" or "invisible" (AAJA 2000, 32-41).

- **Eternal foreigners.** Asian Americans report that they tend to be treated as foreigners regardless of their citizenship. Notes the AAJA handbook:

  > Every adult Asian American, regardless of citizenship, has been asked the "Where are you from?" question by well-meaning people, including reporters. Sacramento is not a respectable answer. Not far from the surface is that, unlike ethnic whites who have become American, Asians, because of their race, cannot be separated from the nations of their heritage." (AAJA 2000, 33-34)

  The Wen Ho Lee case illustrates this point. Lee, a Taiwan-born U.S. citizen, became a prominent international figure when he was indicted on charges that he had transferred huge amounts of restricted information to an easily accessible computer. Justice Department prosecutors persuaded a judge to hold him in solitary confinement without bail, saying his release would pose a grave threat to the nuclear balance. The story was first broken by the *New York Times*, which a review in *American Journalism Review* said "uncritically embraced the outlook of investigators in its breathless coverage of the . . . case" (Fleeson 2000, 20).

  Over the next several months, it became clear that the case against Lee was not so clear-cut. Originally indicted and held without bail and in solitary confinement, Lee eventually pled guilty to one count of mishandling secret information, a misdemeanor charge.

  In a rare move, the *New York Times* published a lengthy page 2 critique of its coverage ("From the Editors" 2000), and followed it with a similar critique on its editorial pages (An Overview" 2000). The issue of race was not raised in either of the *Times*' critiques. In its extensive review of the case, *American Journalism Review* included comments from Henry Tang, chairman of the Committee of 100, a group of influential Asian Americans that includes I.M. Pei and Yo-Yo Ma. Tang was generally complimentary of the *New York Times* for its acknowledgments of shortcomings in the coverage of the Wen Ho Lee case, but did weigh in on the issue of racial profiling: "Racial profiling clearly seems to have been a factor in focusing on Lee, which has contributed to casting Chinese Americans as perpetual foreigners" (Fleeson 2000, 29).

- **Model minority.** Not all coverage of Asian Americans has been directly critical. From as early as the 1960s but more prominently in the 1980s, Asian Americans have been labeled the "model minority." The implication is that relative to blacks, Latinos and Native Americans, Asian Americans have failed to measure up (AAJA 2000).

  Takaki (1998) noted that the model minority designation represents a new myth about Asian Americans; in fact, the high figures for household income correlates with the number of people living in each Asian-American home. And the states with the most Asian-American citizens (California, New York, Hawaii) also are those with higher cost-of-living indexes. "When analyzed for subgroups, such as Korean immigrant men, the individual incomes of Asian men were equal to or below those of blacks and Hispanics and far below those of whites" (AAJA, 2000, 36).

- **Honorary whites.** In noting that racial issues in the United States have generally been framed as black versus white, freelance journalist William Wong contends that Asian Americans have been ignored. Sometimes Asian Americans have been grouped with whites in statistical data. This is true with analyses of college admissions data, as well as of newspaper reports of polls taken in their cities.

- **From nowhere in particular.** Even a cursory examination of the immigration data reflects a wide diversity in source nations from Asia. Often missing from stories is the cultural or historical context. In its dissection of a 1999 *Washington Post* story about the Wen Ho Lee case, for example, the AAJA (2000, 38) noted that "there is no discussion of the improbability that someone born in anti-Communist Taiwan would spy for Communist China."

- **Invisible.** "Because of their smaller numbers in cities and states compared to blacks and Hispanics, Asian Americans are often excluded from public opinion surveys for budgetary reasons" (AAJA 2000, 40). This criticism is similar to that under honorary whites.

Where it differs is in larger cities, where Asian Americans are not polled even when they do account for a substantial percentage of the population. The *New York Times* failed to poll Asian Americans about crime in the city in 1999, and subsequently ran a clarification. The *Los Angeles Times* did not interview Asian Americans in their coverage of the 10-year anniversary of the 1992 riots, even though its large Korean-American population bore the brunt of most of the violence. Said Helen Zia (2000): "Perhaps instead of the model minority, it should be the invisible minority."

Avoiding Pitfalls

Several issues have been raised in this chapter. The review of a couple of cases has highlighted the historically poor treatment of Asian Americans—a history not widely reported in the books read by American school children. The demographic information suggests two important points: (1) The Asian-American population has increased dramatically in the past four decades due to record numbers of immigrants. (2) One must be careful in analyzing demographic information without looking beyond the numbers. (For instance, statistics about household income may be misleading.)

The brief notes regarding coverage of Asian Americans suggest that a general lack of context can lead to embarrassing mistakes of omission and commission. The examples above suggest that journalists must work diligently to avoid pitfalls resulting from ignorance, insensitivity or other factors.

Here are some specific suggestions for avoiding such pitfalls.

Back to Basics

It may sound like a contradiction, but it is important both to recognize differences in Asian Americans and to treat all groups and individuals equally. In other words, it is important to recognize that people from Korea and people from Japan have different cultural roots: Look no further than the Japanese occupation of Korea for a prime example of historical differences. It is important to recognize differences among all types of people.

As suggested by Takaki's comment that "there are no Asians in Asia," Asian Americans do not think of themselves first as Asian Americans.

Many are Americans by birth; others are recent immigrants who may think of themselves as Chinese, Filipino, Vietnamese or Chinese American, Filipino American or Vietnamese American. Some may not yet be American citizens.

This leads to two practical points. First, it is OK not to know where someone is from, and it's OK to ask. But it's important to be sensitive about how and when you ask. If a person's race or ethnicity is not relevant to the story, you need not ask. If it is, it's important to understand the cultural background of the person or people involved. Second, since the days of the Hutchins Commission, the goal of good journalism has been to give "a truthful, comprehensive, and intelligent account of the day's events in a context that gives them meaning" (Commission on Freedom of the Press, 1947, 21). No single journalist can be expected to understand the cultural differences that may be driving an Asian-American group or an individual from an Asian country, but every journalist should remember the basic premise of journalism education. In their discussion of the coverage of Native Americans in Chapter 7, Teresa Lamsam and Dennis McAuliffe, Jr., made this point explicitly.

"I think you have to engage a certain fundamental curiosity in your approach," said Bill Wong (2002). "You start looking at people and asking questions and/or you start attending events. A meeting ... or a celebration ... just to begin your lesson. This can be kind of like a visit to a foreign land in the U.S."

The AAJA Principles

In their handbook for covering Asian America, AAJA (2000) offered three principles: Dig harder, make no assumptions, and don't give offense.

- **Dig harder.** This is one of the fundamental principles of journalism and shouldn't need much elaboration. Looking at stories from all angles, making additional phone calls for information or background, and understanding as many perspectives on an issue as possible are all important everyday goals. This is true universally, but particularly relevant given the complicated situations—historically, culturally and geographically—that are likely being covered.
- **Make no assumptions.** Understanding the cultural differences between the peoples of Asia can be a life's work. Potentially the most

important practical point is to think open-mindedly about the people you interview. All of us are from somewhere. Some of us have never been anywhere but where we are, and some of us are well traveled. Each of us has accepted a certain lifestyle, but it's not the only lifestyle.

Stereotypes themselves are assumptions. For example, during its coverage of the 1998 Olympics, MSNBC posted the following headline: "American Beats out Kwan" after Tara Lipinski defeated Michelle Kwan for the gold medal in figure skating. Oops. Lipinski and Kwan are both Americans. Many of the errors cited in publications like *Project Zinger: A Critical look at news coverage of Asian Pacific Americans* (AAJA 1992) tend to be based on assumptions made either by journalists or editors.

- **Don't give offense.** If the first two principles are followed, this one should be easy. According to the AAJA (2000, 10), "The maxim of American journalism is 'comfort the afflicted and afflict the comfortable.' That does not in any way require ethnic insult. It is pointless. It insults readers and viewers. And, after all, they are the ones who count."

Using Resources

Although the pace of work in American journalism is a potential obstacle, the good news for modern journalists is that resources are at your fingertips. Four important resources are available to any reporter anywhere: the Internet; a variety of national and regional Asian-American groups; local groups, or local chapters of national groups; and scholars who study Asians in America, often housed in Asian American Studies departments of universities.

- **The Internet.** Here's where today's journalists have an advantage over their predecessors. Using any search engine, one can directly locate either specific information about a particular group, such as the Southeast Asia Resource Action Center (www.searac.org) or the National Asian Pacific American Women's Forum (www.napawf.org), or search for background information about prominent individuals.
- **National organizations.** "For any question you want to explore, there's some sort of an organization where you can get a quick overview of the issue in question," says Bill Wong. Such organiza-

tions as political groups, or groups with political leanings, can offer one or both sides of an issue. Asian-American associations, such as the Japanese American Citizens League (www.jacl.org) or the Organization of Chinese Americans (www.ocanatl.org), can give specific cultural information or suggest a source to help answer a particular question or line of questioning.

- **Local organizations.** Of course, these will vary from community to community. In cities with large populations of Asian Americans, there will be formal organizations (e.g., regional business associations or social groups) worth knowing and knowing about. In smaller towns, there may not be. Finding them requires the same type of legwork as developing a story. Make phone calls. Write e-mails. Ask community leaders whom they would contact for information about a particular group or individual.
- **Scholars.** There are more than 20 Asian American Studies programs and institutes in the United States, as well as numerous other universities with faculty members in Asian American studies. An academic association of Asian American scholars, the Association of Asian American Studies, "sponsors professional activities to facilitate increased communication and scholarly exchange among teachers, researchers, and students in the field of Asian American Studies" (www.aaastudies.org). Need some background information or an expert on a particular issue? Many of these people are both accessible and helpful.

What's in a Name?

Properly pronouncing names is a staple of good broadcast journalism. In working with Asian America, one likely will encounter a variety of different pronunciation issues. For example, Indian names tend to be longer, monosyllabic and accented much differently than most European names. In many Chinese dialects, Li is pronounced "lee" and Yang is pronounced "young." However, second- and third-generation Chinese tend to Westernize the pronunciations. When in doubt, ask. It's OK to ask twice or three times to be sure to get the pronunciation right.

The order of names varies widely, particularly among first-generation immigrants. Again, second- and third-generation Asian Americans often adopt Western naming rules. In all cases, it's worth inquiring how any individual would like his or her name presented.

Conclusion

This chapter has focused on Asian Americans, the fastest growing and most diverse group of Americans. It includes a brief historical account of the treatment of groups of people from Asia, a cursory and cautious look at current demographic data, some examples of current treatment of Asian Americans, and a few suggestions for covering Asian America.

The historical perspective is important for several reasons. First, much of the historical information about the treatment of Asians and Asian Americans is relevant to understanding the current demographics. Second, it's important to note that this is not ancient history: Immigration from countries in Asia continues at high levels in the 21st century. Third, incidents such as the internment of Japanese Americans in the 1940s can be instructive in dealing with modern-day issues. Immediately following the terrorist attacks on the World Trade Center in 2001, opinion polls found support for internment camps. A nationwide poll conducted by the Pew Research Center found that 29 percent favored detaining "legal immigrants from unfriendly countries."

Although the demographic information is telling, it should be taken cautiously. It clearly points to California, New York and Hawaii as states with large numbers of Asian Americans. These also are three of the most expensive states to live in, which should be considered in examining mean incomes. The statistics also suggest movement toward greater geographic diversity among Asian Americans. Also note that census figures may not accurately reflect the number of second- and third-generation Asian Americans who married European Americans or African Americans.

Finally, the suggestions for journalistic coverage are presented with the important caveat that Asian Americans are not a monolithic group. What's needed is a watchful eye toward sensitivity to all groups, which can only be accomplished by careful and thorough journalism.

Resources

Internet

http://www.aaja.org/   The Asian American Journalists Association
http://www.apalanet.org   The Asian Pacific American Labor Alliance, AFL-CIO

http://www.apalc.org   The Asian Pacific American Legal Center
http://www.apen4ej.org   The Asian Pacific Environmental Network
http://www.apawli.org   The Asian Pacific American Women's Leadership
    Institute

Books and Article

See AAJA 1992, "Diversity in America: Asians" 2002, McWilliams 1939,
    Wong 2001, and Zia 2000 in the following list of references.

References

AAJA (Asian American Journalists Association). 2000. *All-American: How to
    Cover Asian America.* San Francisco, Calif.

AAJA. Center for Integration and Improvement of Journalism. 1992. *Project
    Zinger: A Critical Look at News Media Coverage of Asian Pacific Amer-
    icans.* Washington, D.C.

"An Overview; The Wen Ho Lee Case." 2000. *The New York Times*, September
    28, p. A26.

Arnold, F., U. Minocha, and J.T. Fawcett. 1987. "The Changing Face of Asian
    Immigration to the United States." In *Pacific Bridges: The New Immi-
    gration from Asia and the Pacific Islands*, ed. J.T. Fawcett and B. Carino,
    105-152. Staten Island: Center for Migration Studies.

Commission on Freedom of the Press. 1947. *A Free and Responsible Press: A
    General Report on Mass Communication: Newspapers, Radio, Motion
    Pictures, Magazines, and Books.* Chicago, Ill.: The University of
    Chicago Press.

De Witt, J.L., Lieutenant General, Headquarters Western Defense Command
    and Fourth Army, Office of the Commanding General, U.S. Army. 1943.
    Japanese Evacuation from the West Coast, 1942: Final Report. Wash-
    ington, D.C.: U.S. Government Printing Office.

"Diversity in America: Asians." November 2002. *American Demographics,*
    24(Suppl.):14-16.

Endo, R., S. Sue, and N.N. Wagner, eds. 1980. *Asian-Americans: Social and
    psychological perspectives,* Vol. II. Ben Lomond, Calif.: Science and Be-
    havior Books, Inc.

Fleeson, Lucinda. 2000. "Rush to Judgment." *American Journalism Re-
    view.* 22:20-29.

"From the Editors: The Times and Wen Ho Lee." 2000. The *New York Times*,
    September 26, p. A2.

Humphreys, J.M. "The Multicultural Economy 2002: Minority Buying Power
    in the New Century." www.selig.uga.edu/

Lee, J.F.J. 1992. *Asian Americans*. New York: The New Press.

McWilliams. 1939. *Factories in the Fields: The Story of Migratory Farm Labor in California*. Boston: Little, Brown and Company.

Min, P.G., ed. 1995. *Asian Americans: Contemporary Trends and Issues*. Thousands Oaks, Calif.: Sage Publications.

Takaki, R. 1998. *Strangers from a Different Shore: A History of Asian Americans*. Updated and revised edition. Boston: Little, Brown and Company.

Wong, K.S., and S.C. Chan, eds. 1998. *Claiming America: Constructing Chinese American Identities During the Exclusion Era*. Philadelphia: Temple University Press.

Wong, W. 2001. *The Yellow Journalist: Dispatches from Asian America*. Philadelphia: Temple University Press.

Wong, W. 2002. Interview with author. 20 December 2002.

Zia, H. 2000. *Asian American Dreams: The Emergence of an American*. New York: Farrar, Straus and Giroux.

Index